Brave New
World Economy

Brave New World Economy

Global Finance Threatens Our Future

Wilhelm Hankel
Robert Isaak

WILEY

John Wiley & Sons, Inc.

Published by John Wiley & Sons, Inc., Hoboken, New Jersey.
Published simultaneously in Canada.

For general information on our other products and services or for technical support, please contact our Customer Care Department within the United States at (800) 762-2974, outside the United States at (317) 572-3993 or fax (317) 572-4002.

Wiley also publishes its books in a variety of electronic formats. Some content that appears in print may not be available in electronic formats. For more information about Wiley products, visit our web site at www.wiley.com.

Library of Congress Cataloging-in-Publication Data:

Hankel, Wilhelm, 1929– author.
    Brave New World Economy : Global Finance Threatens Our Future / Wilhelm Hankel, Robert Isaak.
      p. cm
    Includes index.
    ISBN 978-1-118-00441-8 (cloth); ISBN 978-1-118-03680-8 (ebk);
    ISBN 978-1-118-03686-0 (ebk); ISBN 978-1-118-03688-4 (ebk)
      1. United States—Economic policy—2009– 2. Global Financial Crisis, 2008–2009. 3. Economic policy. I. Isaak, Robert A. (Robert Allen), 1945– author. II. Title.
    HC106.84.H36   2011
    332′.042—dc22

2010047423

Printed in the United States of America

10 9 8 7 6 5 4 3 2 1

To
The G-20
and Its Advisors

But industrial civilization is only possible when there's no self-denial. Self-indulgence up to the very limits imposed by hygiene and economics. Otherwise the wheels stop turning.

—Aldous Huxley, *Brave New World*

Contents

Preface   **xiii**

Manifesto **Democratization of Capitalism**   **1**
          Rescue the Right to Work in Aging Societies   3
          Legalize Black Market Labor   7
          Defuse the Ticking Time Bombs of the
              Welfare State   8
          Enroll 100 Percent of the Population in Pensions   9
          Reduce State Indebtedness   11
          Look for New Answers to Old Problems   13
          Subsidize Start-Ups in Disadvantaged Regions   18
          The Mandate of the Democratic, Constitutional
              Welfare State: Stability, Reliability, Prosperity   19

Chapter 1 **Midas Reveals How to Create Money
through Credit Fraud**   **25**
          Does Progress in Developing Money Equal
              Progress in the World Economy?   26

The State as Accomplice or Controller of the
    Money Economy, or Both?   29
The Illusory World of Finance and the
    Fictional Capital of Banks   32
Will Yesterday's Recipes Help Us Today?   36
The Finance Sector Always Underestimates
    the Risks of Its Innovations   38
Four Fatal Innovations of Global Banking   41
Essential Reforms   45
Four Conclusions from the Financial Crisis   47
Keynes, Properly Understood   51

Chapter 2   **The Great Bluff: The American
             Way out of the Crisis**   **53**
             A Brief Tour of How We Got Here   55
             How American Globalization
                 Revolutionized Finance   58
             Wanted: An Emperor with Clothes   60
             How Goldman Sachs Milked Bubble Trouble   63
             Origins of the Financial Crisis   65
             The Lost Lessons of Long-Term
                 Capital Management   72
             The Government Intervenes; Investors Panic 73
             Obamanomics: Exploiting Crisis, Postponing Costs 76
             The Debt Culture versus Hoarding and Investing   85
             Austerity versus Stimulus: The Trillion-Dollar Gap   92
             Recasting the United States: Domestic
                 Dynamism with Responsibility   100

Chapter 3   **Giant with Feet of Clay:
             The European Union**   **105**
             What Services Has the EU Rendered?   107
             The Euro: Not Dynamic but Dynamite   109
             Is the European Union on Its Way to Becoming
                 a Nation-State?   112
             Do EU Institutions Induce
                 Constitutional Infidelity?   116

Can the Euro Survive? 117
The Three Unknowns of the Current Bailout
of the Euro 121
The Next Financial Adventure: A European
State Bankruptcy Law 123
What Comes after the Euro? 124
The Future of the EU: The Swiss Model 129
Currency "Concubinage": The Currency
Has to Serve the Citizen, Not the
Citizen the Currency 132

Chapter 4   **The *New* New World: Can BRICs
Save the Rich?** **139**
Mimicking Past Economic Miracles 141
The Rise of the BRICs 143
Characteristics of the *New* New World 147
Legitimacy Lost 149
Decoupling and Demographics 154
One BRIC at a Time 157
Debt versus Investment and Savings in BRICs 171
The Group of 20 and Global Imbalances 172
The Roadmap to the New World Economy
Has Changed 174

Chapter 5   **Time for a New Bretton Woods:
Crisis Prevention through Monetary Law** **181**
What Caused Bretton Woods to Fail? 185
"Floating" Exchange Rates: A Compelling End? 191
Living in the "Nonsystem" of
Post–Bretton Woods 193
Keynes with a New Feature: Real
(Not Nominal) Fixed Exchange Rates 197

Chapter 6   **Toward a Brave New World Economy:
Reducing Debt and Unemployment** **205**
The World Economy and Nation: States Are
a System of Communicating Pipes 209
Democracy Begins and Works at Home 210

Pillars of Stability and Self-Healing Therapies
of Modern Society   213
From "Underground" Work to
Lifelong "Retooling"   214
The Old-Age Pension Dilemma   218
The Dilemma of the Overindebted State   222
What Can Be Done?   224
The Three Megatrends of the Global
Economy of Tomorrow   227

Epilogue   Faust and Mephisto on the
            World-Money Stage   231
From Paper Gold to Paper Paper   233
The Narrow Middle Lane of Successful Capitalism   235
From Gold to the G-20   237
Invitation   245

Notes   247

Bibliography   253

About the Authors   257

Index   259

Preface

Modern scientists are like dwarves sitting on the shoulders of their great predecessors and teachers. Even if they do not surpass their forefathers, this great heritage allows them to look farther into the distance, bringing them closer to the problems of today. They can and must continue to update their knowledge.

This book attempts such an update, using the teachings of three Grand Masters of the economic guild as a basis: Adam Smith, John Maynard Keynes, and Joseph Alois Schumpeter. Smith's message to future generations was delivered in his *Wealth of Nations*—note that "nations" are mentioned in the plural. Keynes wrote his *General Theory* "for the assurance of full employment for all countries of the globe," not simply one country. His "suggestions" for the Bretton Woods system of the postwar period (his closing chapter) are as relevant as ever in today's financial crisis. Once again, it is all about creating a "brave new world economy."

Schumpeter's warning that capitalism will turn into limestone as did the dinosaurs if it is not constantly able to renew and reinvent itself holds particularly true for the financial system. For it is the questionable progress and innovations of financial engineering that have triggered this crisis. Capitalism would commit suicide if it allowed these so-called innovations to remain unattended to.

When two authors write a book, they agree on the core statements, but not in every detail. Therefore, there are overlaps here and there, translated by the other author, and small differences in individual formulations. But these change nothing in terms of the content and common message delivered by both authors. Similarly in the English edition the title stresses the "brave new world economy" in the making, while the title in the German edition accents the "domination of money" (*Geldherrschaft*), which must be redirected to the real, job-creating economy in order to make such a sustainable new world system possible. The German author, as former Director of Money and Credit in the German government, president of a bank, and international consultant for central banks throughout the world, contributes fresh perspectives on money and credit and the European debt crisis, while the American author, an international political economist and comparative management specialist on the United States and Europe, provides collective learning and entrepreneurial and public policy insights on job creation, pensions, and sovereign debt dilemmas. It is appropriate that the authors previously collaborated in writing *Modern Inflation* in both English and German at the Johns Hopkins SAIS Center in Bologna, Italy: Once again, the issue of how to maintain a moderate dose of national inflation for the sake of economic growth has become the priority of developed Western economies.

Meanwhile, the world economy is undergoing a revolutionary sea change—away from the West and toward the emerging economies.

The world of the West is out of joint. In the United States, Obama's heroic attempt to bring a European-style social democracy to the country is poised to collapse in the face of a two-front war against America's deep-rooted conservatism, on the one hand, and the inexorable laws of the "hard dollar," on the other. The country cannot simultaneously be a modern social welfare state and a world banker.

On the old continent, the euro crisis has initiated a cold war over the progress of European integration. France and Germany see a unique opportunity to transform the European Union of states into one federal state that they would dominate. The European currency zone, now a centrally planned economic, financial, and transfer union with national characteristics and limited codetermination rights for small and ultimately dependent (heavily indebted) member countries, would be expanded into a Franco-German condominium. The European Commission is deeply divided on the issue: It affirms the goal, but struggles against the Franco-German claim to power. As a result of the conflict, the European Union is apt to emerge as a toothless tiger.

Whatever the outcome, the leadership crisis in the West will once again transform the face of the world economy.

The very viability of the social welfare state is at stake, illustrated by the underfunding of pensions, training for employment, and national budgets. This book relates how the ambiguities of globalization, regional integration, and insufficient reforms in the financial sector undermine the capacities of nation-states to act to foster domestic prosperity and full employment. The emergence of a "brave new world economy" not only begins with radical changes at home, but also requires a major reform of the world monetary system in order to restore confidence among investors and entrepreneurs. Otherwise, the next global financial crisis is inevitable, the dollar and the euro are likely to plummet, the necessary rebalancing between rich and emerging economies will be disrupted, and Western democratic capitalism as we know it will not survive.

The "Manifesto: Democratization of Capitalism" summarizes our suggestions for helping to bring about a civilized, brave new world economy—the steps are further elaborated in Chapters 5 and 6. Then we turn to the stories of the greatest financial credit fraud we have yet experienced, of the Great Bluff of American policy-makers, of the giant with feet of clay in Europe, and of the BRICs and other developing nations that may yet save the rich from their self-imposed speculative extravagances.

WILHELM HANKEL
Königswinter, Germany

ROBERT ISAAK
New York, New York

Brave New
World Economy

Manifesto

Democratization of Capitalism

Beneficial is the fire's power when man tames and guards it.
—Friedrich Schiller, *Das Lied von der Glocke*

While the current crisis began as one of banks and their excesses, it has long since expanded to one of countries and their debts. And it is far from over. Just the opposite: Many of the questionable rescue strategies of crisis managers give the impression that they want to stabilize the crisis rather than to eliminate its causes. It is as if they long to repeat one of the fatal fallacies of the *ancien régime* before the outbreak of the French Revolution: "After us, the deluge."

The epicenter of the turbulence is the old "First World" of the West—not the new, emerging world. The crisis has already changed the face and centers of influence in the global economy today and will show lasting effects in the future. One example is the failure of Obama to transform the United States into a modern social welfare state due to conservative opposition and to perceived

U.S. obligations to remain a hard-currency world banker. Another illustration: the frustrated ongoing effort to use the euro crisis in order to transform the European Union (EU) into a single federal state dominated by a Franco-German condominium.

The world economy of the past three or four centuries, dominated first by European powers, their interests and currencies, and then by the United States, is dead. However, the new global economy has not yet come into being. But we can already anticipate that it will be a "brave new world economy" no longer dominated unilaterally by the interests of money power. Globalization provides the opportunity to balance the still-diverging priorities of old and new economies and to steer the overflowing financial sector back to its "service function" for the real economy. In this manifesto we summarize the steps on this difficult path and some of the major obstacles we need to overcome on the way.

Modern capitalism is not *laissez-faire*. It follows rules—ancient, unwritten, recast anew—whether from market players or from the state, who both share responsibility for the welfare of its citizens. Rules must be adapted to changing conditions. In the long history of the symbiosis between state and society, reforming the rules has rarely been as urgent as it is today.

In the past, nation-states, and particularly their leaders, usually lived quite well from the profits of creative merchants and entrepreneurs. They drew on the resources of these producers for their purposes, the affairs of state, whatever these might be (wars, luxuries, extending power, or the welfare state). Globalization has turned this harmonious symbiosis on its head. Now "global players" neglect national and currency boundaries and their warning signals, and purport to give the state their wishes and demands. In this crisis, banks operating and speculating globally have to be reformed and their extended global markets need to be stabilized with state help. Otherwise capitalism could perish, the same way that communism did some 20 years ago.

Capitalism is not a company. It doesn't allow anyone to avoid claiming responsibility for losses. This applies to countries as well as to banks. No state is so essential to the system, so "systemic," that it can force the world economy to accept forever the collateral damages that arise as a result of its currency privileges; no bank is so big as to persuade the taxpayer that its restructuring would cost him less than its bankruptcy. Capitalism does not die from the heads of venomous snakes which it has chopped off, but of its own negligence in removing heads from the bodies of snakes in the first place.

Rescue the Right to Work in Aging Societies

The current financial disruption looks much like its predecessors. Yet it is an entirely different type of crisis, for systemic reasons. In previous crises, the financial sector served the real economy as an engine of progress. Any entrepreneur or innovator who was ready to take a risk could find a banker to sponsor his endeavor. This crisis was the inevitable consequence of the "extravagance" of the financial sector, which at times failed in its role as catalyst.

The current crisis has other reasons as well. This time, the curves of progress of the financial and real sectors of the economy are no longer in sync. Financial progress targets globalization as a goal; economic and technological progress, in turn, aim to reduce the labor required and the cost of labor per unit of product. The target is the substitution of human capital with capital.

With globalization the financial sector is gradually moving away from national sites of production and workplaces. The result is a deep rift within the real producing, investing, and job-creating economy. Large, global market and export-oriented corporations have nearly become banks; they have turned into financially self-sufficient entities that draw largely from their own sources ("self-funding"): from cash-flow and regular issues. They suffer little or not at all from the migration of banks into the extraterritorial no-man's-land of global financial markets. The victims of this "financial progress" are the medium-sized and smaller companies, the traditional firms bound to their local location and markets. These smaller firms bear the brunt of producing most of the national tax revenue, but remain largely excluded from raising (cheap) capital through the stock market. Their sources of capital are banks, which, exactly when businesses are dependent on them (such as during the present crisis), raise their prices on bank credit and borrowing. For the business focus of the banks has become "investment banking": global securities trading and speculation.

In the middle-sized companies—the backbone of the industrial world and culture—the world of work has been placed under severe pressure. Small and medium-sized businesses are the largest employers and vocational schools of the nation. These firms represent up to two-thirds of all workers and four-fifths of all trainees in the United States, Germany, and other Western industrialized countries. These people rely on finding jobs and income on their doorsteps, or nearby, so that their children's school is at least accessible by public or private transportation. This part of "human capital" is not just limited in mobility. They are not nomads, nor do they belong to the world-language-speaking (i.e., English or Chinese) dominant jet set. Globalization makes those locally bound into victims of techno-economic progress; their social ties and cultural roots constrain their life plans. Instead of achieving social advancement, they are threatened with being downgraded into the class of the working poor.

What is more, techno-economic progress is tied to one's professional qualifications. It is increasingly difficult to keep up with the technical skills and know-how of younger generations. If globalization limits one's mobility, the result is to limit one's technical-economic progress and efficiency at work. One has to constantly adjust and learn or to count on early release into early retirement: and a long life lies ahead after one's working phase is over.

Not only must the industrialized nations of the West help their financial sector out of the difficulties it threw itself into, they must also cope with the consequences of the crisis resulting from the financial excesses: the balance of long-term, rising structural unemployment, the limited mobility of the local labor force, and the rising pressures in the high-tech era of rationalizing and "dehumanizing" factory and office work.

The welfare state could hardly have selected a worse historical moment to confront these challenges. Due to escalating costs of social systems and to an excess of concentrated public debt, its financial maneuverability has, in effect, been eliminated. New tasks and expenditures can hardly be funded from new taxes or loans because in both cases the loads have hit the limit, if not exceeded it. A turning of the screw threatens the danger that the successes of private ownership, entrepreneurial freedom, and initiative (thanks to capitalism) will fall victim to an all-paralyzing fiscal socialism.

The state debt, a problem that the EU and the United States have to resolve together, threatens not only to undermine their credit, but to rob people of this and the next generation of their future prospects.

The United States and the EU countries are facing a generational conflict. The present generation, with their endlessly greedy claims (which ultimately caused today's public debt), has endangered both the habitat and the potential development of their children and grandchildren. Was the leading world economist of the twentieth century, John Maynard Keynes, so thoroughly mistaken when he claimed the opposite in his famous essay of 1931, "Economic Possibilities for Our Grandchildren": more leisure time, more prosperity, more luxury? It depends on the willingness and ability of states and their governments to cope with this crisis and its consequences and to pave the way to a "brave new world economy."

What is involved in this great task?

The financial world needs to find its way back to its true mission, namely to be *at the service of the real economy*. Its function is to transform the real capital of the saver into loans for productive and innovative investors. It is this financial engine that makes capitalism a welfare machine and opens society to innovators and social climbers. However, the financial sector's own innovations have distracted it from proceeding to do this, making it system-alienating.

Banks have turned into trading houses or casinos that speculate on securities and financial assets morphing into investment banks and hedge funds. With their innovative but fictitious products (fictitious in the sense of having little to do with the real world), such as derivatives, bank guarantees, and risky bets, one may be able to earn huge sums of money, but this liquidity fails to create real national wealth, that is, tangible assets and jobs. The "performance" of the financial sector exhausts itself in pushing up prices for dead capital—values of things that already exist such as equities, real estate, and gold—and triggers an inflation of asset prices (asset inflation). Bubble formation in stock markets and other capital markets does not constitute an ID card reading "private and public success" (it could better be compared to a fake ID). On the contrary, this kind of business is a case of misdirecting and wasting capital, because this sort of speculation does not go into real investment and job creation but into the private wealth of a few rather than the social welfare of all. This is what distracts capitalism from its dynamic growth potential and creates social conflict in society, where harmony reigned before. The productivity gains of high technology (the replacement of human labor power and performance through computer hardware and software) call for new strategies for the labor market and for social legislation. The new leisure can—and *must*—be used productively. Joseph Alois Schumpeter pointed out in his prophetic book *Capitalism, Socialism, and Democracy* (1939) that the real source of all progress in society and the economy is the "use of work" in a different, innovative way.[1]

Legalize Black Market Labor

Just as the industrial sector grew out of work vacancies in agriculture, the modern (tertiary) service work sector draws its inspiration from the now-unneeded human labor force. The working society "does not run out of work," according to economist Lord Ralf Dahrendorf.[2] The use of human capital must simply be reorganized. Where this fails, it happens anyway, spontaneously. Human beings, who are made for work and enjoy challenges, do not accept a life sentence of involuntary unemployment. The tertiary service sector has long created an informal *quaternary*, the informal service sector. Black market work (the "underground" economy) continues to be condemned by state social legislation and by the politics of the unions. It is unjustly defamed and penalized by institutions.

In fact, this kind of work closes the ever-widening gap between the increase of age and working life and the decrease of regulated working hours in the formal working world. Manifest in this type of work is the human right to work and the utilitarian opportunity to use personal skills and resources unique to every human being. Such a black market economy allows individuals to work independently as entrepreneurs who labor on their own account and at their own risk, thereby creating real value; the individual becomes a self-sufficient enterprise, a solo business.

The legalization of work outside of the four walls of one's home is a human right: He or she who wants to work should be allowed to do so. It relieves the welfare state (by helping individuals to help themselves) and contributes to the acceleration and continuity of the economic growth process; it is a privately financed long-term stimulus package. This is especially true since the "black" earned income is nearly 100 percent "white" in its output: it is spent in the real economy. The state does not miss out on a cent of this value creation if it adjusts its tax system to meet the demands of this new growth sector—by the conversion of income taxation into increased taxes on consumption (indirect taxes).

Defuse the Ticking Time Bombs of the Welfare State

Two of the greatest challenges facing the nations of the Western world in the first half of the twenty-first century are the financing of social old age security and the public debt mortgage. These two dilemmas could cause the welfare state to fail, and it is, after all, the great achievement of the West, if one excludes democracy and the rule of law. The paradox of the modern welfare state is that only the transition to the financial economy brought it about; for when old people retire from the working world, they can no longer, as in ancient times, be expected to return moneyless to the bosom of their tribe, their family home, to be taken in and cared for. They need their own retirement income. However, despite the widespread opinion in the "capitalistic" United States, this old-age income is not brought about primarily by each worker providing for him- or herself, through financial reserves and savings. This can be shown in a simple calculation: If the supply of sums needed to supply millions of older people with Social Security in the United States, or state social insurance systems, as in most European countries, were combined, this fund would grow to become the greatest owner of capital stock in the economy. Capitalism would "socialize" the institutions of its own old-age security. But the alternative of providing for oneself individually (supposing every person could do so) also reaches limits; it ends in the vagaries of the stock market and capital market. Whoever carries over his savings into retirement faces an uncertain future and takes on high risk. For when the time comes for this pensioner to sell her assets, she needs a third party to buy them, who then determines the price. You need to be almost as rich as Warren Buffett to look forward to a secure retirement in the future, given the risk of not knowing what your assets will eventually sell for. Tens of billions of dollars in private pension accounts were lost in the present financial crisis. And state governments in the United States, for example, are overwhelmed with the burden of between $2 trillion and $3 trillion of unfunded pension benefits (usually based on overoptimistic projections of returns on investments).[3]

Enroll 100 Percent of the Population in Pensions

Nowhere does public accountability manifest itself more blatantly compared to moody, unpredictable market events than in the forms and systems of old-age security. For what counts for the government-insured social pensioners is not the vagaries of the stock market, the volatility of their own accounts, and the risks of invested capital, but only that enough people are paying into the social insurance and that these citizens are fully employed and not without work or income. For then what they pay in, the social security insurance can also pay out.

State social security raises the age-old moral principle that for the effort parents put in to prepare their children for independent living, the children must not give up trying to succeed but give back to their parents that same time and effort later on. Modern society continues to apply the old generational contract, even when young and old are not related. If a society terminates this agreement, it would fall back into the Stone Age.

What happens, however, if the sheer number of claims by parents who have retired from professional life cut unbearably into the legitimate claims of their children?

Who retires and when is not determined by God, and only in exceptional cases is it ordered by the doctor; it is set by social legislation. This social security law determines when the retirement age begins, and who is subject to social insurance and who is not. Two examples should give these social legislators pause for consideration. In Germany, Otto von Bismarck baptized the first social security system (1882–1883), which is still solvent and reliable to this day: After the end of one's working career, there was an average of only five years to finance for only 10 percent of the population in Bismarck's time; a worker entered retirement at 62, and the percent of a worker's income paid in to the insurance was 2 percent. Today, given greater life expectancy, there are over 20 years of retirement that need to be financed. And instead of 10 percent of the population, there are 90 percent to insure, and the pension burden cost for active workers contributing has increased to over 20 percent of income. In view of the widening demographic gap between growth of the elderly population and the same number, or fewer, paying into the pension fund, by 2050 the percentage of income that needs to be paid into the insurance by active workers is expected to rise to 30 percent. In short, the young must sacrifice one-third of their income for the old.

However, the problem could be solved with two steps of reform. The first is to require not 90 percent but 100 percent of the population to enroll in the social insurance system; for the missing 10 percent are the millionaires of the economy; since they take in 35 to 40 percent of the national income, if they all paid into the system, the burden on the young would fall. Whoever wishes to claim that this "people's pension" is pure socialism should look at Switzerland. There this proposal is in effect. The rich are contented with a symbolic pension, greatly below the equivalent of what they paid in; however, they have no problem in wanting to do something for their poorer fellow citizens in the evening of their lives. At the age of 20, the burden upon the young of payment for pensions lies at under 10 percent of income.

The second step in reform is to raise the retirement age. As an example, although the legal retirement age begins in Germany at age 65, the mass of older workers retire and take an early pension at age 59. The companies prefer to let the public pay for them instead of using "collective learning" to improve the older workers know-how through education and training programs. They "socialize" their wage and labor costs—with the active support of the unions. Meanwhile, in the United States, the average age of retirement is 62 with an estimated 18 years of retirement to go (with about of 11 percent of annual income paid into Social Security and pension accounts).

The trend among the rich is increasingly *not* to retire (they are nicknamed Nevertirees); over half of those polled globally never intend to retire (with this number rising much higher in Saudi Arabia and the United Arab Emirates, but dropping much lower in Switzerland and Japan). Raising the retirement age in Germany to 70-plus years and requiring the full adoption of early-retirement costs by companies would theoretically reduce the cost of pension provisions to the level of the Bismarck era.

However, the welfare state does not have to go this far. Even a half-step in this direction would relieve the burden, not only on society but also on all those who *want* to work longer. The answer to the other ticking time bomb of the welfare state is not so simple to grasp.

Reduce State Indebtedness

Although it was possible to deal with the emergency effects of the debt eruption of the recent years by "financing away" the bankruptcy of top institutions in the financial sector in the United

States and Europe, that was accomplished only at the price of bringing these countries a good bit closer to their own declarations of bankruptcy. Euro-based countries in the so-called PIIGS group—Portugal, Ireland, Italy, Greece, and Spain—have already suffered downgrades in their ratings as borrowers, with others, possibly France or England, yet to come.

But not a single problem has been solved by either the state or central bank financed bailout program in the United States for troubled banks, or the rescue in the EU for the risk of insolvency of states in the PIIGS group. The debt burden was not rescued but merely shifted over to the government account, postponing the crisis, not resolving it. Now the states of the West are confronted with the question of whether they want to live permanently in crisis, or to free themselves from the manacles of debt in order to be able to act politically once more.

The democratic welfare state of the West can win back its freedom only by a radical reduction of every tenable standard insolvency. This is more difficult than 80 years ago. After all, in the contemporary world economic crisis, there is no inflationary boom that could accelerate the ascent from the floor of the valley and devalue much of the debt. On the contrary, the upturn, when it comes, will get stuck halfway up. The recovery is not following a V, U, or L pattern, but instead looks like an extended square root ($\sqrt{\quad}$).

Thus, this time, the depressive-deflationary effects are predominant. The overliquidity stemming from the bailout financing is but a momentary snapshot. Bailouts merely secure the balances of the banks in "black holes"; the rest can be collected once the Western central banks come to an agreement on such a policy. The elimination of the debt from the world of Western states can succeed only if the risks posed by their added deflationary effects are neutralized by a positive policy of employment. Government creditors, that is, mainly banks and institutional investors, must maintain the flow of billions of dollars previously skimmed off from taxpayers in domestic circulation. Therefore, the reduction of public debt must go hand in hand with a counterbalancing program of domestic investment and infrastructural renewal. The funds should be drawn from the beneficiaries of debt reduction: banks, insurance companies, funds, and other places collecting capital. Moreover, state investment and development banks (which have existed in the EU since the Marshall Plan era) could be used to mobilize additional resources in the capital market and insert them into the program. It would be a domestic Marshall Plan or a second New Deal (described further in Chapter 6).

Look for New Answers to Old Problems

The world economy of tomorrow cannot dispense with either globalization or the welfare state. Both are milestones on the road of capitalism toward greater efficiency and its indispensable humanization. But the crisis demonstrates that both systems do not function without safety valves, both preventive and those that kick in automatically in times of emergency.

The First Safety Valve: End Global Laissez-Faire

One of the preventive safety valves is to end global *laissez-faire*. This safety valve has to be installed on two levels, namely on that of central bank cooperation as well as that of banks and the supervision of institutions on the financial market.

The global monetary cooperation requires an international monetary law. The Bretton Woods system attempted to pave a way in that direction; its demise in 1973 depicted the precipices that follow when such a long-standing political institution collapses. The Bretton Woods system of 1945 had been a fresh start after the rigid, mechanical rules of the gold standard during the Depression of the 1930s had failed. The "golden brake on the credit machine"[4] tied up not only the banks but also the states in combating the crisis and its consequences. They had to get rid of this bond, and they succeeded.

The new beginning after 1945 was a huge success. John Maynard Keynes had made from the golden brake a "legal" control of the credit machine and monetary nationalism. It was the United States, with its insistence on the dollar as the accounting unit (inside money) of the system that preprogrammed its collapse. In spring 1973, it was not the *system* that was terminated, but rather the unstable value of the U.S. dollar, which was therefore no longer acceptable as the unit of account for the world economy.

A new Bretton Woods, on the basis of a stable, state-neutral unit of account (Keynes's proposed "bancor") for processing transfers between central banks would work. The People's Republic of China and the International Monetary Fund (IMF) have now taken up the Keynesian idea again: In the monetary system of the future an intrinsic "inside money" should take the place of a government-manipulated "outside money"—namely the further development of the "bancor," or the Special Drawing Rights (SDRs) of the IMF.

A globally acceptable international monetary system could be composed of the following elements and based on the following principles:

- The SDR would serve as a reserve currency and accounting unit of the IMF at the central bank level to replace the U.S. dollar. The previous "cover" of the SDRs with a "basket" would be removed, because the SDR as a reference for the exchange rates of currencies, being attached to the IMF, could not be devalued or revalued.
- The countries that join the system agree to keep their "real" exchange rates stable in terms of their SDR-denominated exchange rate. This means that member states reserve the option of combating both internal and external imbalances with their national interest and exchange rate policies. Both

instruments are available in the national armory. A country with underemployment can reduce its interest rates and devalue; the exchange rate is adjusted ("cleaned") for inflation; a country with an inflation problem can revalue instead of increasing its interest rates and thereby jeopardizing its full employment.

In this system, the IMF takes on the role of monetary police and guardian of the financial system. This function goes beyond that prescribed by Keynes's "Clearing Union." The new IMF not only grants stand-by credit to member countries stuck in balance of payments difficulties. It warns of looming dangers and calls on players who foul against the rules with the threat of the withdrawal of credit.

- A new world monetary system makes the exceptional European euro subsystem unnecessary. The EU's Economic and Monetary Union (EMU) could be liquidated according to plan before it "officially" collapses (at a high cost for all participants). The integration of the eurozone into the new Bretton Woods system would allow the return of euro-based countries to their old, traditional currencies in order to improve their chances of combating their domestic crises on their own and relaxing the tensions between the EU states in a manner that can be sustained. The prerequisites for conflict-free progress on integration could thereby be fulfilled.
- The global financial crisis has reinforced the positions of the BRICs (Brazil, Russia, India, and China) and other emerging countries in the world economy and improves the conditions for their process of catching up domestically (through "self-help"). The domestic demand and savings of the emerging economies permitted the dominant and strong-export Western countries to solve their domestic problems faster than expected. Accordingly, the influence of the BRIC countries in the governing bodies of the world economy (G-20, IMF) has increased. The Western world must count on increased competition from

Third World countries. On the other hand, thanks to the crisis these nations see how heavily they are still dependent upon the West. They lose both important export markets and the import of capital and know-how when declines occur in Western industrialized countries. It has become clear that the world economy of the post-colonial era is different from that of the nineteenth and early twentieth centuries. It is no longer the old machine for exploitation of raw materials of backward countries, but rather permits a win-win situation for all participating actors. The zero-sum game in which one's advantages sum to the other's losses is ending and is on the way to becoming a "welfare machine" for all participating nations.

This is the reason why the plans for a brave new world economy and a new Bretton Woods grow on more fertile soil in the Third World than in the First World of the Western industrialized countries. In the former developing countries the political influence of the financial world does not play the same dominant role that it does in the West. There it is not so easy for the banking world and its lobby to block politically desired reforms. On the other hand, the local financial sector there has become strong enough to speed up the internal development process of these countries more self-sufficiently than ever before. It is already apparent today that the new world economy after the crisis will have a better balance between North and South, and West and East, than it has had in the past.

The Second Safety Valve: Bank Supervision and Financial Stabilization

The creation or, more precisely, printing of money is under dual control by the national central banks and by government supervisory agencies that monitor compliance with the law.

In this framework banks are essential for the government and economy. They move the saved capital to the best business and let it "work" there. Banks, writes Schumpeter, are "Ephors" (magistrates and overseers of the kings of ancient Sparta) of the national economy.[5] Just as in ancient Sparta the Ephors reigned behind the scenes, in the capitalist system they monitor the best use of available resources. However, the Ephor is not above the law, but merely guarantees that others abide by the law. What kind of laws do we need for the financial world in its new form?

- The laws must assure clear accounting rules and full transparency of the financial risks taken. Credit creation from "nothing," the so-called leverage effect, should be limited. The investment risks, particularly the off-balance-sheet risks that have caused this crisis, must be fully transparent to any investor.
- The limits and proportions between credit and securities businesses must be continuously maintained and guaranteed. "Investment" banks (a misnomer), were modeled on the since partly reactivated U.S. Glass-Steagall Act, which allows access to cheap credit from the central bank. However, this access for "casino" banks should be prohibited, making a clear division once more between state-insured commercial banks and speculation-driven investment banks. The trade with "dead capital," that is, financial titles on previously existing physical capital, should be limited to the intrinsic funds of the sector.

There is no reason or justification for the socialization of banking losses. Instead, the protection of the deposits of savers should be strengthened and expanded. No bank customer should be harmed by the irresponsible errors of bank managers. Banks themselves are not nature conservancies: Like a privately owned company, the owners and managers are responsible for their losses. No single bank is "systemically vital"; that is solely the role of the central bank. The central bank is the last guarantor of liquidity to maintain the payment system and credit for the economy. Banks should prevent the misallocation of capital. As a principle, it is more important to let banks go bankrupt than to save them. Schumpeter's maxim of "creative destruction" also applies to banks.

Subsidize Start-Ups in Disadvantaged Regions

Like all previous crises, this one will be a proving ground for a combination of learning experiments and engines of progress. Afterward, the world will be politically wiser and economically more stable.

Collective learning is a social process that makes it possible to initiate new legitimate patterns to cope with economic and political change. It is about understanding transformations in the social environment and adapting to them without jeopardizing cultural integrity. Every nation must prepare the conditions to make collective learning possible. The emphasis should be placed upon maximizing national as well as regional benefits, that is, competitiveness, in which entrepreneurs are motivated to apply new methods, to become competitive, to raise the value of work achieved, and to provide jobs. Start-ups for young people are the elixir of the creation of new income and livelihoods.

The middle class is the sector that suffers the most structurally from the financial crisis, and yet which contributes most to providing the training for the next generation of workers. The personally managed businesses of the bourgeoisie typically have no access to an open, cheap, soft capital market; for this group, access is denied to credit granted to the issuer by the bank by underwriting the issue. In Germany, for example, barely over 1 percent of all companies are registered on the stock exchange. And heavier regulations after the crisis in the United States threaten to diminish the opportunities for small to medium-sized enterprises (SMEs) in what has been the world's best micro market for equity financing. Promotion of SMEs through improved access conditions to capital markets is both good labor market and regional structural policy. It counteracts the deindustrialization in disadvantaged regions as well as the migration of workers into overcrowded areas. This requires the creation of local and regional stock exchanges with free access for noncorporations, publicly funded start-up programs, and the establishment of cooperative credit-and-guarantee communities by the sector itself as a collective act of self-help. Last, but not least, the legalization of self-employment (none of which, in functional effect, is really "black market," or should be considered to be illegal) is a component of such programs.

Only collective learning can resolve the conflict between the increasing demands for know-how and job security. This may include learning and training programs in society and business, changes in social and labor legislation, and a new social understanding of unions. The aim should be to deregulate the labor market to such an extent that any worker, if he wants, could become his own employer. What is required is the liberation of work from official as well as union constraints: time and wage guidelines. This made sense as long as armies of dispossessed and nonskilled people were dependent upon mechanical factory labor and were exposed to exploitation.

In the postindustrial society these structural constraints disappear. It permits us to pay out the social dividend from the higher productivity from machines and technology in free time, such as in voluntary self-employment: activity particular to the individual, yet also useful for society.

The Mandate of the Democratic, Constitutional Welfare State: Stability, Reliability, Prosperity

The nation-state is not about to be replaced by anything else, even in the age of globalization—neither by markets nor by processes of integration. But this domestic constitution must comply with the requirements of the times, or be brought up to par. It is a question of the material basis of human dignity: the stability of economy, existence, and income, the reliability of the currency, the good life in society. None of these goods can be obtained in isolation from others or reached by separate paths.

Democratic constitutions are based on the principle of "checks and balances." This requires the "separation of powers" among legislation, adjudication, and government. While this protects the citizen from the danger of the all-powerful state, the individual is vulnerable on another front: The shared form of government is weak, surrendering to the influence of powerful interest groups in society (big business, banks, trade unions). Out of *laissez-faire* comes stalemate.

The basis of every instance of national prosperity is the currency. In a capitalist society the currency cannot be stable and reliable enough. As guardian of the monetary constitution, the central bank is of paramount importance. Or as Schumpeter said, the money system is reflected again in "what a people wants, does, suffers, *is*."[6]

Therefore, the 17 EU nations that divested themselves of their own currencies all share a common risk in their "currency concubinage." Whether or not this risk has been too high soon will become evident in the future.

Ultimately it depends on the central bank whether it is possible to keep the value of money stable, to avoid levels of unemployment that are too high, and to allow the (barely) tolerable inflation rate that boosts economic growth so that incomes rise faster than prices.

Every country is dependent on its material resources and has a duty to ensure that its citizens have enough work opportunities and that income can be generated.

In a capitalist society, this demands not central economic and social planning, but rather a high level of transparency. Markets are efficient only if they can respond to accurate information—what citizens need, want, and can pay for—and are efficient only when the business competition is based upon reliable data that make it clear where its advantages and opportunities lie.

The state has the task of organizing institutional networks of collective learning: schools, training, and continuing education programs, including public media, TV, or the Internet. For the root and key to success in a society is its work productivity. It generates much higher economic growth and far more secure protection against unemployment than overpackaged employment programs and a focus upon abstract targets and goals of the overall economy—a mistake that doomed communism.

Government investment or development banks are an important instrument of public investment guidance and policy. They guarantee that private savings get to where they should to create public and not just private benefits—in infrastructure, business start-ups, and security, or the means for incentives for border regions remote from markets, which, without this help, would wither in an economic desert.

The prosperous society cannot rely only on the resources of private savings to finance legitimate government functions. Still, the development bank is not only an intermediary. It is an institutionalized capital market for long-term future state tasks such as the advancement of youth, families, or science, for which revenues coming in only much later permit credit financing over a long period. On top of that, in times of crisis the development bank is an extremely effective instrument to counter the dangers of oversaving (hoarding).

What must be actively confronted is the general ignorance of people in matters of economics and finance. Although individual destiny and the progress of each individual are dependent on these variables, they remain unknowns for the broad masses. Children cannot learn too early about economics, the role of money and of the financial industry, *and* how social ethics relates to these—that economic means exist to serve the general welfare and are not just ends in themselves—for they will need this knowledge all of their lives. How else will a market and money society protect itself from financial, investment, and pension fraud?

Knowledge of nature and the importance of environmental protection must be provided early in the educational process. This applies not only for products that exist or are grown naturally, but also to those that are industrially processed. And one needs knowledge of the existing natural and mineral resources in the region and society and their uses. Such a background can later lead to ecopreneurship, or environmentally sustainable start-ups—the moral business imperative of satisfying the ecological needs of one's children and grandchildren.

Vocational education and counseling are an essential element of the working world and the welfare state. Young people succumb to the seduction of fashionable professions and the lure of quick money. It must be made clear where society truly offers them a future. Old people can demonstrate their capacities even after their retirement by volunteering in the community. There is no time or age limit for work. As long as a human being lives and can work and wants to work, he or she must be permitted to do so. Human beings have a fundamental right to work.

An important aspect of the priorities of nations and economic sectors lies in protection from unfair competition both domestically and from abroad. The protection of agriculture not only serves the national interest in terms of food security, but is also of increasing importance ecologically. The same applies to the energy needs of the society, its military security, or its young, growing industries (such as solar or wind energy or newly patented methods of production).

Friedrich List, a world-renowned German–American economist, made it clear 150 years ago that the government and the economy form a unity. The state creates the conditions for the use of potential national productivity; the economy turns it to account and creates with its profits the prosperity of the people and the basis for taxation—a marriage that may never end in divorce, for the state or economy alone creates neither conditions for prosperity nor prosperity itself.

The state creates a social system of citizen-friendly services at a distance: In social welfare states such as Sweden, Denmark, Finland, Austria, Switzerland, France, and Germany (among others) this includes pensions, welfare and health practices, protection against hardship due to disability, and care for the elderly. In the case of Germany, the welfare state survived a whole series of crises and disasters: two world wars, two hyperinflations, the change of regimes, mass unemployment, and Hitler. It is not too much to say that it was not the welfare state that survived, but the people, thanks to the state. It gives the citizens security from ever-threatening risks. They do not need to save "too much," but can consume more courageously than in other countries, where this security is absent. A stable social order helps the economy; it can plan more securely, invest, and expand. The welfare state does not burden the economy; it is the economy's growth engine and stabilizer. The government's distribution from higher income (high savings rate) to low (high consumption rate) strengthens the vitality of the capitalist dynamic and entrepreneurial *élan vital*.

Democratic constitutions humanize life in society. They protect minorities, promote the peaceful coexistence of ethnic groups in the same country, and secure a more equitable society. The central bank holds the economic universe together with its commitment to stable money, preserves it from fraud, steers the state's savings rate, and keeps a rein on the banks. Crisis is preprogrammed if politics, the *zeitgeist*, or circumstances interfere with the monetary authorities in performing these tasks.

Now it is a question of networking the economy, states, and currencies so that confidence in capitalism returns—and so that it can survive this crisis as it has before, in the thousand years past.

Chapter 1

Midas Reveals How to Create Money through Credit Fraud

T he world financial system trembles—again. The question is raised once more: Will it survive, and if so, will it be restored to its former self or be totally transformed? The answer depends on whether the revived system continues to contain the basic faults that brought about the latest crisis, or if this time serious efforts are made to eliminate these defects. It is a matter of the separation of the control of money and its influential surrogate, credit.

Since the credit economy has been expanded continually and invariably into globalization, there is no longer any way to get around correcting these structural deficiencies. An expanded and expandable credit system without boundaries means that no state on the earth can protect itself from the consequences of its abuse, and neither can its citizens, its savers, or its economy. Credit fraud is identical with financial innovation born in and through capitalism: It is immanent in the system.

Does Progress in Developing Money Equal Progress in the World Economy?

Since time immemorial money has been "a public good." For several hundred years, money has been led on a short leash by the central banks working on orders of the state. The state is there to guarantee—although not always successfully—that the world of money and goods expands in the same volume and rhythm so that the "purchasing power" of money remains stable. The old perspective that money derives its value from gold was always based on an error. Even under the gold standard it was not the raw material of gold that provided money with its value as an end product, but rather the demand for gold for the purpose of monetization. The reason for the loss of the advantage of the gold standard as a basis for money and credit lay in its limited quantity: No money or credit could grow without being backed up by the precious metal, which economist Joseph Schumpeter called the "golden brake on the credit machine."[1] In contrast, since the gold standard has been abandoned the credit economy has enjoyed a free rein. Banks produce credit within their own regime. This credit creation originates from the business of providing money for investing or saving to third parties that lack capital or are "capital poor" entrepreneurs or firms. These borrowers then use the capital for economic purposes, as well as lending to the permanently money-hungry state, which inevitably finds itself in a conflict of interest, caught between easing its own conditions as a debtor and its duties in protecting the value of its citizens' money.

Money exchange and the granting of credit are among the oldest known professions. Since the existence of a market economy, foreign trade, and savings for retirement and the future, money has been pivotal to all three: a unit of account, a medium of exchange, and a store of ownership or investment. Evidently independently of one another, small communities and highly developed cultures around the globe shared in the discovery of this medium of exchange. Wherever financial capitalism has managed to transform the "lazy money" of depositors and investors into the productive activities of entrepreneurs and innovators, it has instituted highly successful wealth machines.

In recent times, where capitalist practices were missing or inadequately developed, as in communist countries or some Third World nations, local companies operated well below their potential. Even if the people labored for 12 hours or more a day, they could afford only a fraction of the goods and services that could be purchased by the same amount of work in the First World nations. Eventually these countries begin to ask, Why does it have to stay this way?

The West's historical lead in developing and refining the money and credit economy is responsible for its early leap into the modern industrial world, its early dominance in the world economy, its widespread prosperity, and its attractiveness as a social model. Monetary and credit innovations arose first in Europe and thereafter in the nations of the New World: the United States, Canada, Australia, New Zealand, and (later) Japan. People of all nations want to share in the blessings of capitalism, particularly those who have up to this point not been able to. However, the attraction of capitalism as a social model has already been dented by the first global economic crisis, beginning with the Wall Street Crash of 1929 and lasting until the outbreak of World War II in the democratic countries of the West: the United States and Western Europe. The financial crisis beginning in 2007 onward has exposed even more serious fundamental flaws. The inner fragility of the system, exacerbated by the disastrous lack of conscience on the part of many of its actors, is now out in the open. The formerly trusting saver and investor now observes that he can no longer depend upon either his bank or its recommendations.

Those dependent upon credit in the economy, particularly small to medium-sized businesses, have learned how little they can rely upon their local banks for a continuous supply of credit at reasonable interest rates. The present crisis made clear that the financial sector itself was a serious defect and deficiency in the engine of the economy and social progress: It covers the money it borrows on credit, not from deposits, which come in from investors who are creating value in the real economy, but by using resources that the bank itself has received "on loan" from other banks, which can then recall that loan if they are obliged to repay it themselves.

However, this is nothing new. Banks have always done this. They lend out money that they do not, in fact, have. Did this constitute progress in the money system, or transparent credit fraud?

Even Jesus was tormented by this question. The practices of the money changers disturbed him. Why else would he have expelled them from the temple? Perhaps he had heard the story that Herodotus, the father of history, passed down to posterity, a mythical tale concerning the King of the Lydians, Midas, who lived in the seventh century before Christ. He was the richest ruler of his time, and was granted the wish that whatever he touched he transformed into gold. Unfortunately this included the water in the glass from which he wanted to drink. On this "increase in value" of the water, he choked to death.

Midas had discovered that from a limited supply of metal coins, one could produce many more coins if one drastically reduced the metal content of each coin. With this process he liberated the money supply from its arbitrary limitation by a dead substance (available monetary raw materials) and at the same time freed the market from all financial bottlenecks. If the market needed funds, it could get them. Midas's money machine reacted to the increasing demand for its product, making available the additional financial means. Since the era of Midas no natural financial bottlenecks have slowed down the increasing prosperity in the free-market economy. From that time on, the technical progress of money (new forms of financing) and money fraud (the proliferation and devaluation of money) have made their appearances as Siamese twins. But, despite the interest in currency stability, their separation has not occurred up to the present day. Inspite of the common community interest in currency stability, they have yet to be separated. Just the opposite has happened: The more open and unregulated the economy, like the private household going from cash payments to loan payments to billing via bank accounts, credit cards, and bank cards, the more blurred the boundary between money progress and fraud. Coins and banknotes, although legal, are no longer common means of payment, but rather "commercial bank" or noncash loans.

Even Midas could not prevent shrewd money dealers from transforming his coins—which could no longer be weighed, but just counted—into credit, for which interest was paid. Why should he? The demand for the money increased his profits. But when the long-term users of this "light" money (the savers) discovered that the buying power of their assets no longer grew but diminished in value—exposing this financial progress as "fraud"—and when they rejected Midas's coins as a store of money assets, the crisis broke out. Midas's gold was transformed back into pure water!

The State as Accomplice or Controller of the Money Economy, or Both?

Ever since the era of Midas, money itself has remained a public good, under all regimes, for no prince or state has wanted to forgo the profit from its "mintage." In antiquity this was the case for the Greek city-states as well as for ancient Rome, and in medieval times it was true for principalities, or princes. The same principle applies today for modern nation-states and the United States, which—despite its deficits—makes close to 70 percent of its dollar circulation available to the rest of the world as savings or nest eggs. All these state bankers earned and continue to earn enormous sums from Midas's discovery that making money—on whatever raw material basis, be it metal, paper, or plastic—costs only a fraction of its market value. Whoever has the privilege of making money cashes in on the premium of being able to declare it as the legal tender—provided that this money continues to be accepted by the public. Since the rise of the modern credit economy, the state has ceded the same rights to the private banking sector.

These bankers were allowed to use their monopoly on the creation of credit to water down the value of the state's money through private paper or money in the form of chip-based credit cards, just as Midas did with his coins. And the state through its central banks permitted this devaluation of its currency through credit proliferation to go on for far too long.

Why?

Because the state has benefited from the increase in its standard of living through inflationary financing. This increase raises the state's ability to tax and the continual credit inflation fills its coffers with more incoming taxes. The state has always been an accomplice to those offering credit. It remains so today. Why slaughter the hen when it continues to lay golden eggs?

Nevertheless, in the world economic crisis of the 1930s, the first partial operation took place on the Siamese twins—if only at the national level. The German credit law of 1933–1934, together with the banking police supervising the credit, worked on this legal basis and introduced credit ceilings for permissible credit fraud. These became guidelines for similar regulations in Europe and the rest of the Western world. This also holds true for the measures and regulations simultaneously introduced in the United States: the insurance of deposits by the FDIC (Federal Deposit Insurance Corporation) and the Glass-Steagall Act, which blocked speculative American investment banks from access to central bank credits and aid. Unfortunately, President Bill Clinton supported the repeal of this important antispeculation law in 1999, preparing the way for the current financial crisis. President Barack Obama continues to push for resurrecting Glass-Steagall again fully, and not only partially, as has been the case to date.

Clearly these national controls of the money credit market are overdue if global banking activity moves out of state-controlled legal spaces into an illegal no-man's-land of financial markets. Since the International Monetary Fund (IMF) was stripped of power in spring 1972, the financial markets are dominated by the pre-state Midas freedom of private money creation. No controller monitors or interferes with this banking idyll, or at least none did so until recently. The banking world had created its own inexhaustible supply of money. It needed neither the money of savers as suppliers, nor the central bank as provider of "last resort," nor the state as supervisor (or in its eyes, interrupter) of its businesses. Yes, even the real economy itself became dispensable as a secure client of credit and producer of profits. Money could be borrowed and investments settled outside of the actual world of savers, investors, and the use of state control—and all of this could bring in fabulous profits.

The financial sector had reached an entirely new stage of its development: It lived from and with itself. It created its own world beyond the real one that it had served for so long and had once been dependent upon.

The Illusory World of Finance and the Fictional Capital of Banks

This new possibility of interbank debt without boundaries on the global financial market did not just cast aside the old dependencies on the river of savings and the refinancing credits of central banks. Now the building of capital and capital fraud became identical. Midas had to guarantee a minimum of precious metal in his coins. The loan money from banks before the globalization era still contained a substantial residual factor of real capital, or savings. To this extent it represented a transfer of purchasing power rather than the creation of purchasing power out of nothing. In this sense, the credit was inflation–neutral. This was not adequate for the new and globalized bank credit, which came from a *double* credit creation: the passive internal bank credits issued by other banks and the further use of these means in the outside world. But which means? Did the slowly but steadily growing world economy need so much new money, that is, credit? Was it possible to apply the incredible overproductivity of the deregulated global financial sector immediately to real sectors of the economy, accommodating the extent and growth of their gross domestic products (GDPs)? Not at all. Going into the crisis, Figure 1.1 shows the huge overhang of newly produced global financing above the real demand of the growing global economy and its national economies. For a world trade volume (exports, imports, direct investments) on the order of some US$12 trillion (2008), a volume of financing existed approaching US$800 billion. Less than 2 percent of this amount would have been sufficient to satisfy the financial needs of the real world economy!

And for what purpose was the other 98 percent needed?

Lacking sufficient demand for new credit production in the real economy (a world GDP of "only" $50 trillion), the global financial markets created their own facilities at its doorstep. More

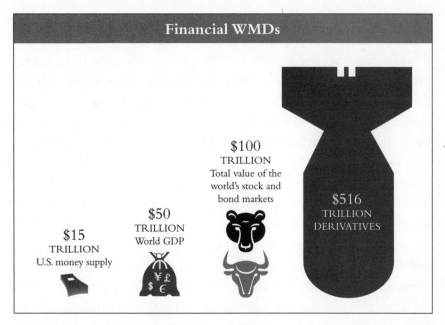

Figure 1.1   Global GDP ($50 Trillion) Compared with Total Derivatives ($516 Trillion) at Start of Crisis in Late 2007 (vs. Global GDP of $64 trillion and Total Derivatives of $795 Trillion in 2010)
SOURCE: U.S. Global Research (www.gamingthemarket.com/financial-armageddon-zombies .html).

and more investment banks, private equity firms, and hedge funds bought up more and more old (stock-exchange-traded) securities and investments, thus creating a climate for asset price inflation ("asset inflation") of the greatest intensity ever seen in recent financial history. The sheer volume of these new derivatives at the end of 2007 amounted to 10 times the real world GPD, or, as Figure 1.1 indicates, over $500 trillion!

The global financial industry does not need the real economy anymore. It divorced itself from the real economy and made transactions with itself: Alone in the United States, the Holy Land of global financial capitalism, its value rose from 2 percent of the national GDP in the 1980s to 8 percent in 2007, just before the crisis. This financial sector has quadrupled in size in the past quarter century and has grown faster than any branch of the real economy.

The financial industry and its hangers-on, ranging from economists and experts to politicians and leading commentators from the media, praised the borderless and unrestrained expansion of the sector and its products (which in reality dealt with the escalation of bank debts and credits without substance) as proof of its strength and superiority: The growth was seen as a dynamic (not as dynamite!) of the market economy, and its advantages were compared to the resources of a state capitulating to numerous problems. The state was granted oversight of the local neighborhood market, but not of the global financial market. It was assumed that the public should be protected from contaminated food but not from rotten credit and the effects of its unregulated growth on jobs and savings.

The old reactionary schools of economics came to life to criticize excessive state deficits and liabilities. The size of the even larger and more threatening private debts was seen as evidence of the debtors' ability to perform in the market rather than as symptoms of a system that was forcing risk upon society. Furthermore, overextended credit was not perceived as a heavy future mortgage being levied on children and grandchildren—as if their education and training as well as a comfortable infrastructure would be self-financing, for any financing for their well-being from the tax system was vigorously rejected.

Leading social politicians and their advisors openly recommended that people invest in the global casino as a secure pension fund for their old age; unregulated funds were presented to be ostensibly as reliable (and as profitable) as the state social system based upon the law and development of income. By these definitions, Germany's welfare state, although still a model for the world, has recently become financially unviable! The fact that profitability, particularly in pensions based on capital investments, is only another term for *high risk* was kept quiet. Now everyone is aware of it.

Today the believers in the fairy tale of the evil state and the good, oh-so-successful capitalists have greatly diminished in numbers. As happened 80 years ago after Black Tuesday (the Wall Street Crash of 1929), and during the subsequent Great Depression, the state is "permitted" to save capitalism, not the other way around.

But which state is responsible for the rescue of global (and stateless) capitalism? None! Nation-states can and must protect the assets of their citizens and firms (which, for tax purposes, are both natural and legal "persons") from banks, funds, and other financial institutions that are threatened with bankruptcy.

However, if the top institutions of the financial sector now expect that governments and central banks take over their risks and inflict themselves with losses based on the notion that they are "too big to fail" (nothing less than a transparent formula of extortion), they abuse the principles of the rule of law, property, society, and market economy: Everyone is responsible for himself. They ensnare the society in the danger of paralysis by "taxflation." Already taxes, which are too high, again have to be increased, and the inflation already looming threatens to be strengthened further.

And why? The financial sector does this to perpetuate one of the oldest and, in the present crisis, merciless structural defects of capitalism, namely, its ability to create real capital from "nothing," even though this is of highly dubious value for society. It is unjust to pardon a notorious and long-since-transformed assassin of the general good of the people, their democratic rights and social welfare state, and their social (not neoliberal) market economy. For the private credit and financial industry is only fighting for the preservation of its age-old privilege: using public money to operate private business. Questions concerning the risks arising from these transactions were countered by the unproven assertion that the collateral damage resulting from the bankruptcy of banks would be still higher: an argument used to demand the system-compromising "socialization of losses," a tactic followed by King

Midas when he watered down his coins. But this has to stop. For only when the credit money of the banks is under the same credit regulations for limits, amounts, and quality control imposed on the state banks regulated by the central bank is there a chance to break through the devilish cycle of inflation and crisis, of money devaluation, of the wresting of wealth from the savers, and the loss of jobs. Only then can the market economy become calculable and immune to crises and freed from the immorality of moneylenders. The present world financial crisis finally gives government leaders the chance to realize this vision.

Will Yesterday's Recipes Help Us Today?

This brings us back to Black Tuesday and the Great Depression 80 years ago. At that time the first systematic bank regulator and control came into existence, simultaneously in the United States and Germany, both states having been heavily traumatized by the crash. The Glass-Steagall Act was passed in the United States. It prohibited investment banks, which were purely speculative banks and had no savings deposits to protect, from recourse to central bank money and aid. So-called investment banks then had to operate their speculative stock market and investment business at their own risk. Just in time for the current crisis, President Clinton signed legislation repealing this law in 1999. As a result, the U.S. central bank could be a player in this crisis. Deposit insurance was created for the banks that took savings deposits and managed them; this is still the backbone of the U.S. banking supervisory system. In Germany, the Kreditwesengesetz (KWG), the Banking Act, came into force in 1934 and became a model for most countries in the world, including the present European Union. For three-quarters of a century the new systems met expectations. However, they could not prevent spectacular bank failures such as the bankruptcy of the Cologne Herrstatt Bank in 1972 in Germany or the savings and loans crisis in the United States in the 1980s and 1990s. But there was no global economic breakdown such as the one that occurred after 1929.

Even larger financial crises could be held within regional limits and controlled—as when the first oil shock broke out in Latin America, or smoldering fires were put out in the old protectorates of the Soviet Union after its collapse. The heated debt crisis of the "Asian Tiger" nations in the late 1990s was contained. Despite the escalation of credit and debt, the Western system of financial capitalism seemed to be more reliable in its operation than ever. This picture changed dramatically overnight. From Washington to London, to Brussels, to Paris, to Tokyo, to Beijing, and to Berlin, the governments of the large industrial and trading states, the so-called G-8, no longer discounted the unthinkable. The global financial system suddenly faced its greatest threat; its meltdown could lead to a dangerous chain reaction of bankrupt firms (of which there are plenty), with socially explosive mass layoffs and black holes in the accounts of the social systems and state budgets as a consequence. See Figure 1.2.

Therefore, the financial system had to be helped, even if it cost a lot of money. Already the G-8 nations had put up trillions for the purpose, an amount reliably estimated at $9 trillion, or the equivalent of close to three times the GDP of Germany. Experts feared that further incalculable sums could follow. One does not know what is more frightening: the sums or the justification. The amounts already constituted the largest public financing in peacetime. The rationale given to the people for this, the most adventurous action ever undertaken by democratically elected governments, would result in the creation of government debts of such vast sums that they could lead to the destruction of state credits, and to the printing of money in amounts that threatened to lead to hyperinflation after the crisis was resolved. The

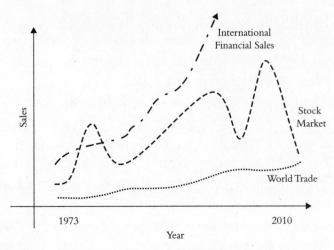

Figure 1.2   Fever Thermometer of Our Sick Financial Economy

argument, however, that the damage to society and the state would be even worse without these means was persuasive neither from a moral perspective nor from the viewpoint of a market economy.

The financial world still assumes that no state can afford to allow its largest financial firms to fail. But they seem not to recognize that it is exactly this condition of being "too big to fail" that is the real threat for the world of nation-states. Nations are learning in this crisis something they did not realize from the previous one—that single actors who are too big, powerful, and influential can extort them and show little reluctance to do so. Only by keeping these financial dinosaurs from failing can a society avoid becoming their prey.

Thus we must consider why the control and warning systems erected since 1929 have failed us so miserably.

The Finance Sector Always Underestimates the Risks of Its Innovations

On a visit to the London School of Economics on November 5, 2008, the British Queen asked: How could this credit crunch happen? She did not get an immediate response, but this question can be answered.

A comparison with former great crises of past centuries makes clear what is new this time, and what is old. Each of the major financial crises of the past was due to financial innovations. The inventors or users of these innovations became so enthusiastic, one could say blinded, that they overlooked or grossly underestimated the risks for themselves and for others. And what role did the regulators or "policemen" of the financial sector play? If they existed, as in the case of the United States and Germany since the 1930s, then they necessarily oriented themselves by their former experience—stretching back 80 years or longer. But the question is: Did the established knowledge of the regulators keep up with the advances in the technological innovations of the financial world?

Can regulators ever keep up with innovators?

Since biblical times, have not the angels of darkness always been brighter than those of light? It is not unusual for criminals to be ahead of the regular police in their knowledge of how to crack security systems or to hack computers. Why should it be different in the financial sector?

But this time it could have been different. For there was writing on the wall before the crisis erupted. The inspectors had the opportunity to prevent it. They behaved as did Belshazzar in Babylon: They did not want to admit what they saw. For this time the *macroeconomic* consequences of financial progress were clearly as recognizable as accumulating explosives for the national and world economy. One could see that for decades the banking world had wandered from the regulated zones of state control to the deregulated no-man's-land of the global interbanking markets. It was common knowledge that the international banking community tested out new financial techniques in this regulation-free zone and replaced the old established and best rules of accounting and evaluation with new and dubious ones.

The consequences spoke for themselves: What one owned ("asset prices") rocketed up higher and higher, forming one inflationary bubble after another in the capital and investment markets. And the inflationary gains in the financial sector did not remain hidden, and not only among top managers. Every macroeconomist could calculate the consequences to be expected from anticipated "second round" effects: Those in the financial sector earned value worth multiple times what the corporate sector managed to produce—but with what? Not with real economic growth, productivity, and increases in capital in production facilities, but always from higher (inflationary) surcharges on real existing assets. That stocks and other monetary investments always became more expensive did not signify that real property and business assets grew in value to the same extent.

Nor did the maldistribution of income remain invisible: The actual earned incomes from companies and earnings stagnated, remaining way behind those in the financial branches. The consequence for economic development was a lack of demand, which continued to weaken. Demand had to become weaker! For the new Midases and Croesuses could not spend so much to put enough money back into the income stream to keep it going.

What actually remained, and was nevertheless not clearly recognized as "systemic" or identified as "bursting" by any of the 20-plus surviving Nobel laureates in economics, was the constant upgrading of ultimately "dead" capital from shares, real estate, and other financial claims on property and investments that had been around a long time: an inflation of capital stocks that already existed, namely the asset inflation mentioned earlier. And ignoring the resulting consequences for the real economy, its laws of circulation and interactions were just as striking and dangerous. Phony but economically effective "excess savings" were extent. The new rich did not invest as much in the real as in the nominal, by putting money into always new, far more lucrative financial investments, and by extension into bubbles that they were continuously pumping up. This money was lost for the financing of new investments in the real economy or for job creation.

However, when the air, which they had earlier pumped into the bubbles, escaped (usually only partially), and what they owned again lost value, they were then bitten by the dog that they themselves had let off the leash. This had been obvious for decades, yet an official warning was never given. Everyone was taken by surprise: politicians, regulators, and the army of experts. Now that the child lies in the well, there is no paucity of ex-post analyses and explanations as to how it got there. Just as in Max Frisch's drama *Firebugs*, the zeitgeist analysts and commentators calmly watched as the arsonists lit the fuse. Each short circuit in their heads could be the spark that set off the fire. And so it happened. . . .

Herein lies the big difference between this crisis and all others. Unlike those crises past, the present crisis could have been stopped by the knowledge of the banking system on the part of central banks, financial forecasters, and qualified gurus in science, politics, and the ever-present media. Accordingly, it is worthwhile to look back a moment.

Four Fatal Innovations of Global Banking

What in the current world financial crisis is so new that it blew the old fuses? The global financial world, domiciled mainly in Anglo-Saxon England and the United States, has been steered since the middle of the 1970s by four basic financial engineering innovations enabled, in turn, by bad policy decisions. These innovations have in common the backdrop of the suspension of the Bretton Woods international monetary system in the spring of 1973 (see the discussion in Chapter 5).

First, globalization and the world unification of financial markets made it easy for the global players, including the leading institutions of high finance, to withdraw from the laws and regulations of their central banks and regulatory offices and to discover entirely new financial products and refinancing techniques. These innovations permitted them the following actions.

Second, global players cut the umbilical cords to their central banks and decoupled their interests from their traditional suppliers, savers, and depositors. In a two-step banking system they could replace the first money circulating function between money-creating central banks and the mainly private commercial banks that brought this central bank money into circulation, with a second, "in-house" function. Instead of having to pump money from the central bank against collateral, they created liquidity through their own production—the lending from bank to bank.

Thus, from time to time the financiers could procure means in their own sector: in their self-constructed global interbanking market. There every bank became indebted to others and paid with new, self-created "innovative products"—the often-mentioned derivatives. Within a few years the highest and most fragile tower since Babel was erected in the extraterritorial no-man's-land of global financial markets—only made up of the paper of unsecured bank-to-bank liabilities.

However, the new market with new products was open only to the leading institutions of high finance. The world of small regional and local banks remained shut out of this paradise of the ability to create money independent of the central bank. The small financial branches were permitted to invest, that is, hand over money, but not to borrow. On paper the national money constitutions still existed, yet only with limited validity.

Once invented, the new world of high finance permitted fantastic sales and profits. In the last year before the outbreak of the crisis in 2007, financiers calculated only in thousands of billions:

trillions. Financial transactions in terms of credit and investment ran ahead of the real world of global gross domestic product with seven-league boots. With their numbers and unreal profits the financial world arrived in the stars, and even though called "global," they left the world behind.

Third, with its new, inexhaustible bubbling sources of profits, the financial sector ended its oldest contract with capitalism—service for the real economy. It became superfluous; one could earn much more from securities trading and portfolio investment activities. One could do without credit customers such as entrepreneurs and outside investors. Why bother to lose time with them if as an investment (or, more accurately, "speculation") bank, one could earn much more on the asset markets of the world (stock markets, real estate, and other financial paper investments) than with bread-and-butter businesses in the real world?

Fourth, the financial sector made an even greater discovery. One could recapture the fixed money and reinvest and reliquidate it. One only had to "securitize" it. Out of the assets already financed one could create new ones and sell them under competent- and secretive-sounding names such as asset-backed securities (ABSs), credit-default swaps (CDSs), and collateral-debt obligations (CDOs) and sell them not only to one's own branches, but through unsuspecting advisors to an even more unsuspecting public. The financial world had discovered a *perpetual motion machine*: Money that could be used for internal debts and then reinvested could be brought back and bundled into securitization of existing commitments! The newly discovered "second" money circulation among banks, savers, or real investors ran like clockwork without the disturbance of central banks and brought in profits that real-world investors dependent upon the products of entrepreneurs could not even begin to dream of. High finance arrived not only in heaven, but in seventh heaven!

Of course, sometimes it became snared and there were losses due to friction in the perpetual motion machine. But there was always a counter that could be brought to bear; one shifted to an ad hoc temporary storage or a general-purpose alternative: Innovation 4a. Special-purpose vehicles (SPVs) could take over at short notice, transforming products that are hard to sell into investments on time. Meanwhile, of course, "on time" had come to mean forever, or in the new language used in the industry for contaminated investments, toxic waste mills. These purchases were made on credit, which the SPV received, because the lenders used the toxic waste as security before its real value was known. The buyers got their money, and their auditors a "clean" balance sheet, which remained obscure for their nonaccounting partners in the sister subsidiaries of the SPV. The organizations for regulatory control (supervisory boards, auditors, and regulators) considered this SPV to represent paying customers. Only when an accident occurred (e.g., if the SPV was threatened with insolvency) did the regulators notice that it was a matter of "illegitimate" daughters of the banks that they had to back up, given the agreements they had made previously. The banks neither consolidated the SPV in the balance sheet of the mother nor accounted for the liability obligations "below the line."

But Innovation #4 was fatal for the previous three. When it suddenly became clear that the new financial products could not be sold, the crisis broke out with the elementary force of a volcano. One market segment triggered the mistrust in the new derivatives: the U.S. housing market. The business in under-collateralized or subprime mortgages collapsed after it had been formed and the resale of these mortgages in the form of massive bundling and securitization sparked widespread distrust. One debacle triggered another. The market for securitized paper turned into a seller's market overnight, and the seemingly inexhaustible bubbly credit donors turned into a huge black hole: All that was to be received and that existed in "interbanking liquidity" disappeared down its throat. The perpetual machine came to a halt with a sudden jerk; the new securities turned into "junk paper" overnight and had to (and still have to) be written down to nothing, or almost nothing. This depreciation eats up *trillions* in equity in leading institutions: It is what is really going on at the very best addresses in global (mainly Western) finance.

The crisis revealed that the most innovative and lucrative banking business in the past 20 to 25 years was in reality the most brazen, obvious, and yet best-organized financial swindle of all time!

Essential Reforms

The nucleus of the systemic crisis was latent in all the financial crises in Black Tuesday of 1929 and the Great Depression of the 1930s (the beginning of the globalized financial economy). It can spread anytime through the global networks of the financial sector, like a flu epidemic. In this context the old crises have become global due to national and social innovation risks. There was never a systemic risk associated with the financial crises of the times before 1929. At that time those who went bankrupt in the financial sector posed a danger neither for the state nor for the stability of the financial system. The gold standard held the world of states and currencies together: It immunized the system from the consequences of a speculation crisis. To learn this again is one of the homework assignments yet to be completed by political elites at the high tables of policy today. The United States is particularly inexperienced in this regard, having joined the gold standard late (*de jure* in 1913, *de facto* in 1914) as the paper dollar could be backed up by gold after the great victory of the United States in World War I.

The first systemic crisis emanating from the financial sector was that of 80 years ago. Not only did it produce official bank control and financial supervision, but this era shapes our understanding of the crisis today—but, alas, with the wrong direction and emphasis. The regulatory laws and, on this basis, the active controllers still view the danger of the crisis to be located in the dangerous interaction between banks and the public they have seduced with the reduction in the costs of speculation. However, the place where the crisis occurs and from which it radiates to the real sectors of the economy is not the same source as in the past. It is no longer the stock market, but the interbank market.

The extent to which anachronistic 1929 imagination still dominates financial market supervision was illustrated recently when the put option of short selling was banned by German financial market supervision. Moreover, a study of the 1929 crisis demonstrated that exactly these policies promoted the decline of prices through the floor. The current world financial crisis teaches a different lesson: It stems neither from the public, which underestimates its speculative risks, nor from the stock exchange, on which its impact has abated. (This is particularly the case in Germany, for example, since only 1 percent of all German businesses has access to the stock market and can take out credit from there.) The trigger and center of the current financial crisis is the globally interconnected large banking system of high finance: They and their innovations are the cause of the crisis—not the public.

Therefore, the present crisis cannot be compared with earlier financial crises, and not with the one following 1929. Because the supervisory authorities, scientific consensus, and a host of financial analysts and banking advisors denied that such a crisis could develop, it evolved without resistance into a global pandemic. And what damage it has caused.

Four Conclusions from the Financial Crisis

Four conclusions can be drawn, which also identify the core principles for a coherent plan for crisis management in order to prevent further crises from developing along these lines:

1. The control of the interbank markets has to be returned to the central banks, which are responsible for monetary and financial stability. The commercial monopoly of money and credit creation founded by global investment banks that began with the liquidation of the world monetary system of Bretton Woods must be ended and its foundations removed, or the crisis will return in the future. It is still unclear how this de facto cartel of global investment banks and its offshoots (investment funds of all varieties, with 90 percent of hedge funds precrisis being registered in the unregulated Cayman Islands) can be controlled or deterred. But it will require a system of global bank supervision or a new world monetary system similar to the gold standard that limits the expansion of financial markets.

2. National bank regulation must become more sharply focused upon *macroeconomic* criteria in the future instead of being satisfied, as in the past, with controls based on legal and microeconomic technical balances. Macroeconomic consequences of error–ridden banking behavior not only pose a systemic threat, but are also easier to detect than the microeconomic discrepancies. From the macro perspective the sinners cannot simply disappear in the maze of their accounting systems, which can be wiped away or retouched. Asset inflation (the building up of bubbles, the dichotomies between financial and real economic growth, the consequences of income and wealth distribution, the numbers and warning signals of the statistical offices and international

organizations) are all in the public record. Any macro-economist can draw the conclusions from this information.

3. However, this macro-oriented process does not make the classical control of banking and balances superfluous. On the contrary, these classical controllers must learn from the most recent crisis and build this learning into their framework. This control must target another powerful, de facto global cartel largely unknown in the public sphere: the *rating agencies*. The three leading rating agencies in the world control 90 percent of the market for the evaluation of bank balances and financial assets: Standard & Poor's (40 percent), Moody's (40 percent), and Fitch (10 percent). These agencies significantly contributed to the outbreak and intensification of the crisis by changing the good old conservative "lowest value principle" (enshrined, for example, in the German Commercial Code of 1897) to the "fair value principle" of the American International Accounting System (IAS)—on their own initiative. The IAS permits the use of variable criteria for evaluating assets rather than keeping reliable, unchangeable evaluation criteria in the middle of the duration period of a contract. The banks could, in consultation with their auditors, determine the risk assessment of the content of their own holdings. Auditors were thus made into accomplices!

By the mid-1980s, corresponding with the acceleration of asset inflation, leading banks in the United States and Germany had shifted to the new IAS accounting rules. The extent to which the IAS has functioned as procyclical, intensifying the crisis, only recently became clear with the fixing of the write-downs in the bank balances: Because too little was written off before the crisis, providing for too little in reserves, one now had to make up for lost time during the crisis. Suddenly, leading international banks and large asset managers had to reveal that because of back-dated depreciation up to this point, as much as two-thirds or more of their own liable equity capital had been lost. These banks and the liable states behind them have worked out an obscure arrangement with the IAS that continues to aggravate the crisis as costs hit both the states cleaning up the mess and their taxpayers. Either the IAS must be reformed in the light of the experience of the crisis, or the institutions of high finance must return to the standards that apply to banks in business outside the front door, that is, people's banks and savings banks. Surely the spirit of the honest businessperson does not dwell only in these local banks and not show up at all in the top institutions of the world financial system!

4. Were the bank supervision institutions in the United States, Germany, England, and Switzerland—the home countries of the largest and most vulnerable individual institutions—really as overwhelmed as they now claim? This can be seriously questioned. No examiner could overlook the superior profits of these institutions in their trading of financial products, particularly the innovative ones. Nor could any expert overlook the fact that for decades these banks were on the verge of abandoning their traditional bread-and-butter business credit customers. For these high-finance institutions the good old "3-6-3 rule" no longer applied: 3 percent was the price of the money paid by the bank in interest, 6 percent was paid by the customer for credit, and as of 3 o'clock one was home or on the golf course!

Once one left the passive deposit business of savings and central banks, the focus shifted to the active business of loan customers. Accordingly, the charted curve of safe interest income of all major players in the industry has gone down over the past decade, particularly at the banks involved in the ongoing "sanitizing" process (from HSBC to UBS to Deutsche Bank). Their fabulous returns did not come from the old respectable banking business, but from the new risky one. No bank examiner could overlook that in all these institutions the credit business related to investing in industry (in relation to total balances and their own equity) had been sharply reduced while the duration and trade related to portfolios of securities and other financial stocks had greatly increased—the lion's share being new and now-toxic financial products.

Under the eyes of the auditors investment banks had become wholesalers in financial titles. They were obviously playing with fire. The auditors could have warned them before they got burned. The European Union also failed to contribute to the safe operation of the European banking system as evidenced in their guidelines adopting the IAS rules. One can be thankful that not all credit institutions followed this precarious advice. Only in the case of off-balance-sheet risks—that fine-spun but fraudulent false accounting technique—could mitigating circumstances be claimed.

If the state is called upon to help people in this crisis, then it should be to aid the victims, not those who brought it about! This help is cheaper for the society than bailing out the banks—both financially and socially. It costs a fraction of what the taxpayer had to put up to take over worthless bank assets and debts. At most, the cost is in the billions, not the trillions.

For the period after the crisis it is important to note that the present distribution of money between the financial and real sectors in the crisis-ridden countries is wrong and must be corrected; it must not be carried forward in any event. "Too much money" in the financial sector caused this crisis. Now "not enough money" threatens to lengthen and deepen the crisis in the real economy (for investment as well as for consumption). The bailout packages of governments struck by crisis-panic on both sides of the Atlantic work toward perpetuating this status of the financial sector, thereby preparing the way for the next crisis. For the transfer of bank debt to government accounts ("bad banks") and the subsidies and guarantees for their battered capital lead not to the salvation of capitalism but rather threaten its demise.

Keynes, Properly Understood

The governments in the United States as well as in old Europe have fallen into adopting the role of system destroyer. They follow Lenin's cynical advice (according to Keynes) that whoever wants to destroy the bourgeois society only needs to debauch its currency. Lenin pursued this actively whereas Keynes feared it would result out of a lack of understanding of those in power and out of a lack of morals on the part of money managers and actors. For it is deeply inappropriate to reward those who cause damage: both to demand it, and then to do it. Such an attitude and policy cannot be justified even in the short run. For the money overhang in the financial sector cannot bring the economy to life, but only trigger the next asset inflation. Therefore, the current shortage of money in the real economy must be eliminated quickly, because it will prevent sustainable recovery, burden the labor market, and drive the country into even higher debt.

Whoever believes that the damaged world of the big banks can save the currency and state finances through unlimited fiscal-deficit spending invokes a different Keynes than the author of his books. It was Keynes who called on the governments of states to put the money economy into the service of the real economy, and not vice versa.[2] Listening to the real Keynes is one of the few ways to determine whether the Midas cult will gain the upper hand or be banned for the sake of prosperity in the brave new world economy.

Chapter 2

The Great Bluff
The American Way out of the Crisis

The circulation of confidence is better than the circulation of money.

—James Madison

The world financial crisis was the result of the Anglo-American vision of globalization: *laissez-faire* free markets, privatization, the razzle-dazzle of deregulation, and creative destruction without limits. The crisis began with risks uncovered in the United States, magnified by its technological and financial innovations. But America's amnesia, its ability to forget the past and then to re-create itself, helped to bring recovery first to the New World. When the global economy appeared most troubled, investments flowed in to stabilize the dollar in the short run, to subsidize past deficits, and to cover the hyperspending of the Bush and Obama administrations and a spendthrift Congress. The high-risk American strategy can be perceived as a great bluff—multiple-trillion-dollar bets made in order to head off

deflation and to introduce health, energy, and other reforms
without real assets to back them up—presaging a high probability
of hyperinflation and a discounted dollar in the future. Whether
the results of Obama's policy finally reach beyond free-market
capitalism "with a human face" to transform the American system
remains to be seen. But what cannot be doubted is that the
initiative was seized by the state from the markets in a credit
meltdown. There was a profound shift in leveraging from the
private to the public sector.

Initially, the great bluff appeared to work and the U.S. economy appeared to begin a fragile recovery in 2009. But then the
Europeans called America's bluff, pushing developed nations to cut
their deficits in order to begin to live within their means and to
keep their government bonds affordable. Meanwhile, long-term
unemployment hit record levels, states and municipalities ran out
of money, unemployment insurance was cut off, and a political
stalemate consolidated around the position that there should be no
new benefits and no new taxes—an unsustainable compromise
given huge debts and the need for stimulus for job creation.

The exploitation of the world's credit and natural resources by
the United States, and its ability to run debts in its own reserve
currency, precipitated the meltdown of global casino capitalism.
But this very same risky, free-rider strategy became the main
hope for correcting the self-inflicted breakdown. However,
success depended upon a delicate balancing act by the Obama
administration: targeting sufficient deficit spending to bring about
economic recovery without overdoing it to the point that
Republican resistance blocked all legislation or that foreigners lost
confidence in the dollar. If, as one pundit put it, the policies of the
Obama administration constitute a rainbow in a dark, cloudy
world, then if the rainbow disappears, the clouds still remain.

Accordingly, the other side of Obama's balancing act remains
the most difficult: how to cut trillion-dollar annual budget deficits

in order to consolidate confidence in the state's solvency and currency while at the same time not undermining the recovery or job creation. Neither his success in getting a national health reform through Congress nor watershed U.S. financial regulation legislation is necessarily helpful in achieving this critical balance. The clouds darkened as the U.S. structural deficit was ranked by the Organization for Economic Cooperation and Development (OECD) as the worst of all developed countries except Japan. The Federal Reserve Bank continued to buy hundreds of billions of long-term treasury bonds to keep the anemic recovery going. Meanwhile, the stalemated U.S. Congress failed to agree on a reasonable policy to cut spending and raise taxes enough to stabilize long-term confidence in the United States in the world markets despite an extension of the irresponsible Bush-era tax cuts.

A Brief Tour of How We Got Here

It was but a few short steps from American supply-side economics to loose loans for unqualified mortgages to the new finance of derivatives to the $55 trillion market in credit-default swaps. Globalization sped this process up in nanoseconds with technology and instant capitalization. Meanwhile Federal Reserve Chairman Alan Greenspan played the saxophone to the tune "Derivatives Can Do No Wrong," and the happy motto of the roaring 1990s— "It's the Economy, Stupid!"—was transformed into a more ominous theme, "It's the Derivatives, Stupid!" It was as if a new set of unelected founding fathers decided to assume a *tabula rasa* in economics in order to build up abstract, high-tech, mathematical models of financial contracts based on the volatile swings in value of other financial assets (derivatives), putting them into practice on a global scale regardless of who understood them or their consequences. The perceptual map of greedy speculators expanded like a balloon until it popped. Nevertheless, global investors sought out the dollar for stability. And Obama's election and economic program acted as tranquillizers for a patient with a heart attack.

Ironically, it was not the overextension of military adventures that threatened to be the turning point in the decline of the American empire, but the financial hubris of high-tech financial derivatives and the "banksters" who pushed them. "Safety through global market diversification" was the elixir of this love fest. But the systemic nature of world financial bets assured that there was no safety in spreading risks, that everything was inter-connected, and that all assets would take a hit at once as people panicked the world over, unsure of what anything was worth. One recalls comedian Eddie Cantor's comment in 1932 when his broker recommended the purchase of stocks for old age: "I did and it worked! Within a week I became an old man."[1]

But how did we get this far? What happened to the checks and balances that are supposed to keep extreme power grabs and revolutionary policies from upsetting the stability of the American system?

The answer seems to lie in philosopher John Dewey's iden-tification of the United States as "a money culture" on one hand, and in the American belief expressed by Thomas Jefferson that "the government is best which governs least," on the other hand.[2] If the government is supposed to stay out of all business and economic affairs while the overwhelming desire of the population is to get rich and to maximize economic growth through any means, no matter how untested, then rampant financial specula-tion and booms and busts are inevitable. This is not to say that Americans do not have values that go beyond money. Rather, to the extent that they do, they are often willing to delegate financial decisions to "experts" and to go on with their lives taking for granted that all will turn out well. But many of these so-called experts were mere marketing sharks: Whether pushing mortgages to people who could not afford to maintain them at the low end, or black-box hedge funds that did not reveal where money would be invested at the high end, financial products were sold massively to clients who did not understand them. Nor did most of the experts, for that matter. Those few who did figured out how to leverage their risks against the U.S. government as the insurer of last resort (Goldman Sachs being particularly successful at this). The U.S. government obliged (with the exception of Lehman Brothers' brokerage firm) and continues to do so. While the government never identified how many companies are "too big to fail," the number seems to be elastic and the Obama administration avoided the suggested therapy of making the banks that are "too big" smaller. Most of the chips in the game have been placed on big government and big banks or companies in an all-out effort to save "that old-time capitalism." Bonuses were but the tip of the iceberg!

Globalization sped up social life to such an extent that few people understood what they were investing in. Financial products became so technically complex that even those promoting them did not grasp their basic assumptions. With more funds than the number of stocks on the New York Stock Exchange, for many time-pressed investors complex investment vehicles became a blur of acronyms where stocks hid their real value behind their labels like old wine that may already have turned bad. Add to this the American tendency to forget history as soon as it is made in order to feel free to do whatever one wants, plus a bevy of unregulated, bright, opportunistic "financial engineers" building obscure leveraged products, and you have the makings of a perfect storm. After all, today about half of the stock transactions on the New York Stock Exchange are comprised of microsecond computer transactions (high-frequency trading) by the richest firms, like Goldman Sachs and JPMorgan Chase, which can afford the best computers and traders—transactions that added little of social value to the economy. The repeal of the Glass-Steagall Act (of 1933) by

Congress in 1999 removed the separation of investment banks and depository banks and set the stage for such speculative bank activities, contributing greatly to the 2007–2010 financial crisis.

How American Globalization Revolutionized Finance

The American preoccupation with money as a surrogate for freedom combined with the nation's constant innovative, technological capacity served to revolutionize global finance. The financial sector displaced manufacturing as a lead sector in the U.S. economy (if one includes real estate transactions, leasing, renting, management, and sales services under financial services). Dollars matter a lot to Americans: They fuel the culture of over-consumption. When entering the financial crisis, consumption accounted for some two-thirds of the U.S. gross national product (GNP). Other cultures such as Japan and Germany avoid discussions of money, while quietly saving it to a fault (Japan and German savings amounted to twice the percentage of GDP as did savings in the United States in 2009, according to the International Monetary Fund (IMF): 23 percent and 22 percent versus 10.8 percent, respectively). The American Dream is often perceived as a very concrete dream with a house attached, which more likely than not is heavily mortgaged. And the temptation to stretch dollars to permit the maximum number of people to participate in this dream appeared as a natural follow-up to the dot-com boom, which gave average U.S. citizens a leg up internationally in technological literacy and e-money trading (often based on home-equity loans). Little did the people in a remote Dutch village know that the value of their pensions was determined by the foolish decisions of underemployed Americans to buy houses with no money down in a speculative binge.

The dollar was once "as good as gold," particularly following World War II, in the era of fixed exchange rates. The U.S. Treasury printed (and continues to print) as many dollars as it sees fit to fuel the global economy, leading to impressive economic growth in the 1950s and 1960s. But since that time, the dollar has become decoupled from gold and anything else concrete: Its value rests only on the faith of millions of people the world over in the U.S. economy. More recently, although this faith has been replaced with skepticism, foreign banks and citizens hold so many dollars in reserves that they cannot afford to throw in the towel on the currency: The United States has the rest of the world by its outstanding dollars! Globally over 60 percent of official foreign exchange reserves are held in dollars.

But then the global financial crisis changed this perception. There was a decline from 74 percent to less than 60 percent of foreign reserves held in dollars in emerging and developing nations in the past decade according to the IMF. The greater troubles of other economies (Japan, European Union, United Kingdom) and other currencies (yen, euro, pound) kept the dollar afloat despite great structural weaknesses in the U.S. economy. The election of 2008 had little impact upon the structural problems that threaten to bring the dollar's value down in the future. America's days of extreme overconsumption—of less than 5 percent of the world's population using up 25 percent of the world's resources—have come to an end. No longer will the majority of the population be able to spend 99 percent of their income and save but 1 percent as they have in recent years. The nation of big spenders has become a country of small savers.

It is unlikely that the Obama administration and U.S. Congress will be able to reverse structural economic difficulties so deep as to cause the majority of the population to lower the standard of living they have so long enjoyed. For in addition to its long-term debt, annual deficits, and projected shortfalls of the Social Security and Medicare accounts, the United States was suddenly confronted with the threat of insolvency of many of its banks to the point that the sustainability of the entire banking system was thrown into doubt. And since the U.S. Treasury served as the "lender of last resort" for the world economy (symbolized by its dominant role in the IMF and World Bank), monitoring the key world reserve currency, the legitimacy of the global financial system was put in jeopardy.

Wanted: An Emperor with Clothes

Which is the more disturbing thought: that the emperor has no clothes, or that there is no emperor?

The United States has not been a conventional empire. Some have implied it is just a republic with a strong case of hubris, or excessive pride and ambition. But no one can doubt the dominance of American military power: The United States accounts for 46 percent of global military spending compared with an average of 4 to 5 percent each by the United Kingdom, France, Japan, and China. Few question that this military power has been overextended, as has happened with all empires in the past. Nor until 2008 was there much doubt that the United States also dominated in financial power, managing the world's key reserve currency and setting the trends in capital investments and techniques. Indeed, it was widely assumed that the United States was the "lender of last resort" in times of crisis—the only country with the financial resources and will to bail out the global economic system in a downturn.

But the world financial crisis of 2008 ended the belief that the United States could rise to the occasion and come to the rescue economically and politically. First, given his record unpopularity and lame-duck status, few granted credibility to the administration of President George W. Bush (no emperor!). Second, many people in the world came to believe that the United States had overconsumed and overspent for so long that very possibly it did not have enough cash to serve as the lender of last resort. In the era of floating exchange rates a currency is only worth what people believe it to be worth. If the superpower seems not to have enough to bail out the world economy, a decline of trust and belief in the entire financial system is inevitable.

Not only did the reign of the ideology of free-market capitalism come to the end of its tether, but the legitimacy of the money system that backed it up did as well. U.S. government officials politicized their own currency and their management of the international system for national interests over the past half century. Consider the overheated printing presses spewing out dollars under President Lyndon Johnson to pay for the Vietnam War and "the Great Society," under President Ronald Reagan to break the financial back of the Soviet Union, and under President George W. Bush to pay for the wars in Iraq and Afghanistan, and the unending War on Terror. And now under President Obama, the U.S. government is placing annual "trillion-dollar bets" that in some decade to come the U.S. government will be able to pay back the massive government spending used to jump-start the American economy. Such abuse of the currency served to undermine the belief in the U.S. dollar and in the competence of American financial and political managers. As a result the world economy in the twenty-first century has become a multilaterally managed system, regardless of whether Americans like it so. At the turn of this century former Fed Chairman Paul Volcker noted that the global economy was kept going by the foolish over-consumption of the American people, and that one could only hope that they would continue to keep it up. This historical phase is over.

The American habit of printing too many dollars goes back years, ever since financial elites began undermining the conservatively designed economic agreements of 1944, signed in Bretton Woods, New Hampshire. Bretton Woods established the dollar as the key international reserve currency, fixed to gold at $35 per ounce. Collusion between American political and financial players used the residue of stability from the Bretton Woods system as a free ride to maximize economic growth and short-term profits. But this implied a huge conflict of interest, with devastating long-term consequences. As managers of the world's key currency and trustee of the global financial system, it is in the interest of the U.S. government to appear as an objective, responsible conservator of global stability in order to maintain its own long-term hegemony. But this hegemony-stability hypothesis is undermined if a free market fundamentalist ideology permits banks, nonbank banks, and hedge funds to use the credibility of the U.S. financial system as a springboard for high-risk financial products and derivatives without any regulation or oversight as to the relationship between equity and leverage. Lord Acton's famous statement that "Power tends to corrupt; absolute power corrupts absolutely" has been magnified on a global scale by American political and economic players. The Clinton and Bush II administrations ruined the credibility of the dollar-based international financial system by permitting, in fact *stimulating*, the creation of trillions of dollars' worth of financial derivatives, free-riding on the belief of the majority of the world's population that the United States would continue to be the fortress of stability in times of global economic turbulence.

New technologies greatly expanded the use of leverage or borrowing by individuals, financial institutions, and governments. From the dot-com bubble driven by technological and financial innovation, the United States led the way to a housing bubble financed by credit derivatives that overshadowed the dot-com boom and bust, as illustrated in Figure 2.1.

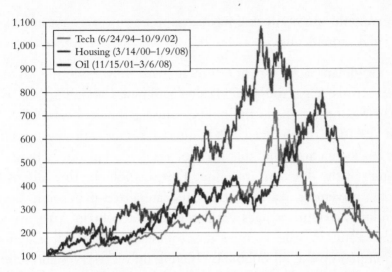

Figure 2.1 A Tale of Three Bubbles: Tech, Housing, and Oil
SOURCE: Data from FactSet, S&P, and Nasdaq as of June 13, 2008. Indexed to 100: Nasdaq
Composite, NYMEX Crude Oil, S&P 500 Homebuilders.

How Goldman Sachs Milked Bubble Trouble

The world's most powerful investment bank, Goldman Sachs,
stimulated and tapped all three of these bubbles for incredible
profits. As journalist Matt Taibbi colorfully summed it up in 2009:

> The bank's unprecedented reach and power have enabled
> it to turn all America into a giant pump-and-dump scam,
> manipulating whole economic sectors for years at a time,
> moving the dice game as this or that market collapses, and
> all the time gorging itself on the unseen costs that are
> breaking families everywhere—high gas prices, rising
> consumer-credit rates, half-eaten pension funds, mass lay-
> offs, future taxes to pay off bail-outs. . . . The bank is a
> huge, highly sophisticated engine for converting the useful,
> deployed wealth of society into the least useful, most

wasteful and insoluable substance on Earth—pure profit for rich individuals.[3]

Goldman Sachs was not content with fully exploiting investment trusts (e.g., the Blue Ridge and Shenandoah trusts) as a vehicle contributing to the bubble causing the crash of 1929.[4] In the 1990s it introduced IPOs (initial public offerings) selling the stocks of companies that had not yet made a profit, stoking the engine of the dot-com machine. This was followed by Goldman Sachs's inventive use of CDOs (collateralized-debt obligations) bundling toxic mortgages with solid ones to obtain AAA investment ratings in order to hype the real estate bubble. Subsequently it pumped up the oil bubble by buying up oil reserves and selling shares, driving up the cost of the commodity way beyond any consideration of supply and demand by using a loophole in the law granted to Goldman Sachs alone in a semisecret letter from the U.S. government. If and when the cap-and-trade carbon tax bubble gets going, do not be surprised if firms pay taxes directly to Goldman Sachs rather than the government, given the bank's huge stake in this next speculative venture and the bank's ability to structure the market.[5] Meanwhile, Goldman Sachs had to settle lawsuits out of court against its practice of bundling toxic mortgages with good ones in order to get AAA ratings on the financial product and then selling it to unwary investors (so-called "dumb money"), while simultaneously betting against (or shorting) its own products!

Meanwhile, in an interview with the *Times* of London, the CEO of Goldman Sachs said he was merely a banker "doing God's work."[6] The assets of the company at that time came to $1 trillion. Later, he tried to make up for this arrogance by tapping Warren Buffett (his largest shareholder) and Professor Michael Porter of Harvard to help decide how to distribute a donation of $200 million to train small business owners in community colleges and another $300 million to provide help for small businesses. This payoff, of course, should have been demanded by former CEO of Goldman Sachs and then–Treasury Secretary Hank Paulson in the first place, in return for the taxpayer's assistance in bailing out Goldman (which did not really need it) and other investment banks (which did).

Investment banks and hedge funds became money machines detached from social value, with speculative capital undermining the Western capitalist system itself as it inundates the potential hot spots of the world economy with capital without any significant state regulatory controls. But let us go back a minute to understand the story of the crisis we are still experiencing.

Origins of the Financial Crisis

That the financial crisis began with thousands of mortgages being issued by banks to Americans who wanted to buy a home they could not afford is beyond dispute. Why this was allowed to occur and to mushroom into credit derivatives that brought down the global financial system as we know it is somewhat more complicated to explain, but a good place to start is the critical role played by former Fed Chairman Alan Greenspan.

In his youth Greenspan was a true believer in the philosophy of Ayn Rand. She was a radical free-market libertarian who argued in novels and essays that government intervention in the economy was a form of collectivism that oppressed the true creative individual, stifling innovative production for the sake of masses of human parasites who sponged off those who produced economic growth. In *Atlas Shrugged*, Rand's protagonist organizes a strike of all the nation's productive capitalists in order to shut down the American industrial system, which comes about with devastating consequences. That a conservative Rand-like Greenspan would appeal to the administrations of Presidents Nixon, Ford, and Reagan, under whom he served, should come as no surprise. Unregulated, privatized free markets were the mantra of Reagan and Greenspan for the sake of economic growth and to push the Soviet Union (the ultimate collectivist state from which Ayn Rand had escaped) to the wall economically and technologically. And the strategy worked! But only at huge economic costs for the United States as well as the Soviet Union. From being the world's largest creditor nation after World War II, by the mid-1980s the United States became the world's largest debtor nation. Free-market fundamentalism was the philosophy that stimulated this development.

President Ronald Reagan teamed up with British Prime Minister Margaret Thatcher to initiate a global revolt of the rich— a globalized capitalism that freed up markets from government regulation so that individuals could maximize their own interests and wealth without limits. Labor unions were crushed and supply-side economics was in full swing.[7]

Greenspan was appointed Chairman of the Federal Reserve in June 1986 and opened the money supply after the stock market crash that occurred three months later. He saw to it that capital was readily available for the dot-com boom of the roaring 1990s. Together with Treasury Secretary Robert Rubin (formerly of Goldman Sachs), Greenspan fended off efforts to regulate derivatives, arguing that they increased economic growth and that the risk of a viral systemic crisis from derivatives, while possible, was exceedingly small and worth taking. This benign assessment of the probabilities of risk to the global financial system stemming from derivatives proved to be disastrous. After all, probabilities in politics and economics are but subjective estimates, mere water logic not based as much on empirical evidence as upon cultural habits of expectation.

After the dot-com boom went bust in 2000 and the United States was attacked by terrorists in 2001 (9/11), Greenspan again opened the floodgates of capital to help stimulate recovery. He did this without enough restrictions to head off the real estate bubble that led directly to the present crisis. Blind to the consequences of massive subprime lending by banks to people who did not have the income to qualify for the size of the mortgages they were taking out, Greenspan continued to cut interest rates and to support the use of credit derivatives based on these loans, which were sliced up and sold to investment banks, institutional investors, and hedge funds the world over.

At a hearing of the Senate Banking Committee in 2003, Greenspan stated: "What we have found over the years in the marketplace is that derivatives have been an extraordinarily useful vehicle to transfer risk from those who shouldn't be taking it to those who are willing to and are capable of doing so." Clearly many players in the derivatives game were not as capable of taking on these risks as they thought!

Indeed, critics of derivatives, whom Greenspan ignored, referred to them as "potential hydrogen bombs" (Felix Rohatyn) and "financial weapons of mass destruction" (Warren Buffett). There was a sense in the U.S. Congress that there was not a political constituency strongly in favor of regulating derivatives. Also, legislators did not want to show how little they understood about these complex contracts by exposing themselves to criticism among their colleagues.

Thus a critical reason for the financial crisis was a mass perception that derivatives were too complicated to understand and should just be left to the markets and the financial experts—all freedom and no responsibility! The short-term incentives on Wall Street to increase personal bonuses in financial firms without penalties for taking on risks that could bring down those firms reinforced speculative behavior with few restrictions.

The basic storyline is not difficult to follow. By setting interest rates increasingly lower and making money more easily available starting in 2002, Greenspan set up real estate and credit bubbles of historic proportions in the United States.

Mortgage brokers offered teaser rates to entice home-buyers with mortgages at variable rates that started low and then went up in later years, when the borrowers, who were presumably going to be receiving raises and earning more in their careers, in fact could no longer make the payments. These included NINJA (no income, no job or assets) loans. U.S. government policy stimulated this behavior by permitting taxpayers to subtract interest payments from their taxes on their first *two* homes! Indeed, piggyback mortgages allowed a combo of two mortgages, eliminating the need for a down payment.

The banks making these loans knew they were high risk and sought to get these hot debts out of their pipelines as soon as they could, pushing the risks onto other financial institutions. The new finance world—driven by high-speed computer models of dynamically hedging risks—made this easy. Banks would simply create structured products made up of portfolios of mortgages, loans, corporate bonds, and even credit-card receivables and sell them on the market. Such portfolios were then transferred to a special-purpose vehicle (SPV), a legal entity created only to collect principle and interest payments and pass on the cash flow from the underlying assets to the owners of three credit tranches: the lowest-risk super-senior tranche, the middle-risk mezzanine tranche, and the most junior toxic-waste tranche—paid only after all the other tranches had been paid in the case of default. The divisions between tranches were determined by specific ratings, for example, AAA for the upper tranches. (The rating agencies were a scandal unto themselves, reaping advantages from close relationships with the very entities they were supposed to be rating objectively.) Then all the tranches were sold to hedge funds, pensions, or SIVs (structured investment vehicles).

This whole process is called securitization—amounting to a wholesale weakening of lending standards and a separation of the borrower from the ultimate owner of the loan *ad absurdum*. Either these structured loan products can be sold directly or the bank can insure itself by buying a credit-default swap, paying a fixed insurance fee in return for a payment by the seller of the swap in case of a default on the products.

Just as the global debt crisis of the 1980s emerged because the banks made loans to developing countries based upon the assumption that the oil price would keep rising and could serve as collateral, so did the banks as of 2002 take on mortgage loans assuming that the prices of housing would continue to rise. When the prices fell, liquidity dried up and the credit crunch was at hand. For in times of crisis, the collateral assets behind the loans that banks have extended lose value and the funding requirements of the financial institutions increase. Rising uncertainty about lending in the future leads banks to hoard cash, not even lending to other banks in need, and drying up the well. So it becomes a negative self-fulfilling vicious cycle of perception, referred to as a *contagion*—like a global flu epidemic.[8]

Having lowered interest rates to 1 percent by 2004, stimulating the housing bubble, the Federal Reserve then raised them over the next two years to 5.35 percent, almost assuring that many cash-strapped mortgage holders with subprime loans (made to home-buyers with poor, or *no*, credit histories) would default on their loans. By the spring of 2007 New Century Financial, which specialized in these subprime loans, went bankrupt with spillover effects around the world in the banks that had purchased some of its products. And by July, investment bank Bear Stearns announced that clients in two of its hedge funds that were heavily invested in subprime products would get next to nothing back after other banks refused to bail out the funds. Soon thereafter Fed

Chairman Ben Bernanke announced the cost of the subprime crisis could rise to $100 billion.

In August of 2007 investment bank BNP Paribas informed investors that due to "complete evaporation of liquidity"[9] in the market, investments in two of its funds could not be withdrawn. The European Central Bank responded by injecting €204 billion into the banking market to improve liquidity. The Fed, the Bank of Japan, and the Bank of Canada also intervened, and the Fed dropped its interest rate half a percent due to concern over the credit crunch. In the United Kingdom lenders started to withdraw subprime mortgages and in Germany, the regional bank Landesbank Sachsen avoided collapse due to investing in the subprime mortgage market in the United States only by selling out to a rival bank, Landesbank Baden-Württemberg. By September, the German corporate lender IKB announced a $1 billion loss on investments linked to U.S. subprime mortgages. And this was followed by a classic run on a British bank, Northern Rock, where depositors withdrew £1 billion and continued to take out their money until the government stepped in to guarantee their savings.

What is striking in retrospect is how little was actually done in this early unraveling of the financial system, even though it was already global in scope! Imagine a tropical storm developing before the global weather service is well enough organized to announce the coming of a major hurricane so people can evacuate. Of course the catch is that the U.S. government did not *want* to have people bailing out of the financial markets! Asymmetric information led the poor and ignorant to take on mortgages they could not afford, which were then sliced up and sold as derivatives to ignorant investors all over the world who, in turn, had no knowledge of the true value of the assets or of the buried risks. The "banksters" in the private sector networked to use their lobbies to get bailed out by the "hucksters" in the administration and Congress who were dependent upon political financial contributions from these very same large financial corporations. Whether Republican or Democrat, the U.S. government was well and truly "bought." The classical principle threatening "moral hazard" kicked in; companies that were too big to fail or too "interconnected," those clumsy giants that could influence the entire financial system, were to be bailed out. The problem was that, given globalization, there were just too many such companies! (In short, foolish speculators consolidate into organizations whose mistakes are magnified by the speed of the new finance technologies and who then desperately try to lay their risks onto other fools!)

In March 2008 the U.S. Treasury Department bailed out Bear Stearns. Then in June 2008 came the largest bailout by a government of a single company: AIG (American International Group, the largest U.S. insurance company) received $123 billion. Given the company's inability to meet calls for collateral on toxic credit derivative loans, the Fed and U.S. Treasury continually had to pump in new money and sweeten the loan conditions in the hope that eventually the best AIG assets could be sold off when the market recovered, in order to pay back the U.S. taxpayers for their billions of dollars of "premium shares." AIG had the U.S. government trapped by the fear that its leveraged loans and its interconnectedness with other insurance operations all over the world would bring down the whole financial system if it went bankrupt.

The government then nationalized the country's two mortgage giants, Fannie Mae and Freddie Mac, in September 2008, to the tune of $5 *trillion*. But, in a huge error in judgment given the logic of the bailouts to date, Treasury Secretary Henry Paulson refused to bail out Lehman Brothers investment bank (first citing market fundamentalist ideology; later arguing he had no legal authority to bail Lehman out), thus unwinding confidence in the entire U.S. financial system globally! What *New York Times* columnist Thomas Friedman called "the electronic herd"[10] disinvested and deleveraged in a mass panic on the computerized financial markets. Within two months, the Standard & Poor's 500 stock index fell more than 50 percent—the greatest stock market crash since 1929.

The Lost Lessons of Long-Term Capital Management

While appearing to have learned from the Asian crisis of the 1990s, when the Treasury and IMF tried to use public means to solve a private market contagion, Paulson forgot the lessons of the collapse of Long-Term Capital Management (LTCM) in 1998 after the Russian default, which would have unraveled confidence in the global financial system without the Fed's coordinated bailout of LTCM's bond hedge fund by 14 private financial institutions.

The most important lesson of LTCM is that without government regulation, financial speculators will take infinite risks with leveraged or borrowed capital, diversifying their speculative investments around the world on the assumption that if something does go wrong, the government will have to intervene to save them in order to preserve the stability of the financial system. The managers of LTCM, in short, were free-riders upon the legitimacy of the financial system provided by the U.S. government. Their own investors were kept in the dark about where the investments were being made and the investments were made upon the assumption that historical trends of the recent past would always repeat themselves. Lack of transparency and asymmetric information were key assumptions in the business model, along with the idea that by taking enough risks everywhere and all the time, one can actually reduce risk and force the government into becoming a silent partner! Moreover, by not regulating such hedge fund activity, the American government was, in effect, free-riding upon the stability of the *global* system. Their flawed assumption was that if everything is left to free markets, the random nature of individual business activity will magically lead to such diversity that stability or equilibrium will automatically be restored over time without government intervention. Of course the billion-dollar bets of LTCM were small potatoes in comparison with the U.S. government's willingness to let an infinite number of investment banks and hedge funds speculate infinitely on borrowed capital.

The Government Intervenes; Investors Panic

No doubt the interventions in the markets undertaken early in the crisis were in part influenced by Fed Chairman Bernanke's academic specialization—the Great Depression and how to avoid another one. The question remains whether the palpable fear of the worst outcome, made increasingly explicit in actions to head it off, does not actually serve to help bring that worst scenario about. Princeton economist Alan Blinder likened Bernanke's actions to a game of "Whack-a-Mole":[11] Every time a new problem emerged, the Fed intervened to whack it down before it had a chance to spread. The ad hoc interventions by Republicans Bernanke and Paulson were no doubt premised on the assumption that it is best for the state to intervene in the markets as little as possible for maximum effect so as not to disturb the economic dynamism inherent in free market ideology.

Such ideological blinders prevented the U.S. government from organizing a comprehensive plan of intervention early on in the crisis, and were clearly at work in the decision to let Lehman Brothers go bankrupt, despite the widespread global implications (a "cleansing" by the markets?). To be fair to Bernanke and Paulson, the problems were new and complex, given globalization and derivatives. They may not have understood the implications much better than anyone else and might have wanted to feel their way to see what worked with the markets.

But when nothing seemed to work and the markets reacted with full-fledged panic reflected in the dropping of first stock prices, then commodity prices, and finally the prices of almost everything else, it became clear that part of the panic was due to the sense that governments (and the U.S. government in particular) were unable to do anything about the financial decline. Everything was spinning out of control. Uncertainty reigned. The month of October 2008 alone illustrates the panic of the mass movement of investors in the markets, followed by a fleeting mass hope that things had turned around as in any other short-term downturn in the stock-market cycle: This registered as the worst month for the Standard & Poor's (S&P) index of 500 stocks since the stock market crash of 1987, yet finished with the best week for the stock market in 34 years, which is counted as the most volatile week in the S&P's 80-year history.

The psychological perceptions of the mass of investors became completely decoupled from what was going on in the real economy, if not once then twice, within a month's time frame! Consumer confidence, a factor that is of vital importance in a nation where the GDP depends overwhelmingly upon consumption, plunged to its lowest recorded level in October of 2008. With nearly half of American households owning some shares of stock or mutual funds, the volatility of the stock market has much more of a psychological effect (e.g., wealth effect) upon the population's perception of spending power than in other nations that are much less exposed to these risks. The fear that spread to the level of a global panic was that *no one* understood what was going on in the world economy. The more an American government—which had so prided itself in representing the ideology of the unstrained free markets—intervened and called for restrictions in these very markets, the more people reacted with the perception that their leaders were confused and powerless, and the deeper the panic. Volatility spiked. The credit crisis was transformed into a crisis of legitimacy.

The great variety of forms of stop-and-go intervention by the U.S. government in the crisis gave the population a sense that their leaders were desperate. This stimulated a "beggar-thy-neighbor" competition among nations to secure their own banks in accordance with their own particular institutions of capitalism throughout the world. Thus, in late 2007 the Fed coordinated action by five central banks to offer billions of dollars in loans to banks. By March 2008 it was providing $30 billion to JPMorgan Chase to buy the fifth largest Wall Street bank—Bear Stearns (wiping out competition, which later would bring JPMorgan staggering windfall profits). In June 2008, U.S. federal authorities began to help out Fannie Mae and Freddie Mac, government-sponsored owners or guarantors of almost half of the nation's home loans, which the government in September 2008 fully nationalized (estimated to cost the U.S. taxpayer up to $389 billion, according to the Congressional Budget Office). The same month, after letting Lehman Brothers go bankrupt, the Fed provided the largest bailout in American history (ultimately $180 billion and counting) for the largest insurance company, American International Group (AIG), in return for 80 percent control. Then the government interventions became truly confusing. After the largest bank failure in the United States, that of Washington Mutual, leaders of the U.S. Congress announced a $700 billion plan organized by Paulson to buy toxic debts from banks in trouble.

The House of Representatives voted down this rescue plan, sending the stock markets into free fall. Then, by early October 2008, both the Senate and the House of Representatives approved a revised version of the $700 billion plan—the largest U.S. government intervention since the Great Depression.

In the same month, the United Kingdom nationalized three banks and Prime Minister Gordon Brown asserted that only by channeling money straight to the banks would the credit freeze be loosened up. Coordinating with the other G–8 financial ministers, Paulson followed Brown's lead and announced a plan to use $250 billion of the $750 billion approved to buy government stakes in a number of important banks in order to stabilize the industry and get the banks lending again. But the stop-and-go actions by Paulson did not stop there. Uncertainty in the markets skyrocketed.

By November Paulson realized that the banks and financial institutions were still unwilling to lend and unfreeze the consumer credit markets and he dropped his original strategy of buying the toxic mortgage assets. He proposed instead a new lending program to be headed by the Fed to use some of the approved bailout funds to help companies lending through credit cards, student loans, and the financing of car purchases.

The government bailout packages were not popular with the general population. The power vacuum in the transition from the Bush to Obama administrations assured that the government could do nothing, further increasing uncertainty. Stock prices plummeted. Oil prices fell by two-thirds from their peak in the summer of 2008.

After Barack Obama was elected President in November 2008, he carefully distanced himself from the specifics of the ever-changing bailouts initiated by the Bush administration, while still, however, being stuck with the responsibility for their effective execution.

Obamanomics: Exploiting Crisis, Postponing Costs

President Obama decided to leverage the Democratic and Republican consensus on paying for the expense of the economic crisis by borrowing rather than cutting spending or raising taxes. The financial crisis was an opportunity not to be wasted to initiate the big changes promised in his campaign. He launched a "Big Bang" economics program including *all* of his major objectives, pushing the budget deficit for his first year in office over the $1 trillion level. How can the government get away with foisting such impossibly high numbers upon the public? Because the state *owns* the money and the printing press. Obama is an emperor *with* clothes, and he lends out coveralls to others.

The beauty of this arrangement is the trick that King Midas— that greedy sovereign who realized he could stretch his wealth infinitely by reducing the metal in his coins while expanding their supply—also understood so well. The Treasury Department decides to lend out billions of dollars at a 4 percent rate of return. People from all over the world flock to borrow the money because it is seen as supersafe, blessed by the magic sparkle of being the key reserve currency under the tutelage of the most powerful man in the world who represents a superpower that always repaid its loans, no matter what else was going on. A $1 trillion loan at 4 percent means only $40 billion in an economy nearly $14 trillion in size in terms of GDP. In 2009 the White House Office of Management and Budget projected a 10-year deficit of $9 trillion. But the end of the fiscal year in September 2009 registered a $1.4 trillion annual deficit (10 percent of GDP), the worst since 1945 (21.5 percent of GDP). And Obama's promise to bring the annual budget deficit down to 3 percent of GDP by 2013 at the end of his four-year term was later revised upward to 4.6 percent of GDP. Only if interest rates stay low would these loans appear cheap from Obama's perspective.

Back at the White House in early 2009, President Obama looked around and thought that perhaps it would be foolish to obsess over financial or housing crises, which were more or less taking care of themselves after the tortuous interventions of the Bush administration and the regulatory follow-ups. So, capitalizing upon the Democratic Party's domination of both the Senate and House of Representatives, he focused full throttle upon his main economic promises:

- Universal health care (Obama's key priority: succeeded in late 2009 in reducing the number of nonelderly uninsured by 32 million, leaving still 23 million of this group uninsured; projected to reduce deficit by $143 billion by 2019 according to Congressional Budget Office in 2010)
- Clean energy infrastructure projects (slowly kicking in)
- Tax cuts for the bottom 95 percent (those earning less than $250,000 annually—a promise inconsistent with Obama's 2013 deficit reduction deadline)
- Expanding unemployment benefits and job creation (too low a priority, until the belated reversal of Obama policy before the midterm elections of 2010)
- Education and training reforms related to expanding Internet access and public service (quietly beginning to succeed with the excellence initiative for schools on the one hand, and poised to double the amount of commercial spectrum available in the country's wireless broadband, on the other hand).

Whereas the thrust of the previous administration was upon rescuing the big banks, dominant companies, and well-heeled managers, and cutting the taxes of the top 1 percent of income earners, Obama (at least in his campaign) wanted to focus upon the middle class and poor, helping out "Joe the plumber." These priorities are represented in the $787 billion stimulus package (later rising to $862 billion) that Obama managed to get through Congress in his first 100 days in office, as well as in the first budget he submitted.

The stimulus package of February 2009 had seven parts: (1) Immediate Relief for Families ($260 billion over 10 years), (2) Modernize Federal Infrastructure ($83 billion), (3) Increase

Alternative Energy Production ($22 billion), (4) Expand Health Care ($138 billion), (5) Improve Education ($117 billion), (6) Invest in Science Research and Technology ($18 billion), and (7) Help Small Businesses ($54 billion).

Alas, as critics have accurately pointed out, not enough of the stimulus spending was targeted precisely enough for job creation. And so for the unemployed (a percentage that rose into the double digits by the end of 2009), not to mention the underemployed, the "Great Bluff" epithet applied to America's response to the crisis took on painful, existential significance. By 2010 the long-term (at least 27 weeks) unemployment rate hit 4.4 percent—the highest since 1948. Between May and the November midterm elections of 2010 the United States shed almost 400,000 jobs. Rather than aiming for abstract increases in GDP (by which recessions are measured), government policy needs to focus much more on creating labor-intensive jobs, such as in the service sectors (education, health and safety, urban infrastructure, elder care, youth programs, and AmeriCorps).[12]

Initially Obama was swept up by the banking crisis, steered by his then main economic advisor, Larry Summers (who worked at a hedge fund for two years before joining the administration), and Timothy Geithner, the Treasury Secretary whose ties to Wall Street during his stint heading the New York Federal Reserve Bank were significant. Not surprisingly, two of the major investment banks with the most influence in the government's recovery plans recovered first from the crisis, showing record profits and awarding record bonuses to their top executives in 2009. In the third quarter of 2009 alone, profits were up 300 percent at Goldman Sachs, which gave a record $16.5 billion in bonuses for the year—an average of $700,000 for each of its 32,000 employees! By letting Lehman Brothers go bankrupt, the U.S. government eliminated the major competitor of Goldman Sachs, setting Goldman up for windfall profits. The same occurred for JPMorgan Chase, which took over Washington Mutual at the government's behest. Big is beautiful!

In March 2009 the Fed announced it would buy almost $1.2 trillion worth of debt to help boost bank lending and to promote economic recovery. While 116 banks went bankrupt in 2009, government intervention helped to stimulate large banks to start lending again by the end of the year (but capital was still not reaching many small firms that needed it desperately to survive, and, eventually, to create jobs). By the end of 2009, innovative intervention by the Fed had resulted in more than $7 trillion being pumped into the economy, ensuring that the Great Bluff would be big enough to avoid even the possibility of a second Great Depression. These innovations included establishing the Term Auction Facility (TAF), to give banks access to loans via competitive auction; the Term Asset-Backed Securities Loan Facility (TALF), to provide loans that banks can walk away from if paying the interest; the direct investment of capital into banks via TARP; and the increase of direct credit available from government-sponsored enterprises (i.e., Fannie Mae and Freddie Mac).

In April 2009 at the London summit of the Group of 20 rich and emerging countries, Geithner called for a heavy increase in funding for the International Monetary Fund for the sake of developing countries, resulting in promises of collective measures worth $1.1 trillion (but much of this money was so slow in being transferred that not all of it arrived by late 2010).

Obama calls his core economic theory "pragmatism, figuring out what works."[13] A University of Chicago (free-market biased) Democrat, Obama is comfortable with the workings of *laissez-faire* economics but focuses on tilting its incentives. Examples include having companies automatically provide 401(k) pension plans that workers can opt out of, and government-sponsored health care for the uninsured. From Obama's perspective the freedom generated by market-based capitalism should be kept while better regulating the risks in the financial sector and those stemming from crony capitalism and the windfall profits of the oil companies.

His complex financial reform package announced in the spring of 2009 called for a simplification of the terms of generic mortgages (i.e., 30-year fixed or five-year variable) so that customers can understand them more easily, while not going so far as to ban exotic mortgage instruments for those who want to take more risk. The aim was to hold Wall Street accountable, to separate proprietary trading from commercial banking (the Volcker Rule), and to protect average Americans from abusive financial practices which, at their peak, allowed a shadow banking system to be financed with some $8 trillion in assets. He maintained these were the goals even after signing the financial reform legislation (the Dodd-Frank Act) in July 2010, fully aware of compromises made with the "market makers," such as permitting the use of hedging derivatives for legitimate business purposes (versus mere speculation) and allowing banks to speculate with up to 3 percent of the equity in their own, specially designated accounts. While banks were forced to spin off certain derivative trading (in commodities, energy, metals, agriculture, and below-investment-grade credit-default swaps), they were permitted to keep derivative trading related to interest rate swaps, foreign exchange swaps, credit, gold, silver, investment-grade credit-default swaps, and "any transactions used to hedge risks"! Even more disturbing, large investment banks were permitted to keep their in-house Industrial Loan Companies (ILCs), which are set up to get around the normal capital requirements and limits on loans normally imposed on banks (although a three-year moratorium was put on setting up new ILCs). Here we are dealing with tens of billions of dollars in loans extended via ILCs by Merrill Lynch ($60 billion), Morgan Stanley ($38.5 billion), and Goldman Sachs ($25.7 billion) in the decade before the crisis—loans to many companies that subsequently fell into trouble.[14]

These loopholes in regulations make enforcement difficult, not to mention the over 2,000 pages agreed upon, planting the seeds for another financial crisis. For example, even after the bill was passed and signed by the president, the government was still sponsoring individual home mortgages at 3.5 percent money paid down (via the Federal Housing Administration). The legislation was muddled in its objectives and did not clearly make the whole derivatives market transparent, address the continuing astronomical bailouts of Freddie Mac and Fannie Mae, solve the "too big to fail" problem, or stringently control Wall Street fraud. As journalist and economic policy advisor Jeff Madrick put it, "systemic risk" is "really about everyone doing the same thing" (e.g., herd behavior), and identifying firms that are "too big to fail" is left up to a new body formed by the Fed, Securities and Exchange Commission (SEC), FDIC, Treasury, and several others who can impose capital requirements, if they will and can do it on time![15] Otherwise, the need for more strict capital requirements for all major financial institutions was just passed on for the Bank for International Settlements in Basel to take care of, which backed down from possible stringent requirements as soon as it viewed the loopholes and vagueness of the U.S. legislation.

The Obama administration is capable of absorbing the positive lessons related to incentives (versus mandates) of the school of "behavioral economics." But whether such micro-incentives are capable of helping to reverse huge macroeconomic deficits is another matter. The initial thrust of the collective learning of the U.S. government was not promising: The aim appeared to be to shore up old structures—of big banks, of insurance companies, of automobile firms (General Motors, Ford, and Chrysler were offered $34 billion in government loans), and even of individual mortgage holders who overextended themselves and could not afford the houses they were in. Stabilizing the old in order to build confidence and to keep existing jobs was a short-term strategy that risked shortchanging long-term investment in the new, innovative job-creating technologies and companies. While Obama has proposed green energy businesses and has launched a small social entrepreneurship initiative, these programs have been drowned out by the attention paid to big banks and companies. Another (belated) exception was the administration's initiative to vastly expand broadband wireless access for commercial purposes in rural areas.[16]

In 2010 preceding the midterm elections in November, Obama quick-stepped with too little, too late in terms of job creation and support for small businesses, which create the most jobs: proposing business tax credits for new workers hired, and signing bills for the HIRE Act Jobs Bill, to temporarily extend unemployment benefits, to reduce tariffs for U.S. manufacturers, and the Small Business Jobs and Credit Act. But in the background Americans were besieged by troubling news: the need for Obama to raise the national debt limit by $2 trillion (to $14.3 trillion); the FDIC announcing the number of "problem banks" insured, which went up from 552 to 702; Goldman Sachs being charged with fraud for selling products designed to fail; the Fed publishing swap agreements for currencies with other central banks given short-term strains on the dollar; the U.S. unemployment rate stuck between 9 and 10 percent; and the official poverty level spreading to affect one in seven Americans.

The implications of the fragile recovery that began officially in the fall of 2009 were riddled with uncertainty—social, political, and economic. The possibility that the Bush tax cuts would be allowed to expire in 2011 either for everyone or for just the top 2.5 percent of income earners made the future even harder to calculate up to the last minute (in 2010) when they were finally extended for everyone—including the superrich—for two years.

It is an open question as to whether the future will be colored more by deflation or inflation. If inflation is perceived by the "electronic herd" to be on its way, debts are then anticipated to become more expensive as interest rates rise and Republicans lambaste the increasing cost of financing the deficit. But, at the same time, the private sector would then push up economic growth, and as the GDP goes up, the annual deficits would shrink compared to national income made available to pay off past debts. King Midas would then be smiling!

But in the short term, a deflationary scenario is more likely. Consider Figure 2.2, which shows that over the past 15 years central banks in developed countries (including the United States) have converged in targeting inflation at about 2 percent and in keeping it within this range.

In addition to this recent record of low inflation, deflation is more likely due to the austerity consensus reached by most

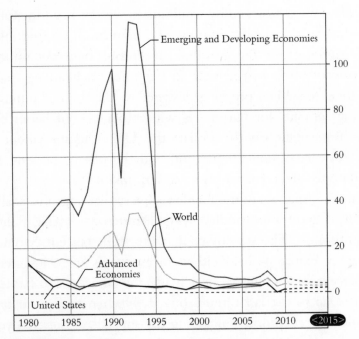

Figure 2.2   Inflation Rates, 1980 to 2010
SOURCE: IMF Data Mapper.

developed countries in 2010, which sought what behavioral economists call "arbitrary coherence" around a joint agreement to cut deficits in European Union nations at once, using the bond markets' negative view of Greece as the "anchor" in terms of "the price" to avoid.[17]

The Debt Culture versus Hoarding and Investing

The argument of the Obama administration that much of the necessary structural repair was due to huge problems inherited from the Bush administration is understandable, and its consequences are unavoidable. So much money has been spent resurrecting old organizations and commitments that there may not be nearly enough available in the future for job-creating investments and innovation—the key to international competitiveness and long-term full employment. Sensing a huge public resentment against the government bailouts of big companies that then gave their executives large bonuses, in October 2009 Obama announced that seven large companies (including AIG, Citigroup, Bank of America, General Motors, and Chrysler) that received billions in government money would immediately have to cut the compensation of their top executives in half.

This was but the tip of the iceberg, and it was too little, too late in terms of public opinion. The tea party movement against big government and bailouts—typically dominated by 45-year-old, white, middle-class males of a Republican or independent persuasion—spread throughout the country in a backlash against federal policy, causing politicians worried about reelection to push even further into an austerity mode. Americans were brought up on a dogmatic liberal ideology of maximizing individual freedom and limiting government and many resent the economic necessity of having to limit freedom and to vastly increase the scope of government for the sake of long-term fiscal stability. Accordingly, with another stimulus package being politically unviable, in 2010 the pressure shifted to the Fed to provide liquidity, even if that meant more cycles of "quantitative easing": buying billions of dollars of U.S. bonds in order to keep down the long-term interest rates.

Obama promised in his campaign to spread the wealth more fairly in terms of income and taxes, given the decades-long stagnation of wages of the middle class, the decline of union power, the proliferation of one-parent families, the low-wage competition from abroad, and the Bush overconcentration on tax breaks for the upper tier of income earners. Income inequality has risen in the United States over the past 30 years to the point where it is the greatest it has been over the past century. As of 2007, the top 10 percent of income earners took in 50 percent of the wages, while the top 1 percent of income earners had captured half of the nation's overall economic growth since 1993.

Given the volatility in the stock market and in the value of the dollar and public resentment of government largesse for those "too big to fail," Obama became increasingly concerned about long-term deficit reduction. He argued for pay-as-you-go legislation in Congress in order to restore confidence and (belatedly) for small-business-oriented policies to stimulate job creation. His health care reforms, designed to be budget neutral, will lower the deficit in the next decade only if no new unfunded health care spending bills pass through Congress, which seems unlikely. As middle-class American families start to earn more, their health care subsidies from the government are scheduled to be reduced proportionally, which could undermine the work ethic. Yet the new health care reform is vital, not only as a stable base of support for young entrepreneurs with families, who can now take risks without losing health insurance, but also giving hope, if not care, to the record number of unemployed and underemployed, not to mention the veterans returning from the two wars in progress. But deep-seated problems linger. Reports kept out of the mainstream press suggest that a number of Americans in Detroit did not have the money to bury their dead, and put them into black plastic bags to be kept in a public freezer, until a former record company executive stepped in to raise money to help out.[18] States and municipalities ran out of money to help subsidize burials for the poor.

Indeed, things became so difficult for Illinois in 2010 that it just stopped paying $5 billion owed to schools, rehabilitation centers, child care, and the state university. The state's pension system is at least 50 percent underfunded, the worst case in the nation—causing the cost of borrowing money to skyrocket. The political system is dysfunctional—a *reductio ad absurdum* illustration for the national stalemate. Two of the last six governors went to jail and a third is standing trial. The legislature refused to cut benefits or raise taxes, leaving town for the summer with a $12 billion deficit behind them (almost half the state's budget). There is no obvious way for Illinois to grow its way out. The fiscal solvency of California and New York is also not assured, underscoring the fragility of any national recovery. With the exception of Vermont, all states in the United States have some form of balanced budget law, meaning that ultimately they will be required either to make spending cuts or to raise taxes in order to get themselves out of any financial hole. But in Illinois, at least, these budget-balancing regulations are not enforced. No wonder there is a tea party movement!

There are a number of other outstanding expenses that will be hard for the United States to cope with: the $11 billion monthly cost of the wars in Iraq and Afghanistan (according to one estimate, assuming there were a maximum of 100 members of Al Qaeda left in Afghanistan by 2010, the United States was paying about $1 billion apiece annually to try to kill them[19]) and the burgeoning costs of the Medicare and Social Security systems given the impending retirement of the baby boom generation. Medicare insurance reserves are projected to be exhausted by 2019 and Social Security reserves by 2041, according to the Social Security and Medicare Board of Trustees (2008). (See Figures 2.3 and 2.4.) Indeed it appears that Social Security and Medicare have promised $37 trillion more in benefits to senior and disabled workers than these programs will be able to cover. By the time this generation of college students retires around 2050, they are apt to find out that close to 40 percent of their payroll taxes will have to be spent for Social Security, Medicare, Medicaid, and veterans' benefits! Moreover, to raise a child in the Northeast of the United States starting in 2010 is estimated to cost $250,000 for a two-parent family and $340,000 for a single-parent family, and that assumes sending the child to a public (not private) university.[20]

Most of the record debt the United States found itself in by 2008 was created before Obama arrived. When President Bill Clinton left office, the nonpartisan Congressional Budget Office

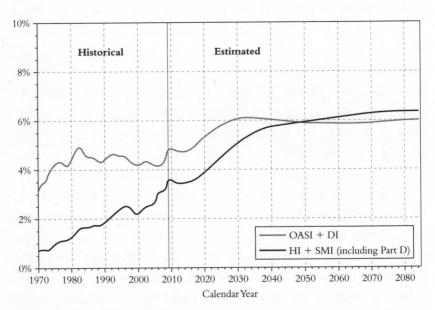

Figure 2.3 Social Security and Medicare Cost as a Percentage of GDP
OASI: Old-Age & Survivors Insurance; DI: Disability Insurance; HI: Hospital Insurance; SMI: Medicare Supplementary Medical Insurance.
SOURCE: www.ssa.gov/OACT/TRSUM/index.html.

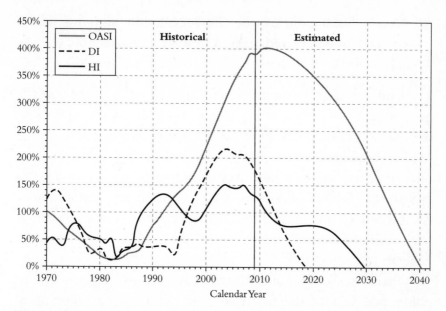

Figure 2.4 OASI, DI, and HI Trust Fund Ratios (Assets as a Percentage of Annual Expenditures)

OASI: Old-Age & Survivors Insurance; DI: Disability Insurance; HI: Hospital Insurance.
SOURCE: www.ssa.gov/OACT/TRSUM/index.html.

(CBO) estimated that the U.S. government would run an average annual *surplus* of more than $800 billion a year from 2009 to 2012. But by 2009, the CBO's estimate changed to a $1.2 trillion annual *deficit* in these years. This $2 trillion shift is attributed in an analysis by the *New York Times* to four basic causes.[21]

1. The business cycle (37 percent): the 2001 and 2008 recessions reducing tax revenue and requiring government spending for the safety net
2. President George W. Bush's policies (33 percent), such as tax cuts and the Medicare prescription drug benefit
3. Bush policies scheduled to expire that Obama decided to extend (20 percent): Iraq war, tax cuts for households making less than $250,000, and the Wall Street bailout (signed by Bush and supported by Obama)

4. New Obama policies: the 2009 economic stimulus bill (7 percent), and new initiatives in health care, education, energy, and so forth (3 percent)

While some of Obama's policies are not expected to cost the government any money (e.g, putting a price on carbon emissions), the big stumbling block in terms of deficit reduction will be the Medicare budget, where health care reform legislation did not include severe enough measures to cut spending (never underestimate the lobbies of doctors, drug manufacturers, and insurance companies). Obamanomics thus risks saving the present generation from serious financial crisis with money borrowed from coming generations.

Obama senses this and knows that only by augmenting his policy priorities of the first two years with a focus upon fiscal payback and restraint in subsequent years might this burden on our grandchildren be ameliorated. Not only are individuals and corporations overleveraged: America as a whole is an overleveraged society! It has become a debt culture. Annual trillion-dollar deficits are projected (by Obama himself) for years to come. According to Ned Davis Research, whereas in the 1950s it took $1.36 of debt in the United States to generate $1.00 of GDP, that ratio has grown in the past decade to $5.81 to generate $1.00 in GDP—with no end to the edging up of the ratio in sight.[22]

Part of the problem has been the effective domination of public unions at the state government level: nationally, in terms of wages and benefits, state and local workers earn $14 per hour more than their counterparts in the private sector.[23]

While the government had a hard time saving, for big companies it was no problem. Corporate hoarding or a "corporate savings glut" became a widespread reaction to the uncertainties due to the financial crisis, government bailouts, and the inevitable regulations of the financial sector to follow. By the first quarter of

2010, nonbank firms in the United States held liquid assets worth 23 percent of debt. With a record $1.6 trillion of deposits (in money funds, bonds, and treasury bills), firms were afraid that if they ran out of money, banks might not be able or willing to lend to them.[24]

Of course as soon as firms stop hoarding and start to hire workers and to invest, governments can more easily scale back their borrowing. Corporate confidence is hard to restore after the financial system collapses, when the old system of firms being permitted to withhold proprietary information is maintained regardless of reforms (making it easier to mask fraud), and when developed countries are bankrupt, and their central banks print money as if there were no tomorrow. Afraid they may not be able to roll over their debt as they did in the past and that new regulations will force banks to keep more of their capital instead of lending it out, firms hoard to hedge against the uncertainty.

Crisis leads to innovation even here: The retail discounter Sam's Club went into the business of making loans to its customers in order to go around the credit crunch. The trend became global to the point that some companies, like Germany's Siemens, even applied for a banking license in order to be able to lend some of its huge cash reserves to clients! Indeed, globally large multinational companies increasingly have so much cash in reserve that they have become their own banks—as British Petroleum illustrated in giving up $20 billion overnight in 2010, without blinking, for a U.S. government fund to cover the potential costs of the oil spill in the Gulf of Mexico.

Obama was lucky to have the financial crisis break out before he took office and has a huge opportunity to create a recovery à la Franklin D. Roosevelt with great social transformations. But he will have to lead a major educational effort on economic sobriety to wean the culture off of its excessive consumption, "dysregulation," and entitlement expectations if he is to avoid mortgaging the future of young people who did so much to help elect him: no pain, no gain.[25]

Within the United States, the debtor (e.g., subsidies for the Midwest farmer) had become more acceptable than the creditor (e.g., the Northeast money man), and now government subsidies of the old establishments risk diverting critical collective learning shifts from investing in the new. Silicon Valley became so concerned with America's lagging innovation that Intel organized a group corporate effort to invest $3 billion in innovation, potentially hiring 10,000 workers in the future. Job creation is at least as important as entitlements if the United States is to pay the piper! An educational and training shift toward emerging job sectors rather than the overwrought sectors of the past, such as finance, automobiles, and real estate, will be critical in this effort to employ the young and to raise the taxes to pay for the entitlements for the old. This is particularly important for the increasingly computerized manufacturing sector, where many who apply for job openings requiring at least ninth-grade levels of math and English skills have only the equivalent of sixth-grade competency. Widespread financial illiteracy also needs to be remedied: After tapping out their home equity loans and their credit cards, some Americans turned to payday loans—writing a check to the lender plus financing costs (15 percent for two weeks) that is cashed on payday, amounting to an annual interest rate of 400 percent. On average such folks use these lending facilities nine times a year, meaning they may end up paying more in interest than the amount they borrowed![26]

Austerity versus Stimulus: The Trillion-Dollar Gap

Debt in the United States and Europe has created a great debate as to whether state policy should reduce deficits and debt with a

straitjacket of austerity, or rather delay such reductions and stimulate national economies in the short term until economic
growth is firmly secured. The austerity camp argues that global
investors, particularly in the bond markets, will not invest until a
clear plan exists to lower state deficits and debts over the next
decade, and that businesses will not risk capital if they believe taxes
will skyrocket in the short-term future to cover the overspending
of the past.[27] The stimulus or "neo-Keynesian" group argues that
the problem is rather one of stimulating demand in the short term,
because businesses will not invest in job-creating growth without
an increase of capital, credit, and consumption in their sector of
the economy. An IMF study, for example, shows that fiscal
consolidation policies in rich countries are typically contractionary
in the short term, rather than boosting economic growth.[28]

Behind this debate—truly the elephant in the room—is the
"trillion-dollar plus" budget gap in terms of what the Obama
administration has forecast for the next decade. According to the
Congressional Budget Office, Obama's fiscal 2011 budget
(announced in February 2010) will lead to close to $10 trillion in
deficits over the next decade, $1.2 trillion more than the Obama
administration has projected, raising the federal debt to 90 percent
of the nation's GDP by 2020. Specifically, the White House
Office of Management and Budget (OMB) projected a $8.53
trillion deficit over the next 10 years versus the CBO's estimate of
$9.75 trillion. When Obama became President the federal public
debt stood at $6.3 trillion or $56,000 per household. By early
2010 it had risen to $8.2 trillion or $72,000 per household.
By 2020, if the Congressional Budget Office estimate turns out to
be accurate, the debt will be $20.3 trillion or more than $170,000
per household, or 90 percent of GDP, up from 40 percent of GDP
in 2008. At the end of World War II, the debt-to-GDP ratio was
109 percent (Greece's in 2009 was 115 percent).[29]

The difficulty with the short-term stimulus argument in the United States is that the money may simply go to paying off old debt (or to building up capital reserves) rather than toward consumption or new business investment. The escalation of U.S. household debt from 72 percent of GDP to 97 percent of GDP (according to McKinsey Global Institute) scared Americans, particularly given all the media talk of barely avoiding another Great Depression. Large institutional pension funds diversified out of U.S. and dollar assets, given the certainty that in the long term Social Security benefits will be trimmed, taxes will go up, and the dollar will decline in value relative to commodities and currencies of countries with less debt per GDP. However, there is some flexibility in that half of Americans paid no income tax in 2009 when the United States had the lowest federal tax receipts since 1950, and the tax rate is among the lowest among developed, industrialized countries.[30]

Furthermore, there is evidence that the "Great Bluff" may have paid off: Economists Alan Blinder and Gordon Rentschier estimate that without the government's response, GDP in 2010 would have been 11.5 percent lower, payroll employment would have been less by 8.5 million jobs, and the nation would have been in deflation. Also, by June 2010 the U.S. Treasury announced that Troubled Asset Relief Program (TARP) repayments ($194 billion) were greater than the debt still outstanding ($190 billion). So the fiscal stimulus, TARP, bank stress tests, and the Fed's "quantitative easing" and other innovative maneuvers may have stabilized confidence, if not quite stimulating enough investment.[31]

Indeed, William Gross (cofounder of PIMCO, the world's largest bond investment company) claims that the government stimulus has largely been dumped "down the toilet" of consumption, rather than targeted toward investment where it is so badly needed for growth (which he anticipates to be less than 2 percent in developed countries in the near future, compared to double-digit growth in the emerging economies).[32]

The United States is caught between a rock and a hard place: New stimulus will increase the debt without necessarily increasing investment or job creation, while austerity savings measures will slow down economic growth and render already historically high long-term unemployment structural, rather than merely temporary (average long-term unemployment reached 35 weeks in 2010). Obama recognized this in his commitment to cut the U.S. deficit in half as a percent of GDP by 2013 at the Toronto G-20 summit in 2010. For as the debt payments come due on the stimulus packages already spent, interest rates rise and crowd out spending on government programs like Social Security. And higher deficits lead, in turn, to a tightening of private credit, putting further job creation at risk.

By November 2010 it was clear that another government stimulus package was not politically viable. The sweep of "tax-cutting" Republicans elected in the midterm elections made this clear. So the same day as the election results were reported, the Fed announced a $600 billion quantitative easing program (buying long-term U.S. treasury bonds) at the rate of $75 billion a month. This was in addition to the $250 billion to $300 billion in repayments to the Treasury from agencies and mortgage-backed securities (MBSs), which would also be reinvested in long-term treasury bills through the first half of 2011. Thus, the total U.S. government spending for quantitative easing (or extension of the "Great Bluff" to keep the weak recovery going) came to $110 billion a month in contrast to less than $50 billion a month of increases in U.S. total economic growth! This was augmented by a December extension of the Bush-era tax cuts for both the rich and the middle class combined with more support for the unemployed and a cut in payroll taxes for two years amounting to over $800 billion. Furthermore, one must calculate as well that the top 36 financial securities and investment services funds paid an estimated total of $144 billion in compensation and benefits in 2010 (a 4 percent increase over 2009).

It is only a matter of time for the credibility of such spending programs to run out with international investors and foreign governments! The heavy spending by the U.S. in Afghanistan will increase given President Obama's decision to extend the stay of troops in Afghanistan another four years. His small symbolic gesture in November of 2010 to freeze the salaries of federal workers for two years will not provide much relief for the budget. Obama's abrupt caving in to the Republicans' tax-cutting program can only be explained as an anticipated election grant for 2012.

It is not just Europeans who are "calling the Great Bluff" but U.S. individual investors and pension funds that are increasingly concerned that the emperor has no clothes. When successful billionaire investors, such as American Jim Rogers (author of *A Bull in China*) advocate getting out of the dollar, teaching your children Chinese, and buying commodities, then one knows that the U.S. political economy needs some radical restructuring. Educating Americans in financial literacy and to make do with less is just the beginning.

Educational institutions must stress Western traditions of political, economic, and scientific thought and resurrect the American heritage of individual mobility through hard work and individual responsibility. Depth of understanding through reading needs to be added to political economic sobriety at home in order to gain respect from other cultures abroad. The American Dream is not something given, but something earned over a lifetime of disciplined work; it is not enough to be *born* equal to *become* so. How long elastic dollar credits and subsidies can continue to flow to those who live based more on high expectations than on their own hard work is an open question.

Postcrisis America may evolve into a healthier place in terms of materialistic objectives. More attention may be paid to the nature of work than to salaries, to leisure time than to the rat race, to friends than to contacts, to spiritual growth rather than to mere economic growth. Slowing things down and settling for "smaller is beautiful" may be just the right recipe for greater human harmony and a "civilizing" of capitalism.

Dollarization

In contrast to Black Tuesday (1929), the present financial crisis did not lead to a worldwide depression. The stock markets did surprisingly well, not to mention commodity prices. Nevertheless, the volatility has sharply lowered people's confidence in currencies and in monetary stability. This concern is valid for the dollar as well, but only marginally. For the dollar is still the key reserve currency. People all over the world need some value to believe in, a commodity that is backed up with some security, a certain store of value. Since the U.S. superpower appears to be too powerful to be replaced in the short term and has always been good for payments on its debts (which are conveniently in its own currency), most people still see the United States as the fortress of capitalism in times of crisis, even if America initiated the crisis in the first place! Any nation that can make mistakes this big must have infinite resources to recover with, or . . . ?

The U.S. Treasury is still the lender of last resort and the dollar is its weapon. As the financial crisis spread outside the United States to foreign markets, investors figured that those markets had further to fall than the American market, where state intervention had been most pronounced, and shifted money back into the U.S. dollar. In a $3–4 trillion daily global foreign exchange market, the

(Continued)

Fed coordinated successive central bank interventions of the group of seven key industrialized states, the G-7, effectively stabilizing the dollar.

If the daily foreign exchange market is a casino and the central banks together represent "the house," currency speculators realize that you cannot win for long by betting against the house!

The U.S. dollar accounts for over 60 percent of reserves and 70 percent of U.S. trade flows. While the euro's share in foreign exchange transactions rose to 26 percent, the dollar is still the favored currency of last resort in times of financial crisis. In the financial turbulence of 2008 Argentineans converted as many pesos to dollars as they could, recalling the economic crisis they had experienced in 2001. Billions of dollars fled Argentina in capital flight as confidence failed in the government's ability to find enough liquidity in the financial crisis.

While the long-term scenario suggests a gradual shift to holding foreign reserves in a basket of currencies to diversify out of the dollar (or into a more stable, neutral Special Drawing Rights system run by the IMF) the "sunk costs" of switching remain so high that it reminds one of the opportunity cost of switching from the Microsoft Office software system in the computer world: the dominant player holds a great deal of latent power. Remember, America has the world by its dollar!

In order to facilitate international investing and to create stability against inflation in their own markets, many national governments have adopted an official policy of "dollarization," substituting the U.S. currency for their own. Thus Ecuador adopted the dollar as its legal tender in 2000 in order to overcome a banking crisis, increasing transparency and economic competitiveness. A year later, El Salvador dollarized its economy as well, despite economic stability and low inflation— improving its country's banking effectiveness. Other countries officially using the dollar include the British Virgin Islands, East Timor, the Marshall Islands, the Federated State of Micronesia, Palau, Panama, and the Turks and Caicos Islands. In addition there are a host of countries and places that have pegged their currencies to the dollar: the Netherlands Antilles, Aruba, Jordan, Bahrain, Lebanon, Oman, Qatar, Saudi Arabia, the United Arab Emirates, Moldavia, Venezuela (hit by a crisis of dollar scarcity due to economic mismanagement!), Belize, Hong Kong, Barbados, Trinidad, Tobago, Antigua, St. Kitts, St. Lucia, St. Vincent, the Grenadines, and Grenada. The dollar is as ubiquitous as Intel chips or Microsoft Windows!

However, if the United States continues to print dollars in the trillions regardless of what happens with the real economy, government debt, or deficits, the quality of the dollar will fall as the quantity rises. Indeed, anticipating this, between 2008 and 2009, the Chinese raised their gold holdings by 78 percent and have been quietly diversifying their reserves out of the dollar. By 2010, half of their new reserve purchases were not going into U.S. treasuries. As the world economy recovers, the dollar decreases in value as investors sell dollars to invest in riskier assets. And as the countries with currencies pegged to the dollar feel the pressure as the dollar falls, they intervene massively to stop their currency values from rising, which would harm their exports; this, in turn, imports inflation at home. Since such intervention rarely does much good given the massive quantities needed to affect global exchange rates, many

(Continued)

countries are under pressure to drop their pegs or to revalue their pegs higher when the dollar falls.

Ultimately, such collective behavior is apt to cause the Federal Reserve to raise U.S. interest rates (or the price of the dollar) under the guise of "an exit strategy" from the massive government stimuli used to stabilize the domestic economy. Obama froze discretionary federal spending and the United States will reduce its deficits. Meanwhile, the Obama administration will continue to push for more free trade agreements abroad, such as the one with South Korea in 2010, in order to take advantage of U.S. exports reduced in price when the dollar falls in value. And the U.S. Congress will continue to press the administration to get the Chinese to commit to a clear-cut rise in the value of their currency rather than going along with their vague, flexible strategy of slow currency appreciation (which is the only thing that makes sense from the Chinese perspective, if domestic wages in China are rising, growth rates are declining, and many jobs depend upon exports). Treasury Secretary Timothy Geithner has referred to this as a threat to the world economy of "competitive nonappreciation" (a term coined by Edwin Truman, a former official at the Treasury and Fed). But in the future, the United States risks being accused of the same fault if it keeps interest rates low to stimulate economic growth and exports.

Recasting the United States: Domestic Dynamism with Responsibility

Why—if the United States has mismanaged its hegemony, has politicized its management of the key reserve currency, has overextended itself militarily and economically—do people the world over look to it for hope, stability, leadership, and even for a way to save capitalism? Perhaps it is because Americans forget their past, rather than being imprisoned by it. They keep coming back to the *tabula rasa*, to reinvent the wheel, to sell and market the new, to discover the future in the present. This ability of the United States to reinvent itself is perceived to be unlikely to occur in another developed country where people have had their brash innovative impulses civilized, traditionalized, ordered, and cataloged, like a museum of embalmed artifacts. To be an American, as Spanish-American philosopher George Santayana put it, is a full-time career. It is not nice, not fair, not social to use all those natural resources to reinvent oneself and one's society each day when one wakes up in the morning, to free-ride upon the credit and greatest opportunities in the world, but it is innovative, stimulating, entrepreneurial, and job-creating. Americans can be counted upon to make something happen with their restless, multicultural energy. That is why foreigners invest in the United States and look to it for new technology, entertainment, and even political leadership.

But if the best and brightest continue to be siphoned off into the innovations of financial engineering and hedge funds, the future takes on a darker hue. The lack of self-denial and the acceptance of self-indulgence "up to the very limits imposed by hygiene and economics," as Aldous Huxley put it in *Brave New World*, do indeed keep the wheels turning in an industrial society, as he forecast. But this occurs at great social cost and, paradoxically, can ultimately limit individual freedom. For in their very desire for freedom *from* individual financial responsibility, *from* facing the structural need to reform their political system, *from* confronting the systematic reduction of their debts and deficits, *from* the need to provide equal opportunity for education up the class ladder, *from* their moral obligation to care for their sick and aged, and *from* the priority of creating work for all who want it—this freedom *from* responsibility undermines a people's own long-term life chances and, even more so, the well-being of their children. Wasteful spending must be cut, while research and development, educational reform, and productive investment in the real economy must be intensified.

Foreign investors will be watching closely to see if the United States can somehow escape its political malaise and successfully focus its collective learning upon "nation-building" at home in terms of education, health care, infrastructure, and retooling for job creation. Mass public anger at the bailing out of big banks and at the seizing of more power by the state threatens to block these efforts in an era when the country needs more statecraft (wisdom) and less market savvy (profligacy). Many citizens have a palpable sense of what "the democratic deficit" has come to mean. A "No Labels" movement has been founded to try to bring the polarized left and right extremes together for common ground in the political center. A third party may evolve (despite winner-take-all electoral laws favoring the traditional duopoly), challenging the perception of political bankruptcy of the main two parties, locked in a zero-sum game that an increasing number of people believe to be more focused on their interest group sponsors than on the national well-being. Those outside the United States are not fully aware of the depth of the structural impasse of the American political system, which will continue to dampen U.S. competitiveness. But if the mode of American recovery should be successful at taming winner-take-all "creative destruction," especially on the part of the financial sector, the United States could again become a first mover, where the soft power of innovative minds goes before it is suffocated by outmoded traditions.

The "Great Bluff" *could* become a turning point for a sustainable growth path after the "Great Recession"—but only provided that American policy-makers restructure their state deficits and transcend the political stalemate, stabilize confidence in a reformed global financial and monetary system, and continue to head off the tailwind of hyperinflation—the potential opportunity cost of trillion-dollar bailouts and deficits. But whether or not Americans are able to transform the nation to maintain its competitiveness, this may very well be the beginning of the end of the U.S. dollar as the key reserve currency (which may have become more of a burden than a privilege). And Americans may increasingly look to Europe and the emerging nations for political, educational, and economic recipes, rather than the other way around.

Chapter 3

Giant with Feet of Clay
The European Union

Two letters have determined the destiny of Europe for the
past 50 years: EU. They represent both the new Leviathan of the old continent and its more mysterious Sphinx.
Without the force of economic interests, the 28-state institution
called the European Union would not have developed from
the post–World War II committee set up to prevent German
rearmament, in the guise of the European Coal and Steel Community. These were the props of supervision used by Germany's
neighbors who, understandably, wanted to fence in a giant so prone
to outbursts of violence, but also whose insight was that they might
be better off working cooperatively than to be free to pursue self-
determination—viewpoints that continue to shape the style, power
distribution, and politics of the EU and its institutions. Within this

framework, the smallest European countries have the most say, while the largest and most populous, namely Germany, pays the most in absolute terms per capital. On top of this structure, the EU bureaucracy developed into a European Leviathan whose three central institutions—the EU Commission and Council of Ministers, the European Court of Justice (ECJ), and the European Central Bank (ECB)—reach deeply and without democratic legitimacy into the capacities and individual lives of their member nations, for the European Parliament (EP) has neither legislative powers nor the usual rights of control over the EU executive.

The "state" of EU is not really a state and may not become one according to the oft-revised EU Labor Treaties. "Union citizenship" is based upon a common passport and the individual's right to live anywhere in the EU. But the EU protects its citizens neither through the democratic separation of powers nor through granting the right for an individual to bring a complaint against the encroachments of the Leviathan in the highest EU court.

Although there is no single "people" of Europe, and there is no individual nation with the voting power to make one possible, the European Leviathan strives to rule openly and without reserve through the EU bodies in the European superstate. Such a superstate is the end goal of the integration process that was set up a long time ago for economic projects. In this pursuit, the EU Leviathan can rely upon a further mythical creature: the EU Sphinx. It is a Sphinx because it formulates its policy in the manner of the Freemasons—behind closed doors without protocol and far from public view.

As long as the labor contracts of the EU involve unanimous decisions, one is obligated to discipline dissidents and critics of publicly organized agitation. This was what member nations such as Austria, Denmark, Ireland, Poland, the Czech Republic, and Slovakia had to experience. Austria was put under pressure when it dared to go into a coalition government in order to make governance possible with a party considered to be "undemocratic" by Brussels; Denmark and Ireland had to keep repeating referenda until the electoral results met with the approval of Brussels. And Polish and Czech Republic heads of state found themselves put on public display in a polemic steered by the EU when they did not quickly and devotedly sign the Treaty of Lisbon. The same thing happened to the Slovak government in the case of the rescue parachutes for the euro: Because it hesitated during the recent financial crisis to help the PIIGS (Portugal, Italy, Ireland, Greece, and Spain), being a poorer nation on average than they were, it was reproached as lacking in solidarity—even though the government had expressed its willingness to help, pending parliamentary approval, which then was not granted.

Under the reign of the EU Leviathan and EU Sphinx, the old continent is in the process of demolishing Europe's most valuable political gift to the world: free democracy and the self-determination of people. In disregard of history, lifestyles, and interests as well as problems, the EU fancies itself as a second, historically belated United States of America.

But this is a fatal misconception. The United States has had a different history for over 230 years than old Europe. Founded by people seeking a new home, which they then carved out, they have long been a unified people and nation. Although the problems of the United States and the EU appear to be similar today, they are not, nor can they be solved in the same way. While each side can learn some things from the other, there are different methods and tools on each side of the Atlantic.

What Services Has the EU Rendered?

The EU Sphinx conjures up a glowing future for its people, who, while very different from the folk of ancient Thebes, still can find a warning of their destiny encrypted in the Sphinx's words. The promise is that the merger of the EU can guarantee peace, the promotion of democracy and economic growth, and now, particularly, protection from the global financial crisis.

Unfortunately, none of this is true.

The peace in old Europe since 1945 owes itself to the consequences of World War II. After this, what goals of war should the peoples of Europe still harbor? The costs of the war rendered them weary of war and incapable of waging it. They could not even pay for wars anymore. Only superpowers can afford it, or regional dictators without legitimacy or scruples, and even they can finance war for only a limited period. The only war that was waged in the post–World War II period on European soil was against a crumbling Serbia—a community action on the part of the United States and EU; the country was attacked, punished, and humiliated without a UN mandate.

The European Union did not trigger any democratic processes after 1945—not in Western Europe, nor in Eastern Europe after the collapse of the Soviet Union. On the contrary: The EU representatives usually reacted to the radical democratic changes at the periphery of the community with caution, if not skepticism. Gorbachev received rhetorical applause for his *perestroika*, but little active support; as to Poland's Solidarity movement and East Germany's peaceful revolution, neither received either one or the other. Earlier in the West, the picture was not any different: Portugal's Carnation Revolution, Spain's liquidation of the Franco regime, Greece's self-liberation from the Obristen dictatorship— all these arose from the people of these nations. In Portugal, the overthrow of an authoritarian dictatorship came from the country's own military. The European Union and its top personnel waited and welcomed the result after the fact. In the case of East German– West German unification into the German Democratic Republic (GDR), even that amount of acknowledgment did not occur. The extension of the European Union to encompass the earlier GDR occasioned no rejoicing, but rather a critical echo. Instead of sharing the joy of the former citizens of the GDR who won back their freedom, one was expected in the EU and its capital cities to take precautions against the increased power of a reunited Germany. Apparently ignored was the fact that the country, because of the integration, had loaded itself down with 17 million new citizens and needed to reconcile a strikingly unequal standard of living between East and West with a generational mortgage. Germany had become poorer (and more plagued with problems), not more powerful. Its per capita income dropped from first to seventh place in the European Union.

Nonetheless, there was a demand—particularly shrill in London, Paris, and Rome—that Germany neutralize the one instrument that would have made it easier to solve its integration problem: its currency. The Deutschmark (DM) was the most stable currency that the nation had ever possessed. Now it should be given up in payment as the price for reunification. It was a decision equally fatal for Germany as for the European Union. For when the German mark was gone, not only did Germany lose its anchor of stability, but so did the European Union.

The Euro: Not Dynamic but Dynamite

Instead of stability, the European Union brought a powder keg into the house: a new common currency, the euro, for soon-to-be 17 highly unequal ("inhomogeneous") member states. This replaced the old, wholesome, monetary discipline emanating from the Deutschmark as anchor currency with a blank check for a policy of debt as limitless as it was irresponsible, used by traditional inflation sinners and soft-currency countries in the EU periphery: the residents of the sunny Mediterranean and the Atlantic coast. With the new single currency, two of the automatic mechanisms for serving to stabilize the exchange rates were thrown overboard: currency competitiveness and currency risk. As long as there were competing currencies in the European Monetary System of 1979 (EMS), the exchange rate functioned as a measure of national economic performance. Appreciation of the currency meant strength; depreciation, weakness. This expression of currency risk had worked as a built-in stabilizer. Deficit or depreciation countries improved their current account through the rising prices of imports and the deterioration of their credit standing; taking the money outside the country became more expensive because of the currency risk.

At the same time, however, this increased their chances on the export market. In the surplus countries, the appreciation worked in the opposite direction: one imported more and more cheaply; if the export was billed in the local currency it rose in price, but only then. The nation derived a "social dividend" from the increased value of its currency; the more favorable exchange rate improved its terms of trade, pushed down domestic prices and interest rates, and raised the general standard of living. Savers and investors from around the world wanted to share in the gains due to appreciation; the capital markets began to flourish; one could import capital as cheaply as one could export it.

Looking back at the European Monetary System of 1979 one sees how well this balance within the EU economies worked. Between 1979 and 1987 there were almost annual devaluations or revaluations ("realignments"); as of 1987, hardly any. The DM functioned as a stabilizing anchor or brake on the inflation train; the current account balances found equilibrium. And the balance was not achieved by accruing debt.

Europe's monetary idyll was abruptly destroyed after 1990 through German reunification. Germany, the leader in EMS interest rates, fell into monetary turbulence because of the "association of inflation" (the growing excess demand from the former GDR). German interest rates at times exceeded 10 percent and brought other EMS partners into difficulty. Some had to devalue (once more) or even leave the EMS, as Italy did and later England.

In the summer of 1993, France experienced difficulties and ultimately demanded that Germany should either leave the EMS or accept the "hypothetical" euro with no ifs, ands, or buts.

Germany's acceptance of the euro (conditioned upon remaining as stable as the earlier Deutschmark, according to the German constitutional court in 1993) was bound to the built-in stability arrangements of two EU treaties (later TFEU): the stability pact of the Treaty of Amsterdam (1997) and the so-called "no-bailout clause" of Articles 125/126 of TFEU.

The stability pact was based on a strict limit on the internal public debt of the new euro nations: 3 percent of gross domestic product (GDP) per year and 60 percent overall. Article 125/26 prohibited any euro state from cofinancing the inner-state budget deficits of any other euro state. Every euro state should thus be compelled to comply with the stability pact.

After 10 years of euro practice, the results are obvious: Neither of the stability measures—the stability pact or the no-bailout clause—has been able to replace the automatic and market-based stabilization mechanisms of the EMS (exchange rate and currency risk). Just the opposite: With the introduction in the old deficit and depreciation countries, these nations were ranked and evaluated as "equally good" as the old surplus and appreciation countries by the European and global financial markets. Moreover, for banks, institutional investors, and other professional financiers they were even more attractive with the elimination of currency and devaluation risk than the stable surplus and former appreciation countries: Due to their higher internal inflation rates, their money and credit lenders gave higher returns with the same currency risks as the others. With the euro one had opened a Pandora's box, which opened ever further with every internal sign of "progress" in inflation. The "catch-up" EU countries on the southern and western edges of the EU—Portugal, Italy, Ireland, Greece, and Spain (PIIGS)—were the most popular investment candidates in the eurozone and accordingly the most highly indebted. It was only a matter of time before this ever more loudly ticking time bomb exploded. See Figure 3.1.

The time has now come.

The euro, which was supposed to bring together the core zone of the EU and rejuvenate and help to build up the peripheral EU countries to the east, has become an explosive rather than potter's clay. What had been pushed as a dynamic currency by those in EU circles has now, in fact, become dynamite! At the moment, after the bomb has exploded, it is no longer a question about whether the EU should be further expanded, to the borders of Russia and Syria. Now it is just a question of protecting Russia and Syria from the fissure. But the question is: How? Are the parachutes expanded to be available for rescuing the euro the appropriate means?

Is the European Union on Its Way to Becoming a Nation-State?

With its policy of making creditor and debtor states equivalent, the European Central Bank system (ESCB—the ECB and its

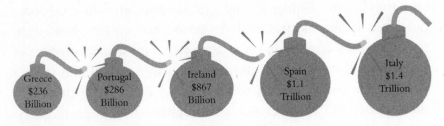

Figure 3.1   PIIGS: European Debt Bombs
SOURCE: Data: Bank for International Settlements. Chart: Suyash Jain.

connected national banks) has maneuvered itself into the beginning of an obvious dead end. For with each currency union equivalence constituting one euro = any euro, for both good (strong) and bad (indebted) members of the currency family, the ESCB opened the opportunity for the group of PIIGS to build up enormous public as well as private overindebtedness.

As the dramatic events of spring 2010 demonstrated clearly, overindebtedness has led the group of PIIGS states to the brink of bankruptcy. The hurriedly put together rescue package for the euro (May 7–10, 2010)—which was in truth a rescue package for the state bank's rotten, threatened creditor banks—pushed beyond the limits of the treaties of the EU. It made the monetary union a liability of cooperative euro states—or more precisely, a liability of their national budgets—and thus represents the official date on which the ESCB-binding stability doctrine was thrown open to question for the euro countries. This raises a number of serious issues of an economic, political, and constitutional nature.

The first question: Will the rescue program for the euro take hold? The answer: for the banks, yes; for the affected states, no, because their debts will remain and be taken over by the rescuers. In addition, this transfer of debt is hooked up to the drastic savings requirements imposed on public finances, placing a heavy burden on the economic growth and social climate of these countries. On top of the inflationary boom of the recent past, the PIIGS will now experience agonizing years of depression. But the dangers of political instability are understated by the bureaucrats of Brussels. For them, the rescue of the euro takes precedence over the preservation of Greek, Spanish, Portuguese, or Irish democracy. Under these imposed austerity measures, it is doubtful that they will be able to rebuild their economies and maintain their democracies with the help offered. For sooner or later, the loans granted will become subsidies lost.

A further question: Will the support funds of 750 billion euros (440 billion euros from other states, 250 billion from the IMF, 60 billion from the EU) initially proposed be sufficient? Here doubts are in order because the consolidated public and private debts involved are estimated to be from three to five times larger than this amount. Every increase in the rescue financing comes up against clear limits in both the contributing states as well as the IMF. Germany alone with its contribution of 170 billion euros has pledged three-quarters of the amount the state takes in annually in tax revenue. The ECB was concerned enough that at the end of 2010 it announced that by 2013 it would nearly double its capital from 5.8 billion euros to 10.8 billion euros.

Such sums, particularly if they have to be increased, are inconsistent with compatibility and acceptance in the politics of finance either by the parliament or by the public. This looks like anything but a serious politics of savings in terms of public policy.

And the EU? It is buying time with this program, but the question remains: for what purpose?

The ability to finance the rescue programs for the euro is intimately bound up with political consequences. Will the process bring the EU nations together or build causes for them to turn against each other? There can hardly be a unanimous response to this question, least of all in the states paying for the rescue. It is possible that in Great Britain—a noneuroland—efforts may increase to bring its own currency under the umbrella of the euro, in order to profit from it, given Britain's own economic and currency weaknesses (the British pound sterling has lost almost half of its value in terms of the euro since leaving the European Monetary System). However, the new government would hardly dare to do this without a referendum, and how that might turn out remains to be seen. If it parted with the pound sterling, England would give up a currency with which it has lived for more than 400 years, the oldest monetary history with the richest tradition in the modern era of currency. And this, in addition, would cause anxiety in England's internal union with Scotland. In turn, France—the secret initiator of the rescue packages, and itself close to PIIGS status—would no doubt agree to any expansion and consolidation of euro parachutes, provided that others pay and that its own influence in the EU bodies is kept.

Germany, the main contributor (responsible for a third of the aggregate liability plus an erosion agreement if other payers fail) sees itself suspended in a double ordeal. Economically, its good "rating" and "benchmark" position in the global and European financial markets is put at risk. It is like the host, who, through giving out too much free beer, goes broke himself! Politically it is a question of Germany's inner stability. The country and the parties represented in its parliament only agreed to the euro against the majority opinion of their voters on the conditions of the stability guarantees approved by the constitutional court.

However, not only will the business rationale of the stability community be taken away with the euro rescue parachutes and the transfer of the fiscal responsibility of states to a liability union, but these actions establish another EU that is not covered by the European treaties or the Basic German Law (GG): a European state with the obligation for intergovernmental financial compensation. To be transparent: Taxes overdue in Greece are now collected in Germany and other euro nations. However, in order to do this the (Lisbon) judgments of the German Federal Constitutional Court (of June 30, 2009), the EU treaties including those related to GG statutes must both be amended. Such amendments require referenda in other EU and euro countries as well as in Germany itself. Should Germany's highest court confirm this state of affairs in an official verdict (the complaint was submitted to the court), then Germany would be removed as the mainstay of the euro. However, should the court revise its position and declare Germany's payments for the euro rescue fund to be legal, the blank check of disloyal euro sinners would be supported in a coup from above. The EU would become a state without a constitutional or legal basis. How this will be received in the civilized world and financial markets, one can only guess. One way or the other, turbulent times lie ahead for the eurozone!

Do EU Institutions Induce Constitutional Infidelity?

Meanwhile, the Economic and Monetary Union (EMU) of the EU is catching up with its predecessors. They broke apart because the state and its currency could not be separated—at least in the era when national problems could be solved domestically. This was true of the Nordic Monetary Union made up of the Scandinavian countries (1873–1931), the French-led Latin Coinage Convention (1865–1926), and finally both world monetary systems, even if for them it was only a matter of negotiated exchange rate regimes: the gold standard, which went under in 1931, and the Bretton Woods agreement, which failed in 1973 as a result of the currency egoism of the United States.

In all four cases, it was internal problems of the member states, specifically obligations to their own citizens, which brought the monetary cooperation to an end. In the case of the Scandinavian countries, it was due to the need to maintain acutely threatened full employment. In the case of the Latin nations, they faced just as acute a threat from the pressure to fight inflation. Even the gold standard and the Bretton Woods system failed due to this hurdle. In nations governed by democratically elected parliaments, domestic national goals and duties have greater weight than the observance of internationally agreed-upon currency rules. In 1931 the stability of employment was at risk in the countries that left the gold standard; in 1973, the stability of the world's money system was at stake when Bretton Woods was terminated. Does narrow-minded nationalism underlie this? No: Nation-states are founded for the self-protection of their own citizens and not the interests of nonresidents. If they respect the welfare of their own citizens more highly than that of aliens, they are acting legitimately to exercise their obligations. The institutions of the European Union must ask themselves whether they are entitled to require members to commit constitutional infidelity. This applies as well to the emergency parachutes for the euro and the PIIGS adopted in May 2010.

Can the Euro Survive?

The answer to the question as to how the crisis that has broken out over the euro will end was given almost 100 years ago, long before the euro came into existence. In 1914, just before the outbreak of World War I, Eugen von Böhm-Bawerk—the head of the Viennese School of Economics, professor, former finance minister of several monarchies, and later a teacher of Joseph Schumpeter—published an article entitled "Power or Economic Law?" His answer: In the long term, economic law always wins. Böhm-Bawerk's conclusion serves as a warning to politicians today.[1]

He proved this with two examples that are still relevant today. If unions demand higher wages than justified by the productivity of the work, their victory over their employers will result in less work and more unemployment. His second example is a lesson for the EU today. If states grant credit to other states or take credit from the capital markets, then the capital markets determine the flow of goods, not vice versa. Böhm-Bawerk's equation: "The capital account commands, the trade balance follows, the balance of payments obeys."

This explains exactly the crisis in which the euro has landed. We have already seen that the euro made all member states into equally good borrowers, although 12 of the 16 proved to be otherwise. Until late 2009 through early 2010, the euro capital markets ignored the overindebtedness of the EU states on the southern and western periphery. Even the European Central Bank (ECB) and rating agencies saw no reason to doubt the same good grades given to all countries in the euro system. The ECB even refused to threaten the euro countries with higher inflation rates, such as the PIIGS, with interest rate penalties or withdrawals of credit.

This not only sharpened the existing inflation disparities and imbalances in the current accounts of the euro countries but, since no euro country could devalue or revalue "its" euros relative to the euros of its partner nations, the *real* exchange and interest rates became more and more visibly out of whack within the eurozone.

In the case of the PIIGS and F (for France), the euro appreciated in real terms, while real interest rates fell to zero or below—which made the taking on of debt from either internal or external sources of credit very cheap and attractive. Foreign and domestic public and private indebtedness boomed, while inflation in the PIIGS outran that of the other euro countries. The ECB ironed out these inflation disparities in its harmonized price of living index (HPI) with its statistical overweighting of the rest of the euro nations into a harmless, average flat rate. In essence, it oriented itself according to a dubious index instead of according to reality!

In the four surplus countries of the eurozone, particularly Germany, this took on a painful division in the economy: the real depreciation of the euro strengthened exports, while the real high interest rates (higher than in the noneuro countries such as Switzerland and the Scandinavian nations) burdened the domestic market and the middle-sized companies, which had to pay more for bank credit. As the strongest country in capital and economic growth, Germany could hold on to its export superiority (one of the top three in the world), but could no longer be a locomotive for growth in the EU and eurozone. Europe had to pay the cost of falsely set exchange rates and interest rates with growing domestic tensions and imbalances. The monetary union did not promote the objective of the "convergence" of national economies, but rather their growing divergence. The PIIGS and France lived well domestically with their practices of overconsumption and luxury "on the credit card." But sooner or later the EMU's capacity as a giant intra-European "customer credit machine" had to reach the limits of its capacity.

This happened in the beginning of 2010: The sleeping but shrewd capital markets discovered the euro's internal debt exposure kept secure by the ECB and the rating agencies. They began to distrust the ECB's guarantee that every euro would equal every other euro, independent of the debt status of the individual euro nations, and massively sold off their euro investments. Since a flight out of the Greek, Spanish, or Portuguese euro into the German euro made little sense, they discovered (or rediscovered) old and new "secure-harbor currencies"—the U.S. dollar, the Swiss franc, and the "small" dollars (Canadian, Australian, New Zealand, etc.). The euro fell, even as much as 25 percent at times.

For the PIIGS within the eurozone, the massive increase in the price of their loans on the capital market went up with the euro's loss in value, with the threat of state bankruptcy within reach. This was particularly true for countries in debt near or above 100 percent of GDP (Greece, Italy, Portugal) but less the case in Spain, Ireland, and France, where credit lies more in the private sector. The ECB had to concede that its policy of "the same interest for all euro countries" had failed. Early May 2010 signaled the failure of the euro project through the reactions to the high-to-overindebted euro nations. National bankruptcy became an acute threat, particularly in Greece, raising the question of a possible exit of the states in question from the European Monetary System and a return to national currencies and the classic sanitizing through devaluations and negotiated haircuts on their loans.

In this dilemma the EU Commission and Paris secretly coordinated a "forward strategy": The ECB and the countries in the euro group should agree to a concerted action to secure the payments of the PIIGS and their creditor banks—the real culprits in this crisis. The rescue program, which is a serious interference with the operation of market forces, provides for the following actors and levels of action:

- The ECB buys "junk bonds" from the PIIGS states, contrary to its articles of association (Art. 22, 28), which ban it from doing so. The amounts involved are open—so open, in fact, that this monetarization of (bad) state debts later could become an inflation threat!
- The governments of the euro countries create a consortium with a new institution: the European Stabilization Fund (ESF). It supports the PIIGS with loans at a 5 percent interest rate if market rates exceed this level. And it will get the money for this purpose either from government-backed loans in the financial markets or directly from government budgets. Its existence is limited to mid-2013.
- The third component is a credit line of an installment of up to 250 million euros from the International Monetary Fund (IMF).

All in all, this program makes available almost a trillion dollars of public funds (guaranteed loans) to rescue the euro and banks. No one can predict whether this will be enough to prevent this long creeping crisis from bursting out into a sea of open flames that the fire department can no longer keep under control. For this depends upon three unknowns.

The Three Unknowns of the Current Bailout of the Euro

First, in terms of law, all the actions agreed upon are illegal. They constitute serious breaches of law and violations of the EU treaties. These specifically prohibit rescue operations from state to state in order not to undermine the indispensable currency morale and discipline necessary for the functioning of the monetary union. The same can be said for the intervention of the IMF, which is in violation of its own statutes. The IMF is supposed to provide balance-of-payments loans in foreign currencies (U.S. dollar or Special Drawing Rights [SDRs]) to central banks, not in local currencies (euro) to states to finance their budget deficits. All of these "emergency plans" require affirmative referendums in all EU countries according to the clear wording of the current "Lisbon Treaty." This requirement, however, has been circumvented by establishing emergency operations and institutions.

Second, politically speaking, a bailout and a "cold" *coup d'état* in the EU amount to the same thing. The EU is taking on many of the vital rights and fundamental attributes of a sovereign state, such as borrowing and financial compensation, which are not provided for in the treaties. Due to this a complaint has been filed in Europe's highest court.[2] A new chapter of the EU may emerge depending on how the cases are decided.

Third, in regard to the amount of money coming from the ECB, ESF, and IMF, the sum of almost a trillion dollars of "fire-fighting liquidity capacity" may not seem so great after all. When it comes to escaping from the flight out of the euro into "safe-harbor currencies," it is not enough. For then it is not just a question of the registered state and private debts of the countries at risk of insolvency, but of *all* savings that seek a safe currency harbor. Although these sums are incalculable, they far exceed the billions that are available for the rescue.

France is clearly behind all these emergency plans for rescuing the euro, and, as a highly indebted euro country, must be concerned about falling into a situation similar to the PIIGS. It takes Germany to task for a lack of "solidarity" in its behavior, arguing that with its surpluses (consequences of its strengths in productivity) it does not compensate for the deficits of its partners, but helps to bring them about. Germany should pay as before and operate with a domestic inflation policy in order to bring life back into the economies and exports of its partners—a demand that economists of the left support, for they see in this a chance for sustainable wage increases.

Ten years of the EMU and the euro have clearly shown that the euro did not bring Europe's nations together, but exposed their historical, cultural, and structural differences even more strikingly. Different lifestyles and habits cannot be smoothed out with a common currency. The hope of European politicians that they could use the euro bill to buy a ticket for the streetcar named Desire, their vision of a "Europe united and made equal," was not to be. The peoples of Europe prefer to stay "individual and distinctive."

All that remains is to state the interim balance: The euro has neither increased the future prospects of Europe as a whole nor improved the situation in the national welfare states. On the contrary, the separation of community money from the national politics of budgets markedly reduced the efficiency of national economic and social policies.

What weighs the most heavily is the asymmetric load distribution of the euro mortgage. The PIIGS are the beneficiaries of the euro, while the "good" and disciplined euro countries provide them with their available savings. Now the beneficiaries are upset that they have to pay back their loans. The euro crisis has become a test for the sustainability of European solidarity.

Europe's top economists will come to realize that Eugen von Böhm-Bawerk was correct: The economic reality always prevails over political illusions. However, Europe's politicians must realize that their well-known "money-integrates-nations theory" was only a beautiful dream, and anything but a reliable compass for the safe navigation of ships of state as they enter shallow waters.

It is tragic, however, that Europe, which has suffered for a thousand years under the "imperialist power" of the leading nations that sought to compel unification through force—first Germany, then Spain, France, England, and most recently, Germany again—now sought an instrument of peaceful convergence that has not worked: money. And Germany is psychologically torn: Just as it was prepared to leave behind its exceptional record in history and politics, it had to discover that its monetary nationalism in the gestalt of the German mark (DM) was the best guarantee for its fortunate postwar era, as well as for Europe as a whole. But the road back to national currencies in the EU lies in the stars. For the EU Commission is not prepared to withdraw from its misguided monetary adventures.

The Next Financial Adventure: A European State Bankruptcy Law

The next financial adventure is already fixed on the agenda. States without their own currency must always reckon with the possibility of becoming insolvent in difficult times. The euro—a "foreign" currency of each euro nation—has, in the meantime, driven a dozen of them (in addition to the PIIGS) into precarious proximity to bankruptcy. Therefore, it seems naive, if not ridiculous, if EU policy attempts to cure this evil through an EU-wide state-insolvency law.

The threat of bankruptcy in these states is a built-in part of the euro system, even if it has not been seen as such! The planned bankruptcy clubs have new rules aimed mainly at hiding the fact that one is willing to continue the euro rescue policy even when the rescue parachutes collapse or their funds are exhausted.

The affected, euro-impacted countries could get rates that are cheaper and more appropriate for the system if they were free to return to their old, national currencies than relying on the "haircuts" and negotiated rates with insolvency creditors envisioned by the insolvency clubs.

A state with its own currency *cannot* become insolvent, but it can always threaten to devalue in order to force concessions in the regulation of its debts. The overindebted state protects its domestic creditors (depositors, investors) by transforming its domestic debt 1:1 into the new currency. In terms of foreign creditors, some of the value of their loans would be written down, which is nothing more than a partial insolvency, although the country has the choice of depreciation as a stimulus to negotiate with respective creditors a bankruptcy quota, a debt cancellation (haircut), or an extension of time (moratorium).

There is no need for "Berlin clubs" with new means for the settlement of pending state insolvencies in the eurozone. The old clubs (in Paris and London), the best in the business, have a half-century's worth of experience with the IMF, and are sufficient to satisfactorily resolve the problems created by the EMU and the euro.

What Comes after the Euro?

Whichever way it goes, the euro is a currency on demand. The failure of the planned rescue efforts is in sight. The legal framework already exists: the Lisbon Treaty, Article 50, allows member states to withdraw from the EU. Consequently, this also applies to members of the Economic and Monetary Union (EMU), which is a component of the EU. The only open questions are as to which date, the course that will be taken, and the resulting scenarios.

Let us recall that within the EMS there is a hard core that functions well, the so-called D-Mark zone (Deutschmark zone). The members have functioned as an informal currency union (no contract, no currency agreements formally secured it), since all participants have had the same interests and followed the same goals. The mutual interdependence of the trading among partners was high, up to 65 percent and more; the maintenance of currency stability was their common goal. This de facto currency union functioned because there was no reason for changes in exchange rates. The exchange rate thermometer always read "stable"—no partner had any interest in changing it; for depreciation would have meant inflation, and appreciation would mean, in contrast, a loss of competitiveness in the market.

The following sections lay out alternatives for life after the euro.

Alternative I: Continuation of Euro-Currency Union as a Hard Currency Block

Only if the euro is streamlined to include a monetary union of equals, with identical interests and goals—an enlarged D-Mark zone with a different name—can the eurozone be perpetuated. The euro would then be as it was initially planned to be: a D-Mark on the European level, the eurozone at the core of the internal market with open access opportunity to all EU countries that meet the entry conditions for the euro club. For the countries leaving the euro, there would be an open opportunity for rehabilitation and recovery of their lost competitiveness on their own without outside pressure or tutelage. They would return to their old currencies (setting their domestic euro assets and liabilities at 1:1 on this basis) and sharply devalue the "new" old currency in terms of the exchange rate with other nations. Within the euro entry hall, the remaining 11 EU nations would pass over their own national currencies into Exchange Rate Mechanism II (ERM II). From there they could negotiate their insolvency quota (or "haircuts") with the help of the IMF, the EU, and its diverse clubs (Paris, London). Their creditors hold bad cards in this situation: They must accept these suggestions or leave empty-handed.

All debt crises in the past 25 years (but also in the past 2,500 years!) were resolved this way—so why should this not be the case this time around?

Moreover, the ex-euro countries would have the satisfaction of getting out of the swamp of debt without the aid money from the rescue packages and without a visit from the IMF and European taskmasters who (like the reparations agents in Germany after World War I) check on their compliance with the aid loans, and more or less force them to continue cheating—an economic absurdity.

Alternative II: A Soft Euro–Currency Union of EU Southern Countries (with or without France)

If a transformation of the eurozone into a hard currency block à la the old D-Mark zone does not come about, the soft variation of a residual eurozone of soft EU countries could remain. This would be a rebirth of the old Latin Coinage Convention once led by France with almost the same members (excluding Switzerland), but without a gold base as in those days. It would remain open as to whether France once again would take over the leadership.

Another open (semantic) question is, no matter which of the currency blocks emerged, the hard or the soft, whether or not it should henceforth be called the "eurozone."

Alternative III: Orderly Transition to National Currencies

This alternative would make the most sense by far for all euro countries. After a (lost) decade of experimentation with the false integration vehicle (the currency), the EU countries would return to the golden 40 years of European integration history following the Treaties of Rome in 1958 and lasting up until the beginning of the euro era in 1999: the Europe of nations and its stability based on competing national currencies.

For Germany, this return would mean the end of the Deutschmark "reparations" on the altar of Europe. This D-Mark II would appreciate and serve as a kind of stability anchor in relation to the other European currencies, and would have to be devalued if necessary. For Germany it would be a return to what Karl Schiller called the economic "social dividend."[3] The gains from revaluation would benefit all Germans (households as well as firms) in relation to imported goods and services or the consumption of bananas, gasoline, or holidays overseas. They would receive more goods and services for their money. Real income and the assets of all households would increase. The economy would once again benefit from the lowest interest rates in Europe. The export sector would not be damaged as in the past; it would save on the purchasing side what it would eventually lose (if invoiced in foreign currency).

The greatest gain, however, would be in the euro debts on the fiscal side in Germany. It could pay off its euro debts with newly revalued German marks; for in Germany, the specter of another national bankruptcy could set up another round of ghosts.

Nevertheless, Europe would still receive monetary coopera-tion. It would be concentrated as it was before the euro era in the EMS on the exchange rate policies vis-à-vis the dollar and other international currencies. The euro would become the successor of the earlier "ECU" unit of account and reference for exchange rates, a symbolic European currency. The ECB and the new institutions of the planned fiscal, transfer, and liability union could be abandoned.

There is not much time to realize these alternatives. Tomor-row's panic reactions of uncertain savers could determine the time frame and outcome. So far, the flight from the euro has been held within limits and moves in conventional forms: investments in gold, real estate, and solid stocks. But even these legitimate forms of private savings and asset protection cause severe economic losses: The savers invest in "dead capital" rather than in new projects, jobs, and income. At the same time the propensity increases to invest in stock market and financial instruments, raising the prices of assets (asset inflation). The gold boom is a flashing warning sign, and should be taken seriously.

With these developments, the risk grows of short circuits on the part of EU grandees. The first two—the elimination of cur-rency competition and the exclusion of financial markets from state financing and redevelopment by the rescue fund—could result in a third: the restriction of capital transactions with foreign countries up to the point of prohibiting them. Article 64 of the Treaty would give them the handle. Why not use it?

But this would be tantamount to shooting oneself in the foot. The euro would become a domestic currency à la the Third World. The citizen uses the euro to cover daily expenses. But to save and invest, she looks for another currency, a "black market" one if necessary. However: A form of money that no one keeps for private investment or savings no longer brings prosperity to everyone in the community!

Things must not be permitted to get that far. The hard euro is still not lost as a currency (Alternative I), but only if the captains, already past the point of needing to use binoculars and radar, see the visible iceberg on the horizon and change course to sail around it.

The Future of the EU: The Swiss Model

It is still too early to speculate on the future of the European Union. Here the Keynesian wisdom applies: It is increasingly difficult to detach oneself from old ideas in order to develop new ones. But the double crisis of the West (global and European) has made clear:

- The EU is not a shield against the crisis. On the contrary: It has increased it in-house.
- The EU has not made the old national social and welfare state unnecessary. On the contrary: The nation-state is challenged more than ever in the crisis.
- The EU has not grown together through the euro. On the contrary: The euro countries have diverged in their development in terms of the common currency; inflation rates and internal current account imbalances are wider spread than in the era preceding the euro.

The future of the EU lies neither in a continuation of its territorial expansion nor in its expansion into a European superstate. Equally irresponsible is the expansion of the monetary union into a fiscal union in which the states (still) able to pay are stuck with those that are no longer solvent. It may seem as if the step from monetary socialism to fiscal socialism is short and consistent, but it ends inevitably at the wall of a well-trodden dead end!

The end of the euro does not mean the end of the EU. On the contrary: The EU is delivered from the threat of a powder keg that would have blown up sooner or later. European politicians have the time and opportunity to reflect on the future of the EU in a world situation that has been transformed. What will make the EU still attractive for its member states tomorrow? How should their business card appear for this world?

Behind the euro debacle is more than just a failed monetary experiment. The domestic politics (including currency policy) of democratic states is and remains integration-resistant. It is solely up to the discretion of the local citizens, voters, and their parliaments and not "unpatriotic" Eurocrats. If it were any different, they would shrivel up.

The end of the euro frees the ECB and ESCB (and the politicians of the so-called Euro-Group) of the false ambition of trying to turn a stateless currency into a "second dollar." The central banks of the world need short-term usable government securities in order to invest their reserves securely and to keep them liquid. As long as the European Union is not a state (it never will be), the euro is and remains disadvantaged compared to the IMF's Special Drawing Rights (SDRs) or even U.S. dollars. Germany could make up for this shortcoming with a new DM. It would not be the worst service that it gives to a united Europe (as it did before).

So what remains of the old European Union? The past cannot be a model for the future; for the problems of the past 50 years are either solved or they endure. Europe has eliminated its war damage and worked through its war memories, and the scars have healed. There is no threat of war nor danger from a hostile ideology outside the front door; communism and the Cold War are history. There is no need to fear their comeback.

The future of the West (United States and EU) is overshadowed by global issues affecting all of humankind (environment, climate, population, and migration pressures) and the upheavals of the new world economy (new competitors, loss of market share), and more than ever before it is up to nation-states to do their homework: battle the crisis; curb inflation, overindebtedness, and unemployment; cope with the aging of the population.

The EU really only has a "say" in the latter two groups of problems: the global market and the state.

In the new world economy, both Atlantic coasts pull together closer than previously. The United States and EU can afford neither a trade war nor a currency war with each other, and also cannot afford fighting over votes in the old and new global governance bodies: the IMF, the World Bank, the G-8, and the G-20. On the state level it is less a question of old goals than testing new instruments in order to realize them: Will security be reached through more market maneuvering and competition or through more statecraft and control? How does one deal with the financial sector? How can the financial actors be tied more closely to the real economy? How much debt and debt servicing can a society bear? Which innovations are relevant for growth, which must be promoted, and which are self-financing?

In answering all of these questions in the EU of the future it will be less a question of "acting" than of advising, clarifying, and coordinating.

The EU of the future will be much more analytical, making problems evident, rather than an active solver of problems. As with the United Nations (and formerly the League of Nations), the greatest weight of the executive (Commission, Council of Ministers, ECB) will be put on the level of communications: the European Parliament, the periodic meetings and discussions of the decision-makers on the spot in the member countries. The milieu of the new EU will be more contemplative than the old. Instead of political action, it will be all about debate, dialogue, development, and the transmission of ideas.

From these building blocks the image of a new "Helvetic" Europe will be formed. Policy will be made below, in the autonomous cantons of the comparable states. Up above in the EU bodies, the great lines of external representation and common action can be designed.

This EU must not exclude itself from nonmembers like Switzerland or Norway or from Russia. The last residue of European particularism, the difference between the European Economic Area (EEA) and the European Union, will disappear. This EU can do without symbols or nonparliamentary institutions, leaders, and representatives.

A qualified expert secretariat would organize the meetings and agendas of political leaders, the conferences and debates of the delegates, and the testimony of experts on the issues at stake. This enlightening rather than acting European Union is the future European Union. When a wise head (he was called Oedipus) wrested power from the Sphinx, power that she had accrued through her superior knowledge, she committed suicide. Because she had lost her knowledge? Or her rule? One could also say, because she had realized that her time was up.

Currency "Concubinage": The Currency Has to Serve the Citizen, Not the Citizen the Currency

A state without currency is forced to declare bankruptcy just like a company or bank that becomes insolvent in the case of poor management. Were the neoliberal founders of the EU treaties of Maastricht (1992) and Amsterdam (1997) conscious of this when establishing the Economic and Monetary Union (EMU)? Of course not.

Otherwise, the current euro crisis never would have occurred.

The monetary unions of former times merely constituted agreements on national exchange rates, some of them unilateral.

Giving up national currencies was never a subject open for discussion. The global gold standard of the nineteenth and early twentieth century was an international exchange rate convention derived from the National Coinage Act of that time. It was a Euclidean world monetary system according to the theorem: If two measures are equal to a third (in this case, the statutory threshold amount of gold), they are also equal to each other in proportion to their parities with gold. Even the Bretton Woods accord after 1945 agreed that "international monetary law" did not refer to national currencies, but rather to their exchange rates (see Chapter 5).

The same was true of Europe's regional subsystems of the pre-euro period: the Mint Union of the Scandinavian countries (until 1933), the Latin Monetary Convention led by France (until 1926), and the European Monetary System of 1979, the immediate precursor of today's EMU. When it came to currency crises due to balance-of-payments deficits and tensions (which always occurred), neither the states nor their currencies were under fire, but solely their fixed exchange rates whether determined by gold coverage or contractual obligations. The inevitable result was exchange rate adjustment—currency devaluation in a crisis. This adjustment replaced state bankruptcy, which was never really threatened or seriously considered.

The exchange rate adjustment to the inner realities of the economy (inflation, current account deficit)—if it turned out to be convincing enough—reconstituted the confidence in the currency, restoring both equilibrium in the balance of payments account and the lost international competitiveness of the recovering nation. The nominal external value of the currency was adjusted to its changing internal real value. And one could depend upon the success of this compensatory mechanism. It proved to be successful even in the EMS of 1979, to the satisfaction of the European currency partners (although requiring extended bandwidth for the "breathing" of exchange rates as of 1993). Whenever currency crises occurred in the pre-EMU period, they were always resolved monetarily, never escalating into state crises!

But this was drastically changed with the euro currency "concubinage" of the current 17 EU states; in the final stage of the European integration process all 30 states are anticipated to share a common currency. Within the eurozone there can no longer be exchange rate adjustments and corrections. The EMU is monetarily already a state, but not in political reality where the EMU constitutes neither a state nor a constitution. In the final analysis it is always national parliaments that decide on legislation and state budgets. The prime right of democracy and its parliaments is to have the final word on collecting and using public funds (through taxes, debt, expenditure)—and this still rests with the EU states, not with the EU institutions. Nothing is permitted to change in this regard, as the German Constitutional Court (in its "Lisbon verdict" in the autumn of 2009) reaffirmed once again—unless the nations of the EU decide otherwise by referenda and constitutional amendments.

Nevertheless, EU institutions and European policy steadfastly pursue their intention of changing this legal and constitutional situation by maintaining a single currency and the adjustment processes triggered by it—including crises! The euro currency is designed to serve as a "locomotive" for the trip to a Europe modeled after the United States; for this purpose it should be used and continually developed. The business basis (and justification) for this is articulated as the "constraint theory" of the EU grandees, aimed at the public spheres and the media in order to convince them that there is no alternative to this policy as its protagonists continually affirm. The European Central Bank (ECB) practices this theory by reporting the data of the eurozone in toto, keeping its national causes and components under wraps. This process worked to help obscure the euro crisis for a long time: Few saw the crisis coming due to a lack of illuminating figures, not to mention the opportunity to take timely countermeasures.

After 10 years of experience with the euro, one can no longer ignore:

- The euro experiment is in its most serious crisis to date and appears doomed to fail. Twelve of the states with a common euro currency are highly overindebted both privately and publicly—four of them being the so-called GIPS (Greece, Ireland, Portugal, Spain), where debts are so heavy that even their impending state bankruptcy cannot be excluded.
- Instead of leading to a joint objective of a policy of monetary stability, the common currency has resulted in the unleashing of a wild redistributional struggle within the EMU—a beggar-thy-neighbor policy, which is unprecedented in the 50-year-old history of the EU. It is as if the EMU is a Pandora's box that has been opened. Not only have the GIPS abused the system by taking advantage of credit and interest gifts thrown into their laps (they received the same ratings as the good and stable euro countries, and the interest rate on their credit was cut by a third or more beyond), in order to live robustly and recklessly the means justified by their gross domestic products—and this at the expense of their faithful contractual currency partners, who paid their deficits by allowing them to use the euro abroad. Above all, Germany paid.

This did not make much of an impression upon the GIPS. Greece expanded its government mismanagement, Ireland "hypertrophied" its now insolvent financial sector, Portugal put its overdue structural reforms on ice, and Spain financed its biggest housing bubble since the looting of Peruvian gold and silver mines. After the discovery of these mines, Spain declared bankruptcy due to the religious mania of Philip II (1596). Since then motives and financial techniques have changed. Yet

like the old colonial powers (France, Italy, Belgium), the euro
countries misused the euro as their bonanza.

- The eurozone countries have thus made themselves hostages
of the laws of the currency concubinage that support the
financial and banking world. Because the EMU was not
threatened by monetary losses (a softened GIPS euro was
always valued at 1:1 in a hard German or other euro), it paid
off for the deficit countries to buy cheaply (that is, at low real
interest rates and revalued real exchange rates) and to take
credit from the surplus countries. For investors and depositors
from the surplus countries, in turn, it was a good deal to leave
their capital with the GIPS at their higher yields without any
risk of inflation or devaluation. Alone the transfer of capital
from Germany (the nation richest in capital in the eurozone)
came to an estimated 1 trillion euros via euro money and
capital markets—an enormous withdrawal effect upon this
economy, because these means were then lacking for domestic
circulation. With this capital, Germany would have been able
to rehabilitate its state budget, its welfare state, the middle class,
its infrastructure, its cash-strapped municipalities, and the new
German states. However, so-called experts try to outdo each
other in the assertion that Germany was the main beneficiary of
the euro—arguing that the country owes its export surpluses to
the (weak) euro. But the truth is that without the euro, the
country would have accurate (i.e., lower) real interest rates and
higher real currency exchange rates—as good as those of
Switzerland, Sweden, or Denmark. So Germany would have
been just as well off without the euro, or even better off!

- Meanwhile, the bank debt in the GIPS and other euro deficit
countries is four to seven times the domestic GDP, in contrast
to 2.5 times in Germany. It is this combination of public and
private indebtedness that leaves the financial world and EU
leaders at a loss. The financial world wants its money back as

soon as possible without "haircuts," while government policies need to prevent this in order to protect against the threat of state bankruptcy!

- The lesson for both sides from the disaster brought about by themselves could not be more depressing for the old continent and its values. Conventional politics calls for severe sanctions for the states that have jeopardized the euro and does not recognize that these austerity obligations (be they from cuts in expenditure and income or from tax increases) are senseless macroeconomically (although not morally). Such policies merely perpetuate the crisis in GIPS and other EU member nations and freeze old and new loans. In the meantime, with its refusal to participate in massive debt restructuring and "haircuts," the financial world not only further demolishes its reputation, but throws its very rescue by the states into question: Unscrupulous traders and evil speculators cannot be of any help to the (neo)liberal state.

- And what about the states themselves rescuing the euro? Politicians must recognize that the currency—regardless of whether national or European—is not at the disposal of the state and its goals, as desirable as this may be. The currency is solely a means at the disposition of the citizen: for his or her right to liberty, to property, and for a self-directed future.

The EU and its community of states lose their democratic legitimacy and indispensable support from European citizens and voters if they try to change (that is, to *break*) contracts that have been misdesigned or have proven to be inadequate (such as the debt of the banking system ignoring the Stability and Growth Pact of Amsterdam—a relic of the limited neoliberal vision of its inventors, or dismissing warnings against impending national bankruptcy: the intent of the "no-bailout clause" (Articles 125/ 126) of the EU labor contracts of Lisbon. Or if they expose the celebrated independence of the ECB from government directives as a farce by mandating that this institution buy worthless junk bonds of GIPS states ripe for bankruptcy and pay for this with freshly printed, but highly inflationary euros.

The EU puts its overall endeavor at risk if it believes it can save the long-failed monetary "concubinage" of the eurozone countries by means of a fiscal rescue package: a "currency Socialism" (à la Vaclav Klaus) brought about by the now newly minted financial socialism. The EU becomes its own suicide bomber when it forces its citizens to support their own currency with their tax pennies. Such a currency is not worth a thing. It may circulate as legal tender for a while and be used in the supermarket, but it will fail as an investment or asset for capital preservation. Europe's economies are forced to save in "dead capital" (gold, foreign currencies, tangible goods). This is bad for Europe's prosperity and its growth prospects, not to mention the ratings and the ability to pay off the guarantors of the euro who have to vouch for the currency (and the debt underlying it)—such as Germany.

Have the EU, EMU, and the euro come to their end? The answer is yes, if the old policy is continued; but no, if it is revised. Europe has to find its way out of the present impasse and go back to its beginning—back to the good old EMS: from the failed currency union to the trusty exchange rate union, back to currency devaluation as an alternative to national bankruptcy. This means that the euro could play the role of the old "ECU" as a reference unit for exchange rates as Europe's symbolic "gold."

Chapter 4

The *New* New World
Can BRICs Save the Rich?

T
he *New* New World will be dominated by the sea change of economic dynamism shifting away from the West to the emerging economies, led by the exploding middle classes in the nations known as the BRICs (Brazil, Russia, India, and China). The West seems old, indebted, and politically stalemated in comparison to many emerging nations, where an increasing share of the world's economic growth and institutional investment will end up. Indeed, by 2020, the BRICs are forecast to contribute twice as much global growth as the G-3 (the United States, Japan, and Germany). In the sectors of automobiles, mobile phones, and commodities, the BRICs are leading the way.

With 40 percent of the world's population, the BRICs already account for 25 percent of global GDP and are intensely increasing

their trade with one another, often in local currencies, and becoming more independent. They are much less dependent on
exports than most people realize (exports account for less than 15
percent of GDP in Brazil and India, not to mention China). In
June of 2009, the BRIC leaders met with representatives of the
Shanghai Cooperation Organization (SCO; including a number of
former Soviet republics) in Yekaterinburg, Russia. In addition to
coordinating on global financial regulations, this meeting also
focused on moving away from the dollar as a key reserve currency
in an orderly fashion and restructuring the International Monetary
Fund (IMF) in order to make Special Drawing Rights (SDRs)
more significant as a transition to a multipolar basket of currencies
as the basis for a new international monetary system. They are also
quietly focusing development on environmentally sustainable
projects and processes and are likely to surprise the developed
world with their competitiveness in sustainability.[1]

The excesses of the financial sector among the rich nations go
back to imbalances in the world economy that have long been
recognized. Those emerging economies that are most successful in
international trade (i.e., the BRICs) are precisely those endowed
with large domestic markets and resources capable of being developed. Global imbalances (on the unlikely assumption that causality
can be so easily attributed) are largely the result of surreptitious
export-led growth strategies of states—above all China, in addition
to Germany and Japan. A nation imports the necessary development
capital, although it "has it" or could mobilize it at home because
the savings are present. It is a new version of the old concept of
mercantilism. At that time, gold was lacking, which was needed
for the production of domestic money and credit; therefore,
a nation had to bring it in through export surpluses in order
to succeed—taking money and credit hostage, according to the
theories of Hume and Smith, among others. Today the BRICs,
Organization of Petroleum Exporting Countries (OPEC), and

other commodity-oriented countries lack essential institutions in order to transform the wealth of savings into productive investments: capital markets and banks, both of which are under-developed. Thus, a nation finances a large part of its investments and development through foreign reserves. But the conversion of foreign reserves into domestic money and credits is highly inflationary: pure money and credit creation. Because this process must be kept under control, a large residual basis must remain in accumulated reserves that cannot be used, particularly in China.

These residual reserves serve to finance the huge deficits of the U.S. financial superpower (due to the role of the dollar) as well as the deficit nations of the EU—because these reserves are stored in the currencies of these deficit countries. The overdevelopment of the Western financial system (overbanking connected with risky financial innovations and know-how) resulted in heavily supporting this wrong-headed financial development process of Third World states, diverting them from attacking their own financial underdevelopment. Foreign money and credit were easier and cheaper to obtain than money and credit that were available domestically! And yet it was due to high financial reserves that a nation was deemed creditworthy. The crisis signals the end of this seemingly comfortable but profoundly uneconomic mode. The indebted United States and European Union countries are no longer creditworthy or good debtors. The BRICs, OPEC, and others must invent other strategies and investment vehicles for their surpluses. The old mercantilism failed, because not all nations can export at the same time.

Mimicking Past Economic Miracles

Now the crisis forces rich but highly industrialized countries into more savings, and the two old masters in exporting (Germany,

Japan) will have to expand their domestic markets. From the perspective of the old world, the *New* New World is not more "beautiful," but more painful, for it must shrink and share its export markets with new competitors. However, the world economy as a whole will become more stable in the process.

The emerging economies have already attempted to imitate those that formerly had "economic miracles" (such as Japan and Germany). They observed the effectiveness of postauthoritarian stability aimed at commercial results through export-oriented growth, trying to keep politics and security issues in the background in order to attract investment and trade. Being underbanked, they were not as hard hit by the near bankruptcy of the global financial crisis in comparison with the overbanked rich countries of the West, which were suddenly weighed down by their domination of financial sectors that created no new social value, but merely charged higher prices for old capital. The financial reserves of the emerging nations helped to bail out Western institutions with which globalization had permanently interlinked them. The global transformation was underscored at the Copenhagen Climate Summit in December of 2009, where President Obama and his Secretary of State Hillary Clinton found it necessary to crash a private meeting of the BRIC countries in order to solidify a compromise promise of transparency—a result far less significant than the power shift implied by the process involved in this particular negotiation!

Developing countries are no longer seeking out the old rich nations of Europe or North America for models, but are looking rather to Singapore and China, the "bricks" among BRICs. The only exception, paradoxically, appears to be the financial sector: The underdeveloped countries seek to mimic many of the wealth-creating features of the wealthy, even after witnessing the inevitable booms and busts that must follow from such speculative behavior.

The Rise of the BRICs

During the Cold War, the world was split in half with two main players. The key source of information concerning the Soviet bloc for the Western world was the U.S. Central Intelligence Agency (CIA). In the twenty-first century, the world is divided into 20-plus parts (the G-20) and the key institutions shaping information are large multinational companies (such as Google and Goldman Sachs). In 2001 the thesis of the Goldman Sachs economic unit was that given their rapid rates of development, Brazil, Russia, India, and China—which chief economist Jim O'Neill of Goldman named "the BRICs"—could eclipse the economic clout of the richest countries by 2050 (see Figure 4.1).[2] By the time of the London Summit of April 2009,

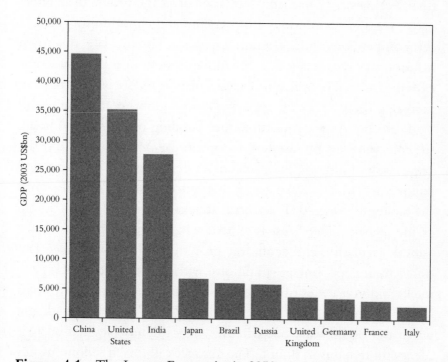

Figure 4.1   The Largest Economies in 2050
Source: Dominic Wilson and Roopa Purushothaman, "Dreaming with BRICs: The Path to 2050," Goldman Sachs Global Economics Paper No. 99 (2003) (www.gs.com).

the BRICs had accepted the appellation of Goldman Sachs, had combined into a political alliance, and were in the economic position of being asked by the IMF to contribute billions of dollars in order to bail out the financial system of the rich countries. What goes around comes around. . . .

Underlying this political and economic sea change is a deep, global, anti-Western, antimodernist trend that has been centuries in the making. Not only the Islamic world but traditional societies throughout the globe have become skeptical if not adamantly antagonistic to the decadence of the Western, democratic capitalist way of life, which dominates the rich countries. Fascism was one extremist revolt against the banality of this mass materialism and atomistic individualism. Communism radically attacked the structural weaknesses of individualistic capitalism and provided an alternative socialist state model. Both fascism and communism failed in the competition with Western capitalism. In the late twentieth century, the apparent victory of Anglo-American capitalism led to extremes of materialistic financial speculation and social polarization, preparing the way for the spread of a third global revolt: Islamism.

From the Arab perspective, the founding of the state of Israel, the interventions by Western troops in the Middle East, and the imposition of Judeo-Christian and Western lifestyles on traditional cultures led to a massive backlash from the Islamic world—with the September 11, 2001, terrorists attacks representing only the tip of the iceberg. The West is experiencing a rejection of its materialism, secularity, and economic growth for their own sake. The undermining of vintage traditions with the technological gimmicks and vulgarities of modernity is not tolerated in many Third World countries. Capitalism may have "won" in 1989 with the fall of the Berlin wall, but whether or not democracy has been as successful remains in doubt. The abstract call for "freedom" is not in itself persuasive: Societies must demonstrate that they deeply understand and are committed to individual liberties, the protection of private property, and the rule of law and are willing and able to enforce democratic limits against the interests of any one interest group, power clique, or set of multinational companies that seeks to dominate the national polity.

In terms of the classical Western economic model, the question has become whether or not the West can afford to pay for the freedom of its own corporate and government speculations. For example, the debt-to-GDP ratios of the top 20 richest countries are twice as high as those of the 20 largest emerging markets! For how long will the emerging countries be forced to help pick up the tab? The Chinese and other emerging economies are quietly diversifying out of dollar reserves (i.e., buying U.S. treasury bonds, which support U.S. overspending). Indeed, the foreign exchange reserves in Asia and emerging markets—particularly China, Russia, Brazil, India, and Taiwan—have exploded, significantly outstripping those of the United States and Europe. See Figure 4.2.

No longer trusting the United States or the IMF as reserves of last resort, emerging markets have concentrated on savings to the extreme, contributing to significant global economic imbalances matching in proportion the imbalances caused by overconsumption in the United States and developed countries.

A related issue is whether or not the classical model of free trade will fade out as a process of "regionalization" around each of the BRICs is developed. Perhaps the largest controversy here is the aggressive export policy of the Chinese, stimulated by an undervalued currency, against which other developing countries, not to mention developed countries, seek some protection. The Chinese exporters, on the other hand, see the "free trade philosophy" of the World Trade Organization as a cipher for their individual freedom and are clearly enthusiastic about it. Shrewd policy-makers in China are exploiting the differences between the free trade rules of the World Trade Organization (WTO) and the voluntary compliance rules of the IMF. China pushes for strict

Figure 4.2   Reserves of Foreign Exchange and Gold
SOURCE: Data: CIA, *The World Factbook*. Chart: Suyan Jain.

enforcement of the free trade rules (for the sake of its exports),
while ignoring the IMF because it does not borrow from the IMF
and therefore is not officially subject to any of its recommendations in terms, for example, of letting the Chinese currency float
upwards (which would hurt its exports by making them more
expensive).[3] Neomercantilism comes in many flavors!

From 2000 to 2008, direct net exports contributed just 1.1
percent annually to total Chinese GDP growth (or about one-
tenth). However, in the same period, investment rose by about 8
percent—the real driver of GDP growth, helping to explain why
China was not hit that hard by the 2007 crisis. But the Chinese
dilemma is that to keep high growth rates the nation must either
shift toward radical domestic consumption (against a tradition of

high savings rates to make up for a weak social safety net, to finance family education and pensions, etc.), or rely more heavily on an export-growth-oriented model (motivating the government to keep the currency somewhat undervalued in order to keep their exports more competitive). The Chinese are not likely to turn to the West for a domestic policy model.

For Anglo-American globalization has so sped up the capitalist process of creative destruction that the traditional communities of all societies are overwhelmed: Citizens who are confronted with more change than they can cope with reach for the comfort of old habits and values, a psychological conservatism that can also take the form of religious conservatism or extreme nationalism. Moreover, the industrialized "overbanked" peoples of the West most afflicted by the housing bust, the debt resulting from the crisis, and the threat of terrorism are more likely to stay con- servatively stuck in place than are people in the more dynamic, emerging growth economies. A poignant example of indigestible change is the daily volume of "high frequency trading" of U.S. stocks that makes up half of the transactions daily: Such trades can be carried out in 400 microseconds, or 1,000 times faster than the human eye can blink. No wonder traditional communities assume that this computerized economy not only is inequitable, but undermines traditional "human" values!

Characteristics of the *New* New World

The characteristics of the *New* New World have come increasingly into focus, disconcerting the elites of the Old Rich and "Old" New World. The *New* New World is:

- *Emerging*, comprising a tectonic shift in power and wealth from the West to the East, and from slow growth, old rich industrial nations to high growth, emerging economies.

- *Bi-multipolar.* Countries create shifting alliances for economic, political, environmental, and security objectives with the "G-2" (United States and China) being the dominant players *if* they are permitted to participate.
- *Traditional.* National traditions and employment are preserved as key priorities, even if this means protectionism.
- *Capitalist with speed limits.* Capitalism will be kept to the extent that it can be combined with national traditions and slowed down by state regulations; it is necessary in order to compete in the global economy with the leading economic countries, which are all capitalist in one form or another. Developing countries will refuse to be bound by new regulations that the developed would impose (e.g., in the financial sector). Regional agreements also serve to modify capitalist modes.
- *Technocratic* more than democratic, in the sense of Jurgen Habermas's notion of "purposive rationality," using scientific means. The elite will use all means to try to catch up. "Frugal innovation" and "reverse engineering" are two of the major trends.[4]
- *Energy resourcing* to assure access to scarce sources of energy abroad and to maximize the economic utility of domestic endowments. "Sustainable development" is a fashionable leitmotif.
- *Self-confident* in terms of national pride, particularly in successful emerging economies.
- *Corrupt*, particularly given the difficulty of distinguishing corruption from lobbying even in the industrialized world (e.g., Berlusconi's seizing of privileges for his media empire in Italy, Goldman Sachs in the United States, and Opel in Germany). And corruption in the developing countries as well: International law defaults to sovereignty and national leaders do whatever they deem to be expedient (i.e., in North Korea, Venezuela, Iran, Zimbabwe, the Sudan, Egypt, Israel, and China). There is no international court to hold them to

account (the United States, for example, does not recognize the legitimacy of such a court). Indeed, increasing multipolarity inevitably results in increasing opportunities for corruption. The normal objections to corruption seem to be eclipsed to the extent that a power clique can sell itself as "too big to fail": "Systemic stability" covers all political rationalizations in presumably democratic states.

These *New* New World characteristics appear to be inevitable for two reasons:

1. Demographically, the old rich industrial countries (and soon China) are aging so fast that the emerging majorities of older people will want to hang on to the old system and its benefits ("systemic risks"!) even though they may mortgage the future of their children economically and environmentally to do so.
2. Emerging economies are tempted to use all means at hand to consolidate economic and political power, figuring that they have little to lose but their poverty, massive unemployment, and dependence; they will embrace capitalistic growth, but not necessarily the Western democratic models often associated with economic growth in the West.

Legitimacy Lost

Legitimacy derives from deference produced by force and awe. For example, the key reserve currency of the nineteenth century was backed by the British navy, the Industrial Revolution, and respect for British financial services. The dollar was initially backed by gold, victory in World War II, superpower status, and respect for the U.S. information technology revolution and innovative financial services.

But the gold-based Bretton Woods standard collapsed due to excessive spending and printing of dollars by the U.S. government (see Chapter 5). The credibility of the financial system has been devastated by the unregulated extremes of financial speculation resulting from *laissez-faire* economic innovations. The Anglo-American dominated globalization system seemed to implode without anything to replace it. And American superpower legitimacy has not been increased by its frustrated interventions in Vietnam, Iraq, Afghanistan, and Yemen and failures to halt nuclear weapons proliferation. Rather, these impotencies have appeared to speed up the decline of the American "empire." The United States' transformation from the world's greatest creditor country to the world's greatest debtor has but reinforced this loss of status. Like a young pop star, the U.S. superpower sports the danger of expiring prematurely due to excessive consumption and risk-taking.

So while developing countries may envy America's wealth, military power, and innovative capacity, they no longer see the United States as an ideal model for their own development—if they ever did. Nor do they look to European countries, limping toward regional integration and a coherent foreign policy, to find a clear-cut path to follow. The Nazi experience in Germany tainted and delegitimized the subsequently successful German "social market economy" in advance: This system is based on a sharp contrast between economic order (state "structure," social benefits) and economic process (free-market entrepreneurship, consumer democracy).

While not yet on the rocks, the West seems to have lost its anchor as well as its bearings. Western schoolchildren and students increasingly fail to learn the ideal political and economic traditions of classical Western thinking as they are pushed toward pragmatic adaptation to short-term technological training and fleeting job project assignments in the private and public sectors.

For example, few Western politicians, much less those of younger generations, are familiar any longer with the principles of the ideal democratic republic of Aristotle in his *Politics* (upon which the stability of the U.S. Constitution is based). First, Aristotle described the classical Greek cycle of government in which power corrupts: the good form of rule by the one (benevolent monarchy) displaced by authoritarian dictatorship, thrown over by the good form of rule by the few (aristocracy), corrupted in turn into a mere oligarchy, turned over by the good form of the rule of the many (democracy), which soon was fated to degenerate into "mob-rule," eventually exploited by a demagogue, who created another rule by the one. To trap stability in this cycle, Aristotle advocated a "mixed form of government" balancing the good rule of the few (aristocracy) with the good rule of the many (democracy) in his ideal of "*politea.*" American Founding Father James Madison picked up on this model, preferring the stability of the Roman republic to the fragility and short-lived direct democracy of the classical Greek city-state as the framework for the U.S. Constitution. Madison was, above all, concerned about the political domination of cliques or key interest groups (i.e., corporate lobbies today) and the discrimination of any majority against any weak minority.

As the American system shifted away from any credible form of representative democracy toward the corporate plutocracy it has become, few people at home or abroad find anything close to an ideal model of governance in the United States. Any system that permits a billionaire (Michael Bloomberg) to change the rules to permit himself to become mayor for a third time in the major city of New York and then to buy his reelection by spending over $100 million of his own money can hardly be called a "democracy." And that it takes millions of dollars to successfully run for the Senate, and nearly as much for many campaigns for Congress, just illustrates the transformation to plutocracy and rule by lobby rather than by representative democracy. Money without limits poisons democratic capitalism. Corruption by interest groups with deep pockets has been institutionalized, legitimized by the Supreme Court and bolstered by an eighteenth-century constitutional framework. The spreading independent tea party movement—a populist patchwork coalition against the domination of American politics by big business and big government and more regulation—rejects the existing plutocracy without understanding the political cycle implied by it or defining the appropriate responsibilities of the government. Moreover, the use of gerrymandering (redistricting) by elites to divide up voting districts to assure one or the other of the two dominant political parties an electoral advantage has contributed to polarization and stalemate, making the country almost impossible to govern, much less to serve as a democratic model for others.

As historian Louis Hartz pointed out long ago, Americans truly understand only the Lockean *laissez-faire* liberalism that they have experienced and believe in: Having never experienced feudalism, or the reaction to feudalism in the form of socialism, or the reaction to socialism in the form of fascism, they do not understand these strange ideologies, but only their own form of dogmatic liberalism. And today they do not understand the roots of this "checks-and-balances" form of liberalism, and can articulate only abstract devotions to individual freedom without being able to explain the political framework upon which it is based!

Moreover, leisure time as the basis of culture in order to cultivate the bases and political framework for individual dignity seems to have disappeared. There is no time for depth in the era of high-speed globalization Western innovation has created. It is no accident that students no longer take the time to read books, much less finish them, so distracted are they by the Internet, video games, and other fast-moving media and life distractions. Due to globalization and technology, this cultural attention deficit disorder is spreading rapidly to emerging nations as well.

Not surprisingly, the BRICs and other developing countries are looking to their own traditions—rather than to the West—for a model of development. There are significant "sunk costs" in terms of mainstream habits and values that guide new efforts much like the tectonic plates guide the flow of water under the Earth's surface. And if individual lives and human rights are shortchanged with people becoming just so many cogs in a socioeconomic machine, so be it. . . .

Studies of the so-called national "economic miracles" among developing countries over the past half-century reveal that "post-authoritarian unity and political stability" frequently characterize these successes. Chinese economic clout, for example, has emerged as an outgrowth of postauthoritarian structures from the past that are still in place, though often hidden from view, providing a taken-for-granted stability and unity from which concentrated economic growth strategies can be launched (such as the huge 2008 economic stimulus). Chinese "market authoritarianism" has permitted the country to absorb foreign capital and technology while making very few "democratic concessions" in terms of the Western perspective. Other characteristics of "economic miracle" performance include efficient agriculture; high rates of investment; government subsidies for savings, research and development (R&D), and exports; entrepreneurial opportunities; government modernization of infrastructure and population controls; sources of cheap (skilled) labor; education and training improvements; currency reforms; cultural homogeneity, privatization of state-run companies; a "hunger" or vitality of the people; and, last but not least, catching a wave of global economic growth.[5]

Less successfully than leaders in China, Vladimir Putin attempted to resurrect Russian pride and economic power by leveraging commodity prices on their way up: Alas, when they go down, the Russian economy sometimes looks as if it is in a free fall. Putin's successor, President Dimitry Medvedev, acknowledges the need for radical change, even to the extent of approving the attempt to create a Silicon Valley near Moscow.

India's technological successes stem in part from the "liberal authoritarianism" of the state's creation of prestigious engineering institutes (but also benefiting from the government's initial failure to pay attention to the software business—giving it freedom from regulation to develop). Even Brazil's surprising recent economic growth can partially be attributed to a strong state philosophy based upon national traditions and efforts to achieve more equity in the society. Western *laissez-faire* liberalism has not been the dominant feature of the BRIC approaches to economic development, and the global financial crisis has further discredited this model.

Decoupling and Demographics

The decoupling theory asserts that emerging markets can become an engine of growth no longer dependent upon exports to the industrialized West. However, it is but a half-truth: that is, it seems to be true about half the time. For example, in 2008 the stock markets of the emerging economies plummeted with the onset of the crisis: Brazil (–55 percent), China (–68 percent), India (–62 percent), Indonesia (–57 percent), Mexico (–40 percent), and South Korea (–56 percent). But what a difference a year makes! By the end of 2009, the trend had reversed with huge financial flows into the developing world, and the stock markets exploded: Brazil (+142 percent), China (+125 percent), India (+88 percent), Indonesia (+114 percent), Mexico (+56 percent), and South Korea (+61 percent).[6] To take the BRICs alone, Brazil, Russia, India, and China accounted for 45 percent of global growth between 2007 and 2010 according to Goldman Sachs, twice as much as in the first six years of the decade.

The surprising economic strength in the developing countries after the crisis is reinforced by UN demographic trends showing a greater projected decline in the working-age population in developed than developing countries over the next four decades, as well, of course, as a greater percentage growth of the "old old" (over 80) in the developed countries than in the others.

Japan, Europe, and the "New World" (United States, Canada, Australia, and New Zealand) are aging fastest (average age 35–41) and shrinking as a part of the world population (Europe and the New World going from 29 percent in 1950 to 17 percent today to a projected 12 percent in 2050) compared, for example, to Africa (going from 9 percent of world population in 1950 to 14 percent today and projected to make up 22 percent in 2050), where the average age of those in the sub-Saharan countries is 16–18 years old. East Asia is also aging fast, with an average age of 35. But most of Latin America, the rest of Asia, the Near East, and the five Mahgreb countries of northern Africa have an average age of 23–28. The potential human capital for economic growth is clearly building in the developing countries, where longer-term investment capital is tempted to flow.

In terms of demography, the BRICs significantly differ. India and Brazil are in a much better position than are China and Russia. India will benefit in the next two decades from increases in the working-age population—growing by 240 million (or four times the present population of the United Kingdom). Brazil's working-age population is projected to grow by nearly 20 million. But in Russia, by 2030 this cohort will decline by 17 million, according to the UN, while in China it will peak in 2015 and gradually taper off. Indeed, by 2030, India will overtake China as the world's most populous nation.[7] See Figure 4.3.

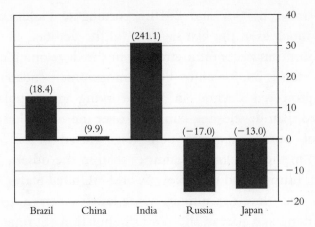

Figure 4.3   Working-Age Population Percentage Change, 2010–2030 (in parentheses, change in millions)
SOURCE: United Nations data.

The key here is the ratio between the dependent population and the working-age population in a country (e.g., "population dividend"): As the initial burden of the large youth population becomes a huge young-adult population, savings ratios go up as well as potential investment. China has been most successful in training such populations as productive, export-oriented manufacturing workers, while Brazil has experienced difficulties given a past heritage of inward-oriented economic policy and a capital-intensive commodity sector. The fiscal drag of being on the wrong side of demographic distribution (in Russia and China, for example) can be partially offset by the large available capacity left for "catching up" in terms of technological development and capital accumulation (no longer an option for developed Japan, for instance). So the greatest human capital potential of all is in the least developed countries in terms of young people capable of entering the workforce, but whether the absorptive capacity in terms of skills, infrastructure, and jobs will be sufficient to satisfy this potential is an open question.

The financial crisis served to hyperstimulate a trend for institutional investors and pension funds in the developed countries to hedge their bets by investing heavily in high-growth emerging markets, where interest rates are higher and there are booms or bubbles to take advantage of. As increased financial regulation threatens the West, the motivation to park capital in the East where there may be less regulation also becomes stronger. The Great Recession thus performed a valuable service of redistributing economic growth to the emerging world. Here the "deepening of capital" is apt to bear the most fruit, *provided* that the financial sector, infrastructure, and educational skills can be updated fast enough to absorb the avalanche of potential investment.

This may be of little immediate consolation to the billion people who are going hungry in the world. But even for them, a shift of capital flows to the emerging economies may bring hope, unless all the money ends up being recycled once more to cover overconsumption in the developed nations of the West. This is one reason why it is so vital to correct global imbalances characterized by too much consumption in developed countries and too much saving in developing nations.

One BRIC at a Time

Economic development is spontaneous, indigenous creation within a nation, not something forced upon it from outside. Since the BRICs know this well, they are not about to become dependent on Western capital or models, and have no problem with selecting free-trade and free-market recipes *à la carte* while attempting to develop as much as possible outside the theories of the Western mainstream. Literally, they believe in constructing their economies one "BRIC" at a time!

What Western policy-makers often have not comprehended is that the BRICs are not *wrong*. If slower economic growth is the price of keeping their indigenous integrity as national units, so be it. They strive to keep their trade and money within the national fold (or at least their own region), to keep jobs at home, to protect key strategic economic sectors until they are mature enough to compete globally, and to take their own good time in pursuing these objectives. The pushy, abstract, self-righteous economic models of the West are often left outside the door, where they may paw and scratch to no avail! If legitimacy is based on force and awe, there is widespread global recognition that the West cannot afford force and can no longer automatically demand "awe" or respect. The shine has lost its luster.

China: Model or Enigma?

Meanwhile, a red star is rising in the East. With a 15 percent share of global GDP, China is poised to take off and is replacing Germany as the third-largest economy in the world—leading a dynamic East Asian region of dancing "tiger" nations. Goldman Sachs predicts that by the end of the first decade of the twenty-first century, the four BRIC countries will account for half of global consumption, with China accounting for 30 percent—more than the consumption growth of the G-3 (the United States, Japan, and Germany).

It is clear that to rebalance the global economy, the three large surplus economies—China, Japan, and Germany—will need to spend more and save less to make up for the decline in U.S. consumption. Only China appears to be willing to fulfill this role. In contrast to the conventional wisdom, in the past decade net exports accounted for only 10 percent of its economic growth. Its large $585 billion stimulus package of 2008 increased government spending on infrastructure (and repairs of earthquake damage in

Sichuan) but may not have enough impact on household consumption. Corporate savings rates are higher than family savings rates. In the rural areas personal savings rates are much lower than in the cities. Unless a social safety net is created to cover basic health care, pensions, and education, the people are apt to continue their habits of saving for these family necessities. The national government moved in the right direction, doubling the spending on education, health care, and social security between 2005 and 2008, but this still is only some 6 percent of GDP, compared to an average of about 25 percent in the Organization for Economic Cooperation and Development (OECD) countries. The official national policy was to provide basic health care for 90 percent of the population by 2010, but the people will need time to realize this when it happens and to change their savings habits. Consumption as a percent of GDP is half what that of the United States has been: 35 percent, significantly lower than the typical 50 to 60 percent of other Asian economies.[8] Although the surprising spread of plastic credit cards among the young (which Chinese parents feel obligated to cover) is a motor of consumption, that could also become overheated—as it has in the West. Aware of this, the Chinese leadership intervened to slow down credit distribution and to dampen potential bubbles in the economy.

Meanwhile, however, Chinese workers are earning more and striking more frequently for better pay and conditions, particularly at foreign multinationals within China (reflecting nationalism). From 1995 to 2005, labor costs tripled and productivity per worker quintupled. Even though manufacturing labor costs are still a fraction of what they are in the United States or Germany, the average wage of the 130 million migrant workers rose 17 percent to $197 per month between 2009 and 2010. Still workers' share of national income fell in the past two decades, making an eventual shift from cheap laborers to new consumers almost inevitable.[9] Creating more money for consumption among workers will help to balance the global economy as the Chinese increasingly buy more exports from the United States, Germany, and elsewhere.

Zhang Xin, one of the wealthiest entrepreneurs in China (who studied at Cambridge and previously worked at Goldman Sachs), criticized the return to too much state control by the government during the crisis and the state's narrow regulations against ideology, health care, and spirituality. "If you take away the market, we are back to the planned economy. . . . We are only allowed to make money, nothing else."[10] She believes that to be whole, a human being needs the spiritual as well as the material. From the perspective from Soho, the real estate development firm she founded in 1995 with her husband, she anticipates a crisis precipitated by growing disparities between rich and poor, which lead to labor disputes and massive social discontent.[11]

China's challenge will be to shift government spending on infrastructure to private consumer spending and stimulus for employment. This will require significant reforms of the financial system in order to shift the dominant lending from large banks at the national level to local and regional banks in rural areas, where credit is desperately needed to fund entrepreneurship and job creation. There is a national experience of such rural finance in the 1980s that ideally could be tapped to inspire new rural banking structures in the twenty-first century. The dilemma economic policy-makers face is to regulate the heavy lending at the national level to limit the number of bad loans while expanding the facilities at the local rural level, where the government has been focusing its development targeting anyway. After tightening its economy before the Western financial crisis hit in order to cool off real estate and economic growth, China's economy stalled in late 2008, leading to its great stimulus package and subsequent boom (typified by a 15 percent rise in GDP in the second quarter of 2009—compared with 10 percent in South Korea, 21 percent in Singapore, and 5 percent in Indonesia). This success overshadowed

notable stimulus packages of some 4 percent of GDP in South
Korea, Singapore, Malaysia, and Taiwan. Indeed, by the end of
2009 the gap in growth rates between the emerging Asian
economies and the Group of 7 industrialized countries had never
been wider—over 5 percent growth versus some 3.5 percent
contraction.

When China more or less repegged the yuan to the dollar in
2009 out of fear of undermining its export markets, it created a
situation in which the currency inevitably became undervalued
when the dollar fell. This increased dependency is a paradox given
China's call for the world economy to break away from its
dependence upon the dollar as the world's key reserve currency.
But a deeper "sunk cost" is also exposed: the classical export-led
growth model that served China so well in the past may not be
effective in a future in which Americans may radically reduce their
spending on imports.

Still, the Chinese have imported not only a full range of
technological development, but the capacity for their own technological innovation. The conventional assumption of Western
policy-makers that Western-developed countries can specialize in
high-tech areas that can be balanced by Chinese manufacturing
may not work out as planned:

- The Chinese have enough levels of development and enough
  people to staff *all* of these levels in order for them to keep most
  jobs at home, as well as most investment.
- They already produce 60 percent of the world's solar panels!
  China is testing how far it can regulate loose lending, which has
  flooded the domestic market with liquidity, without having to
  radically raise the value of its currency and interest rates (and
  thus dampening exports), which is apt to follow.

Underdevelopment saved China's banks from exposure to
toxic subprime lending in the United States. And even in their

"underdeveloped" banking system, the Chinese are proving to be more resilient than many anticipated. Between 2004 and 2010, China went from having zero to four of the world's largest banks in terms of market value. For example, the Agricultural Bank of China has 320 million clients, a staff of 441,000, and a multitude of branches. Learning from the aftermath of the 1999 Asian crisis, the Chinese elite cut out the middleman in 2008 and demanded that the banks supply more credit: The loans grew from 102 percent of GDP to 127 percent within a year! Even here other developing countries are looking at the Chinese model in contrast to the hoarding Western banks (whose so-called "stress tests" are concerned with bank survival, not with providing needed credit to the real economy). Still, the Chinese are in a learning phase with perhaps as many as a third of the outstanding loans in doubt: From 1998 to the present, the government has pumped $420 billion into the five biggest banks alone. But Chinese policy-makers have the reserves to cover all such problems, along with the resolve to target credit for investment in the domestic infrastructure in a sustainable fashion.[12]

Meanwhile, China has led a successful charm offensive to exploit the strong interest in intraregional cooperation in Southeast Asia. After China was perceived as saving its neighbors from a devastating weakening of their competitive position by initially refusing to give in to pressures to depreciate the renminbi, China has pinned down the China-ASEAN Free Trade Agreement (CAFTA). CAFTA covers China and six members of the Association of Southeast Asian Nations (ASEAN) and will expand to cover all ASEAN countries by 2015, leaving the United States without a substantial role in this multilateral framework. The basic structure was put in place with the Greater Mekong Subregion (GMS) agreements of economic cooperation for water transportation (with Laos, Myanmar, Thailand, and Vietnam) and railroad linkages (with Thailand and eventually hooking up with the Singapore-Kunmin rail project). Indeed, the lack of sufficient potable water in the country is emerging as a critical resource issue in China, as it is as well in India. And China's charm offensive abroad loses luster at home and abroad when the solution to tensions in Tibet is to flood the region with Han immigrants, presumably for the sake of faster economic development, but deliberately diluting Tibetan culture and even the job prospects of the natives in the process. On the other hand, the state's targeting of Shanghai for educational development led to striking teenage achievement in the OECD Program for International Student Assessment (PISA) examinations of 2010! But now China confronts the challenge of employing its overeducated "ants" (as unemployed college graduates are called) who have burrowed into small city apartments or have returned home to rural areas.

The Kaleidoscope of India

Chinese development in manufacturing is often contrasted with software development and local entrepreneurship in India. And one reason for the frustrating diffusion of Indian efforts is presumably that India is the largest democracy in the world. Like a multifaceted kaleidoscope, India's many layers of tradition, region, language, and economic disparities appear on the surface to militate against a strong, central development of global comparative advantages in the classical Western sense. Yet one-party central governments can make disastrous political decisions in terms of economic development (i.e., Mao's "cultural revolution") as well as leading to "economic miracles" (i.e., Taiwan and South Korea in the 1960s). And so India's democratic culture of experimentation and adaptation has greater potential than many assume, as the software industry in Bangalore has demonstrated, not to mention three years running of GDP growth rates of over 9 percent before the financial crisis. India was also somewhat buffered from the global crisis since it was less export-dependent than many other economies. On the other hand, it came into the crisis with more public debt than many countries.

India's structural problems have more to do with a dependence of over 60 percent of the population upon jobs in agriculture than with democracy per se. There is a lot of local innovation in the agricultural sector, but not yet a systematic policy enabling agricultural efficiency to be so increased nationally that labor is freed up for development in other sectors—as occurred, for example, in England in the middle of the nineteenth century. Massive educational restructuring at the primary and secondary levels of schooling, as well as increasing the availability of university training (particularly for women) are critical in permitting India to transform its economy in order to become more self-sufficient.

One vital trend in this direction is "frugal innovation" or "reverse engineering," leading to the production of the $2,400 Nanu car by Tata Motors and the development of the portable Mac 400 by General Electric–India, which permits electrocardiograms to be taken for only $1 each. Indeed, 6 million Americans have already gone to India for "health tourism"—many for open-heart surgery, for just $2,000 a pop![13]

However, the continuing dependency upon the agricultural sector exposes India to the constant instability of droughts, typhoons, and increases in the cost of food and other resources, pushing the inflation rate to double digits despite a 4 percent target by the central bank.

In terms of banking, underdevelopment protected India from the subprime crisis, as it did most developing countries. And as the banks develop, they want the freedom to maneuver that the United Kingdom and United States enjoyed until they become globally competitive. Given their stability in the crisis, India's Finance Minister, Pranab Mukherjee, citing praise for India's banking system, opposed any sort of taxes on the banks to discipline them, which developed countries with zombie banks were pushing. This Indian position against any bank tax for funding bailouts in the future was vindicated at the June 2010 meeting of G–20 leaders in Toronto, where it was agreed that any such tax should be left to the individual countries to decide. However, underlying the official spin, the cost of banking intermediation in India is higher and the penetration (in terms of customer segments and geography) is lower than in other markets. In the future, India will have to work on a more effective institutional enabling policy and regulatory framework given a fragmented industry structure, restrictions on capital availability and deployment, restrictive labor laws, weak corporate governance, and the inability of managers to improve capital allocations and productivity in service platforms.[14]

Just as a series of five-year plans worked in the economic development of France, they could prove to be effective in India as well. While the recent focus upon infrastructure development (70 percent state-financed and 30 percent private sector) is necessary, it does not reduce India's energy or resource dependence, as China is aiming to do with its strategic investments in Africa, Latin America, and elsewhere. The key issue for India may be to create a critical mass of transformative economic development of strategic sectors through targeted rural financing, education, and development coordinated with dynamic metro centers. The government's promise of 100 days of "public" work annually, paid for by the state, for everyone in rural areas is a bold initiative (despite the difficulties of financing it in the long term). The resistance of the country's lobby of lawyers to the presence of any foreign lawyers working in India is less compelling, and does more to isolate India from the international legal community than to preserve jobs at home.

In order to acquire sources for their heavy energy demands, Indian policy-makers might observe the imaginative policies of China abroad carefully in order to determine which alliances might help them on their way to more sustainable energy self-sufficiency in the long run.

Laid-Back Brazil

Brazil seems to have avoided the extremes of the financial downturn by neglecting to force through "Anglo-American" reforms in the banking sector, where the state still has a dominant regulatory role. While historian Eric Hobsbawm referred to Brazil as "a monument to social neglect,"[15] this very indolence appears to have had positive consequences in terms of cushioning Brazil's economy from the global financial collapse. For example, huge reserve requirements for private banks and taxes on funding that pushed up prices of loans discouraged the wild (West!) risk-taking typical of richer countries. There is a global pattern here: Countries that have restricted capital flows, such as China, India, and, in this case, Brazil, have suffered less exposure to negative turbulence in globalization, while still managing to benefit from the positive systemic upturns.

To fully understand Brazil's surprising strength (indeed its financial banking system appears to be in better shape than that of the United States), one must look backwards briefly. In 1985 when Brazil resurrected its democracy, its inflation rate floated between 100 and 150 percent annually. The system was plagued by "inertial inflation," in which individuals behaved as if inflation would rise no matter what steps the government might take. Then, in 1993–1994, Fernando Henrique Cardozo, a sociology professor from a wealthy family, as Finance Minister introduced the "Real Plan," which solved the inflation problem, suddenly reducing the inflation rate to 2 percent a month. And soon thereafter he rode to being elected President on this basis, after the elites of Brazil learned that voters like low inflation and that low inflation wins votes. After advocating privatization of state-owned firms and attracting foreign investment, Cardozo became the first democratically elected leader to be reelected in the history of Brazil. He was followed by Luiz Inácio Lula da Silva (Lula), who also was elected to the Presidency twice in a row (giving the country significant political credibility). Lula maintained a stable anti-inflation policy (despite earlier prolabor rhetoric) by keeping conservative macroeconomic targeting. Yet at the same time, he moved away from market-oriented liberalism, keeping state control over key industrial sectors, and advocating a progressive commitment to social policy to militate against the great inequalities that still plague Brazil.

While industrial production fell 12 percent in December of 2008—the largest drop since the federal statistics started tracking it 17 years ago—Brazil has been somewhat protected by its reduction in public debt below 40 percent of GDP. Given that, atypically for Brazil, inflation has been kept low and monetary policy has been able to keep interest rates low. However, public spending increases before the 2010 presidential election threatened public debt reduction and with it future prospects for continuing low inflation.

Accounting for double the amount in goods and services compared to Russia and for about half the output of Latin America, it is little wonder that Brazil has cast itself as a leader of the global "South." Under President Luiz Inácio Lula da Silva (elected in 2003), 13 million people were lifted out of poverty and progress was made in rectifying income inequalities. The *Bolsa Familia* (family grant) policy paying mothers a small sum as long as their children stay in school 85 percent of the scheduled time and get medical check-ups proved to be successful at reducing child labor in rural areas, despite the supplementary support that is necessary for similar results in more expensive urban zones and *favelas* (slums). This policy is the poster child, the largest, of the conditional cash-transfer (CCT) programs in poor and middle-income countries (costing 0.5 percent of Brazil's GDP), and serves as a model even for New York City.[16]

Brazil's social and economic success helped to legitimize its tougher, somewhat anti–American edge based on a national self-confidence in pushing for a developing country bloc. Brazil continues to consolidate its leadership in Latin American integration through Mercosur, the regional trade bloc excluding the United States, as a springboard for growing Brazilian global leadership in meetings of the North–South Group of 20. Led by Brazil (with over 7 percent growth in GDP for 2010), Latin America is largely experiencing a growth surge (4.5 percent in 2010). Moody's has forecast a stable outlook for the banking system of Brazil and a sustainable credit cycle given favorable demographics, the social mobility potential of the population, and robust domestic demand and job creation.[17]

Russian Realism: "Dead End"?

The least successful BRIC is Russia. In fact, some believe this leading bloc of developing nations should be called the BICs, not the BRICs, given Russia's economic free fall after the crisis: a contraction approaching 10 percent in 2009 after an average annual GDP growth rate of over 6.8 percent over the previous decade. This great decline is due to its dependence on exports of oil and other commodities, which dropped in price with the decline of global demand, combined with high corporate debt and the failure to restructure the economy under President Putin. The so–called "realism" of Russia's efforts in the era of Vladimir Putin to resurrect the country's great power status has served to mobilize national pride, but at the risk of reintroducing Cold War animosities based on weapons and threats rather than sound economic development and prowess. Initially this hard–line stance against the West and NATO appeared to work, but since the Russian invasion of Georgia, the strategy has hit a threshold of diminishing returns. It is one thing to fear Russia, but quite another to make Russia attractive for foreign investment, without which it cannot become free of its almost total dependence upon exporting commodities. Authoritarian commodity-based states have been shown to have significant competitive weaknesses in the high-speed, innovative, technological economy of the world today.

In its last major economic crisis in 1998, when Russia declared default, the ruble lost two-thirds of its value overnight, which paradoxically helped Russia to recover within six months given its export-driven economy. However, a decade later, President Dmitry Medvedev announced in a national radio address that Russia could not develop the same way any longer, that this is "a dead end," and that the crisis would force policy-makers to restructure the economy away from its dependence on exporting hydrocarbons and natural resources. This recognition contrasts with the viewpoint of Prime Minister Putin, who places most of the blame for Russia's economic performance on the external global crisis rather than on domestic conditions. While Russia was able to tap its $600 billion reserve fund to help bail out businesses "too big to fail" and to recapitalize banks, by failing to push responsibility to these institutions economically, Russia created the same future conditions of "moral hazard" all too familiar in the United States. The Russian banking system stabilized after the 2008 crisis but more financiers in Russia anticipate stagnation than expect any Brazilian-like burst of growth.

Foreign companies think twice before establishing a large presence there because of the potential for bureaucratic harassment and legal difficulties. When Ikea in 2000 announced before setting up in Russia that it would do business as usual there, not paying any bribes, the authorities turned off the power at its grand opening. Motorola faces such troubles daily, but stays put. However, the Kremlin began to confront the issue, concerned about the loss of foreign investment, when in late 2008 capital outflows reached $130 billion. The Russian market is so large, many multinational firms cannot ignore it.[18]

Putin's expressed goal of Russia's becoming one of the world's top five economies by 2020 is unlikely without further economic integration with Europe and the restoration of a sense that a predictable rule of law prevails in the country that Russia's neighbors can count upon. Nevertheless, the Russians appear to be willing to use whatever bargaining power they can muster to achieve this goal. For example, former U.S. Secretary of the Treasury Henry Paulson claimed that in 2008 Russian policymakers proposed to the Chinese that the two nations should sell Frannie Mae and Freddie Mac bonds in order to force the U.S. government to bail out these huge mortgage finance companies.[19]

Given diminishing numbers of workers due to demographic trends, corruption in state-run businesses and bureaucracies, and the ineffectiveness of top-down management techniques in remaining competitive globally, Russia will need radical restructuring in order to recover its former high economic growth rates. National policy will need to create incentives for Russians to invest their own money in the Russian economy, for local businesses to create alternatives to the commodity-export trade, and for management educational systems to adapt to these objectives if a positive investment atmosphere is to be fashioned from the pessimistic stalemate of the status quo. Otherwise, the estimates by analysts at Bank of America Merrill Lynch that Russia will have an average annual growth rate of only 3.5 percent between 2011 and 2020 are likely to become a self-fulfilling prophecy.

But as oil and gas prices creep back up with global economic recovery, the political motivation to break away from the status quo model may diminish. Unless, of course, the price of oil reaches the $150 a barrel threshold when alternative green energy technology suddenly becomes an attractive economic alternative to oil! It is no accident that the most sophisticated developed economies are hatching strategies to seize the global sustainable energy market as it develops and to employ more of their people in this sector. However, they may well discover that the BRIC countries counter them in sustainable enterprises in order to keep jobs at home.

Russia's increased influence is in no small part due to the West's provocation of putting NATO forces on the Russian border, on the one hand, and based on the West's dependence upon Russian oil and gas, on the other. The Russians will continue to push for pricing oil in a currency other than the dollar. To the extent that the West has humiliated Russia in the past, Russia will be motivated in the future to slant its national pride in an anti-Western way in order to leverage animosities at home and fear and uncertainties abroad concerning Russian nuclear and military power. But without the radical economic restructuring that Medvedev has called for, Russia's economic influence will wane and the BRICs may become the BICs after all. Intimidation and threats are not recipes for creating a positive model of development that other nations would like to mimic. That elites refer to Russian foreign policy initiatives as "operations" has the echo of a dark, Cold War version of the intelligence services, as evidenced by the 2010 exposure of a Russian spy ring in the United States. In a pinch, domination by Goldman Sachs may be seen as preferable to more individuals globally than domination by the KGB.

Debt versus Investment and Savings in BRICs

With Greece flickering in the Western twilight, the austerity versus stimulus debate takes on a different color in the BRICs than it does in the developed world. With much lower debt-to-GDP levels in the BRICs, there is a strong temptation to point to Greece as a poster child for "misdevelopment" Western-style as well as to further distance one's own model of development from that of the West.

Consider household debt between 2000 and 2008 in the BRICs, for example: In China household debt rose from 4 percent of GDP to 12 percent, in India from 2 percent to 10 percent, in Russia from 1 percent to 10 percent, and in Brazil from 6 percent to 13 percent. Meanwhile, in the United States, household debt rose from 72 percent of GDP in 2000 to 97 percent in 2008! Historically, "deleveraging" from such debt takes an average of six to seven years from the time it really begins (post-bail-out stimuli).[20]

Meanwhile, there is a good chance that India or Brazil may design the right policies to encourage investment in productive capacities, which could yield high growth rates from low bases of capacity utilization. Given that Brazil has had a much lower rate of savings than its BRIC peers (and the lowest productive capacity per worker), its share of foreign direct investment has also been low, giving it an unusual opportunity to shift policies toward savings and investment. But the risk is that Brazil may settle for the "laid-back" status quo of benefiting from commodity exports and the recent opening up of its markets rather than developing a dynamic growth strategy.

While India has the lowest per-capita income of the BRICs, its policies have been beneficial in opening up regulations to attract more foreign direct investment. But it needs to continue with labor and infrastructure reforms to encourage a shift from small manufacturing units to larger firms that can benefit from economies of scale and scope, as the Chinese have.[21]

The Group of 20 and Global Imbalances

At the London G-20 Summit in April 2009, the rich countries stood as the accused for their sins and not the poor. This anti-Western, antimodernist transformation had been long in the making in the developing world. By the time of the Toronto Summit of the G-20 in June 2010, the rich nations found themselves obligated to promise to cut their deficits in half by 2013. Otherwise, they were afraid the bond markets would turn against them as they had against Greece, locking them into a deflationary debt-trap. After all, at this point the G-7 countries had the highest debt-to-GDP ratio that they had experienced in 60 years.

The BRICs will continue to coordinate their own regional blocs for the maximum impact in meetings of the Group of 20. And their agendas will be driven by national interests and self-conscious pride that may not be in accord with Western expectations. For example, while the United States and other Western countries recognized the declaration of state independence by Kosovo in 2010, the BRICs (and most African nations) did not.

Western policy-makers go on the assumption that the Group of 20 must work to alleviate global economic imbalances. If the United States tilts toward becoming more of an export-led growth country, others must tilt toward importing more to help balance current account imbalances. If the U.S. dollar goes down, facilitating this shift, other currencies, particularly in Asia, must go up in value. If the United States no longer plays the role of lender and importer of last resort, other countries will be forced to pick up some of this slack—including emerging economies represented by the BRICs. But this Western textbook rationality is apt to be frustrated.

For the BRICs are increasingly looking outside the wealthy West for sources of capital, energy, and markets. It is in their interest to block Western initiatives in the short run in order to tilt the game toward their views in the long run. The neoliberal vision of global free trade is being transformed into a bumper-car experience of stop-and-go: Nations cut regional and bilateral deals, inspired in no small part by the regional privileges claimed by the

European Union, on the one hand, and by the bilateral realism of American economic policy (pushed so strongly by the Bush II administration), on the other hand. Few pure neoliberals, if any, are left standing. As Professor Timothy Shaw put it, "the nightmare of the Washington consensus" has been pushed aside by an emerging "Beijing consensus"—with China, the "BRIC" of BRICs, leading the way.[22]

The recent crisis of capitalism has resulted in a major redistribution of wealth and power from the West to the East and to the emerging economies. This sea change holds the promise of greater global equity and human harmony for all concerned, if international institutions can be transformed in order to codify and manage the radical shift. Then the emerging economies can "save" the developed nations in a win-win global system. In the meantime, however, it is worth taking a look back to see how projections of development recipes today could evolve differently from expected, as anticipated in part by prescient economic thinkers in the past.

The Roadmap to the New World Economy Has Changed

One of the paradoxes of the future of the new global economy that emerges after the financial crisis contradicts written theory. John Maynard Keynes invented the name "developing countries" at the Bretton Woods currency conference of 1944. The United States was dead serious at that time about its war goal of decolonialization in contrast to its British allies. The British fought tenaciously for the inventory and maintenance of the British Empire. Nevertheless, Keynes, as leader of the British delegation, worried about how the capital needs of the postcolonial world could be covered, after their eventual severance and independence from the sources of finance from their mother country. Conventional financing on the international capital markets was not an option. The markets had to be built up after the war and were overwhelmed. In addition to the development of Third World countries, it was necessary to finance the war-damaged industrialized countries and their reconstruction. Also, capital market conditions for these "underdeveloped" countries would have made the amounts unpayable. Keynes proposed a mix of funding from public and commercial sources for the new "aid for development": a special fund from which the subsequent World Bank (WB) for "reconstruction and development" emerged. The WB should take on this double task with subsidized soft loans. (See Chapter 5.)

But now, a half a century later, it is clear that these benevolent intentions constituted a distraction from the real problems of developing countries. In meeting the capital needs for even the most poor and backward economies, it is not a question of capital injections from the outside, but of the development and expansion of even sparsely flowing sources of capital inside the country: the organization of institutions for the promotion and utilization of savings and their transformation into loans to finance their investments. In short, it is a question about the development of an efficient financial sector within the country. The argument that in poor countries there would be no savings was never accurate: Savings are always there, and with surprising constancy. The subsequent analyses of the World Bank always came back up with the same result: that even in the poorest countries in the world, the savings rate (in percent of national income) is seldom less than 5 percent. This domestic source must be expanded and made more fruitful.

It was this obsession with capital assistance from the outside from all concerned, from the capitalist right to the Marxist left, that steered development theories onto the wrong track. Even though their corresponding approaches contradicted each other ideologically, both came ultimately to the same conclusion: Without assistance from outside, it is difficult to impossible to get a process of indigenous development under way. Some recommended copying the Western capitalist model with an argument blind to history: No other option would be available. On the other hand, for supporters of the left-oriented *dependencia* theory (popularized by Argentinean economist Raul Prebisch) outside assistance constituted a kind of repentance payment for the sins and crimes of the West during the colonial period.

The conservative development model (formed by the revolutions in Europe and the United States, and spread and popularized by industrialization) was confused with "development" by the progressive illusions of the Western bourgeoisie and its intellectuals. It was oblivious to the fact that humankind had "developed" free from external influences since the cultures of the Stone Age, and in all parts of the world at that, only at different speeds and in different directions. The left-oriented model, in turn, transplanted the revelations of the Marxist worldview of legality (and the resulting organization to "plan") in human history—already refuted at home—to the Third World. With the help of "development plans" and their predictable "capital gaps," which had to be closed with development aid, it should be possible to set a process of self-sustaining development in motion in developing countries made dependent in the colonial period and to eliminate their dependence upon the markets and needs of the industrialized countries.

Fernando Henrique Cardoso in Brazil was not the only, but was the most successful, reformer in breaking down the fixation in both theories upon the Western world's experiences and ways of thinking (or "rationality," in Weber's sense) and in refuting them. Development is a comprehensive social process, which comes from and is shaped by many historical sources, and certainly not just by financial factors. Every society is capable of development if the necessary preconditions are there and the appropriate incentives are set "from above" (be it through religion, government, or politics). This was confirmed by German "stage-of-development theorists" in the footsteps of Friedrich List, the great German-American economist of the first half of the nineteenth century, as well as by the work of twentieth-century American economist W. W. Rostow.

But one factor motivated and ultimately drove all development processes that were researched historically and theoretically analyzed: taking on the underlying growth of population. This was made incontrovertibly clear in the work of the Jamaican economist Sir Arthur Lewis (the first Nobel Economics laureate from the Third World, in 1979). From today's perspective, measured against Lewis's criterion, the People's Republic of China already has its recent sensational development leap behind it. By 2016 at the latest, a brake on China's population will kick in: The growth will decline of not only the population but also of the influx of people from the agricultural rural areas to the urban industrial centers. From that time on, one must anticipate a sharp increase in the expected growth of wages, which, although not stopping the growth process, will slow it down considerably. Above all, China's integrating into the world economy due to low wages and the competitiveness of its exports will weaken significantly, as has been apparent for decades with its rival, Japan.

India holds the best cards for the future among the BRICs, according to the Lewis criterion. By 2035 the UN estimates that India's population will increase from 1.2 billion people to 1.5 billion, or 26 percent; its labor force will grow by 33 percent, up to around 1 billion people (almost 10 times the population of Japan). Goldman Sachs concludes that with every 100 million increase in new workers expected in the next 10 years, India's GDP will increase by an additional 4 percent annually. India's biggest challenge in the future is to provide the necessary training, education, and employment outside of the agricultural sector—a daunting task, but one that can be achieved if collective learning can be coordinated with the release of private initiatives.

Russia's opportunities are significantly restricted in comparison with those that the other three BRICs were able to achieve on their own. It is transforming its economy from a mineral-exporting economy to a natural resources manufacturing economy, not based on financial aid, but relying upon cooperation with the West (and especially the EU), particularly in terms of know-how in the development of an efficient financial sector and management. Only if its economy becomes viable in the future will Russia be able to resolve its problems of a shrinking population that will have to support an increasing proportion of elderly people.

The rise of the BRICs has long been a bright spot for the darkest of all developing continents: Africa, especially south of the Sahara. Trade between the BRICs and Africa has increased from $22 billion to $166 billion between 2000 and 2008— that is, by nearly eight times annually. China's share of this volume is about two-thirds. Taking advantage of its language edge, Brazil is the most important foreign investor in the former Portuguese colonies of Angola and Mozambique. President Lula visited Africa several times, opened up new embassies, and explained that the strengthening of Brazil's relations with Africa was an integral part of Brazilian policy.

China and Brazil are in a position to provide Africa with much cheaper investment than can the old industrial countries, including Germany. "The Chinese build three streets for the same price as the Germans ask for one," declared a minister from Ghana at a recent economic conference on foreign investment in his country.[23] Nevertheless, African politicians warn, and not without reason, that one must be careful not to swap the old colonialism with a new one. For the new interest of China, Brazil, and India in Africa is not without imperialistic tendencies, which cannot be ignored. The focus of BRIC investments is located in countries with rich mineral resources: petroleum (Ghana, Sudan), coal (Mozambique), iron ore (Angola), copper (Zambia), precious metals (Congo). As for the BRIC countries, these mineral resources are the basis of new wealth if it is possible to process them domestically and to develop them further industrially. In sum, Africa's natural resources are the basis for the establishment and development of processing industries, in order to bring its own countries prosperity and jobs. Africa is entitled to expect help in this endeavor from both the First World and emerging economies.

Chapter 5

Time for a New Bretton Woods

Crisis Prevention through Monetary Law

F unds, currency, and financial crises are all endemic to the success story of capitalism. Why? The initial reason lies in the individual's right to dispose of her money freely: spend it, invest it, or save (hoard) it. Too much money spent leads to inflation; too much money hoarded leads to deflation. Only saved money simultaneously invested in the real economy leads to a path of balanced economic growth, free from inflation and deflation. This path is as narrow as it is rare. It is the exception in a system riddled with outside influences such as political forces and natural catastrophes, as well as the tendencies or altered behaviors of the owners of funds.

But there is a second—systemic—reason for financial crises: the limitation of funds available for goods offered, because whatever the national economy produces and displays always is waiting for a customer. This purchasing power derives from the costs resulting from production: wages, salaries, and interest; for these costs are at the same time incomes from work, investment, and use. Whether these incomes are then spent up to 100 percent and used to consume the goods offered is another question. Money can also be saved, invested, and hoarded, leaving the producers involuntarily sitting on inventory. Economists required centuries to understand this and to discover how to organize and adjust available funds and their substitute, credit, in order to avoid unpleasant surprises.

However, the availability of money and credit cannot be left to the discernment and arbitrariness of banks, much less to greedy, profit-oriented professional money-brokers and lenders. Two *different* levels of control and steering precautions must be met, because the relationship between money and credit must be in sync, as well as the relationship between volumes of loans and funds, on one hand, and of the available supply of goods, on the other.

Therefore, in the modern monetary economy, wherever it exists, there is a two-tier organization. It consists of the "internal" funding cycle between the state-commissioned activities of the central bank and the mainly private banking system: The central bank provides the banks with their money as a means of the "last available liquidity." In the "external" funding cycle the banking system transforms the money into credit as the most common means of financing of the economy. But money and credit are as much "public" as they are "national" goods. Central banks provide their economies with the necessary means of finance in national, not foreign, currency. But the more the goods markets skip out of the domestic framework of the national economy and its national regulated monetary and credit system (and they have always done so, even in the distant past), the more that another problem rises in the selection of a money and goods economy. In addition to the national rental price of money (the loan interest rate), the price of converting the national money into a foreign currency (the exchange rate) appears.

The interest rate and the exchange rate create a unity in the global network of goods, money, and capital markets—the sum of present financing costs or risks. Without reliable, calculable costs of financing and risks, no world economy can function, especially not with the rapidly accelerating growth of the past 200 years. In the meantime, both the number of global economic actors (firms, banks) and the quantity of products traded and financed in the world economy have increased to a breathtaking extent.

What's behind all of this? What drives this globalization and progress? Ultimately, the answer lies in the technological progress of our times—the most recent and enduring being the explosion and spread of the electronic industry, its media, and products.

The resulting radical reductions in the costs of transportation and communication have put goods and services that were formerly only nationally produced and sold into the worldwide market. As we now all know, parts and raw assemblies of products are often produced thousands of miles away from the final assembly, and accounting systems have been relocated to countries where labor costs account for only a fraction of the cost of the computer. Old market boundaries (drawn by transport costs, lack of information, unpayable currency risks) have largely evaporated. Within the large multinational corporations, they have all been lifted. They continue to exist only in the old state and monetary currency zones, although in many cases they are pooled, as in the Economic and Monetary Union of the EU. Not only have the issues of exchange rates and the associated currency risks remained, but during the recent trend toward globalization these problems have dramatically worsened.

That there are exchange rates that pose a currency risk problem is not a new notion; it was already recognized by the Phoenicians. What is new are the dimensions of the problem: Volatility spills over from exchange rates to currency risk and back without governability. For with the explosion of the global economy has come an implosion of its instruments of regulation, steering, and control. It is almost incomprehensible, but true: Just when these regulatory mechanisms are needed the most, we have abolished them!

Let us try to trace what has happened.

There have been large-scale, organized efforts to solve the exchange-rate problem since the early days of the nineteenth century. Once upon a time there was the gold standard, which worked almost perfectly until the outbreak of World War I, and only sporadically thereafter until 1931. Under the auspices of the gold standard, the modern capitalist world economy came into being. The second large-scale experiment was launched after World War II: the so-called Bretton Woods system. The birthdates of these systems share a key feature: Both world monetary systems were responses to catastrophes. The gold standard was the reaction to the chaos that Napoleon left behind in Europe; the Bretton Woods agreement sought to reconstruct financial systems that lay in ruins following World War II.

But just as revealing as the birth certificates are the death certificates. Both systems died of the same cause. Their carriers and operators, the states, were immersed in internal difficulties and gave their own solutions priority over the implementation of the monetary rules they had agreed on. National interest trumped the rules of the currency club. The states refused to be subject to these rules as they had previously been. They needed the monetary instruments to do their homework—in the case of the gold standard, to fight against mass unemployment; in the case of the Bretton Woods system, to defend against the inflationary tendencies of the outgoing dollars streaming from the United States.

But in the current crisis, there is a much more serious issue: Can the global economy (and Western capitalism) survive without a world monetary system of the old variety? Because it is obvious that the vacuum existing since the death of the Bretton Woods system in the spring of 1973 helped to trigger the current existential crisis of Western capitalism. And if it is true that the new emerging economies in the world economy and other "catch-up" countries in the development process are dependent on this "welfare machine" (as J. S. Mill in the nineteenth century baptized it), then the answer to this question is high on the agenda of the twenty-first century.

However, in order to answer the question, the reasons for the failure of Bretton Woods as well as for the crises of the post–Bretton Woods era must be clarified.

What Caused Bretton Woods to Fail?

Go back to the summer of 1944 in the winter sports center of Bretton Woods, New Hampshire, where the world monetary system was created at the end of World War II. The conference was based upon "Plans for an International Clearing Union," drafted by John Maynard Keynes, Advisor to the Bank of England and head of the British delegation. Despite the watering down of some elements of Keynes's blueprint by the U.S. delegation, led by Henry Morgenthau Jr. and Harry Dexter White, the principles and basic ideas remained intact:

- After the war, the world trading nations would return to the principle of free trading. But the international capital flows would remain under state control because they pose an incalculable risk for the balance of payments. Behind this stood a concrete pragmatic argument. The influence of "political" capital transfers, such as the removal of war debt and the capital starvation in the postcolonial, independent, abandoned "developing countries" (a term Keynes created and introduced at this conference), could not be calculated for decades to come.

- The national central banks would receive an International Refinancing Window for limited credit in order to meet their contradictory dual function: domestic full employment and price stability to assure stable external rates of the currency. This was to be accomplished through a new "Clearing Union" (CU), a type of central bank of central banks (proposed by Keynes). But the U.S. delegation adamantly rejected the idea of a CU associated with automatic assistance. The Americans insisted on strict verification in individual cases under restrictive conditions imposed on underlying national economic and monetary policies (conditionality). They contended that no "bank" was needed, but just a "fund" established with ad hoc payments of member countries, for which they proposed the name "International Monetary Fund" (IMF). The United States gave the IMF its initial endowment of US$800 million.

- The newly developing countries should be integrated in the world monetary system of fixed exchange rates through supporting loans. But because of their particular situation and need for capital, they would receive special and long-term sources of raising capital: "The International Bank for Reconstruction and Development," known today as the World Bank (WB). This organization, in turn, obtained its funds from the budgets of developed countries and lent them on the capital markets on "soft" conditions of long-term, low interest rates, thereby guaranteeing the status of the WB-rich countries to offset any losses. During a transition phase, war-ravaged industrial countries were also eligible to receive WB help.

Free trade, fixed exchange rates, controlled and regulated capital movements, and central bank assistance in case of payments difficulties were the four pillars of the Bretton Woods system that dominated the global economy for the first quarter of a century following World War II. As in the era preceding World War I, the gold standard led them to a golden age. Under their aegis, the war damage to the industrial countries was overcome, and the developing countries integrated into the new global economy under the rubric "Third World." As in the nineteenth century, the monetary system functioned as a welfare machine for the nations included. Once they had consumed their war profits in struggles for independence, an ever-growing number of Third World nations reached for the support of the IMF, the WB, and the organization created in the meantime by industrial countries for official development assistance (ODA), while they devalued their currencies when they came under international pressure. But harrowing crises like the current one did not materialize.

If one asks for the reasons why an advantageous system such as this one began to falter for all nations involved in the early 1970s, and had to be abandoned under pressure from the EU countries at the time (France in particular), the answer lies ultimately with the cuts in and changes of the "Keynes Plan" forced by the U.S. delegation in 1944–1945. What seemed like a victory of political pragmatists over unrealistic economic theorists turned out to be a lightly laid fuse on a powder keg.

Keynes had prescribed a system of two "automatic stabilizers," which were designed to secure the agreement's equilibrium as well as to serve social justice within nations (and enable its acceptance in times of crisis):

1. To exclude any privilege of a single currency (no currency should be "more equal" than others), the IMF should be used as the basis for money credit and the calculation of exchange rates: a neutral unit of exchange in terms of all states and national currencies as opposed to the gold standard in pounds

sterling or, later, U.S. dollars. Keynes had proposed the name "bancor" for this systemic, artificial money (derived from the English "bank" and the French for "gold"). The use of the bancor would have deterred both the privileged status of the United States and the denaturalizing of the system into a pure dollar standard.

2. Equality of treatment of debtors and creditors, should imbalances arise, would work to serve both the internal equilibrium as well as the acceptance of the system by its members. For Keynes it was a question of the laws of logic: In a closed system (such as Bretton Woods), the deficits of one member could provoke the surpluses of another, but also vice versa: The surpluses of one could bring about the deficits of another. Therefore, both causes of imbalances should be treated equally and placed under the same legal system of fines or sanctions. Excessive surpluses were to have the same interest penalties imposed as excessive deficits! Keynes had foreseen the later abuse of the system from extreme surpluses (Germany, Japan) as well as extreme deficits (United States) and sought to prevent them. But as a would-be permanent surplus nation after the war, the United States was not interested in any surplus punishment. So it went along with the old (rather theological) perspective that debts are debts and, therefore, sins to be punished. Creditors, however, are paragons of virtue who please God well. The United States moved away from this bigoted attitude only at the end of the 1960s, when it was transformed to become the debtor of debtors in the system.

Neither of the two pillars of stability of the Bretton Woods system found the approval of the United States. The bancor was replaced by the U.S. dollar. The responsibility of creditors for system imbalances was deleted without any replacement. What remained was the prejudice of past centuries: Debts are identical to mismanagement and harmful for any system—as if there had ever been economic growth, innovation, and social progress without the credit financing of debt!

Even two decades later, when confronted with a sharp fall in its world market share and challenges to its global leadership, the United States found revenge in identifying the Bretton Woods system with its own interests and the dominant role of the dollar. The weakness of the U.S. economy and the dollar was transferred consequentially to the world monetary system, infecting it with the disease from which it eventually died. For the IMF was not the main supplier of liquidity in the world economy and "lender of last resort"; it was the United States. Even the IMF had to raise U.S. dollars for the assistance loans it granted. The United States was both a country which now and again needed assistance and the world banker who granted it where appropriate—a crazy design. It was only a matter of time before such a system fell into distress and had accidents.

While all indebted countries with current account deficits on their balance sheets had to cut back, devalue, or plunder their reserves if they wanted to receive IMF assistance, this was not the case for the United States. As world banker, it could give aid to itself, with money it printed itself. The United States as world banker exported its inflation, which the rest of the world had to import. This went well for a long while, but not forever.

The system suffered from a double asymmetry: of that between deficit and surplus countries and, more seriously, of that between the privileged debtor, the United States (at the end, the largest in the system), and all others. Asymmetry One set up the system for risk of abuse by the creditor nations, while Asymmetry Two subjected it to exploitation by the leading nation, the United States.

While not without complaining, the weaker, deficit member nations acquiesced to the abuse by the stronger, export-surplus nations of the system. Although the "export-led" growth in the surplus countries drove them deeper and deeper into deficit and disabled their own process of catching up, they remained loyal to the system. They drew upon the goods, the know-how, and the capital imports of highly productive economies. On the other hand, the privileged position of the United States disturbed the Third World less than it did the other Western industrialized countries. In particular, the present EU countries (at that time called the EEC countries) were not willing to accept "imported inflation" (U.S. dollar flows) from the United States over the long term. This was above all true for the Federal Republic of Germany, which brooked no compromise on its policy of a hard Deutschmark. For a period of time, it was possible to diffuse the conflict between "soft" dollars and "hard DM" through the revaluations of the DM. The not-to-be-devalued U.S. dollar was devalued in terms of DM, but not against the other currencies of the IMF. But in the end this was only one way of buying time; the procedure could not be repeated forever. From a European perspective, a shift away from fixed, U.S.-dollar-denominated exchange rates was inevitable. The leading neoliberal school held this shift to be "a major reform."

Two mutually exclusive options were available.

1. *Either* one saved the system and its fixed exchange rate (or rates) by changing the reserve currency and unit of account (as Keynes had proposed) for the IMF's state- and currency-neutral unit of account, a new version of *bancor* procreated in the 1969 reform of the IMF's newly introduced "Special Drawing Rights" (SDRs).
2. *Or* one followed the neoliberal recommendation and went to flexible exchange rates determined by supply and demand in the currency and foreign exchange markets.

In the currency turmoil after 1971, which was, in principle, a U.S. dollar crisis, Option Two dominated: The duty to support intervention in foreign exchange rates was eliminated, abolishing the fixed exchange rate system. Although it continued, the Bretton Woods agreement had been deprived of its central element. The global exchange rate mechanism was dissolved. It was not the Third World that terminated the system because of the disadvantaged position of deficit countries (Asymmetry One), but the First World of developed countries that undermined it, due to Asymmetry Two: the privileged position of the United States and the dollar. Other nations no longer wanted either U.S. inflation or the threat to their own domestic stability and the export-led growth upon which it depended.

"Floating" Exchange Rates: A Compelling End?

The transition to the nonsystem of "floating" exchange rates was anything but smooth. As of the end of old standards (1931), the leading industrial nations were initially on the brink of a currency war. Just as then, the time came for "competitive devaluations," only they were less the result of government-sponsored trade and export-mercantilism, but more due to rapidly growing speculation on global capital markets without regulations or government interventions. In the EU, according to Chancellor Helmut Schmidt, these erratic exchange rate fluctuations became an opportunity to prepare for a European exchange rate mechanism (ERM, described in Chapter 3, the precursor of today's Economic and Monetary Union). Keynes had already predicted the end of the world monetary system diluted by the United States at the Bretton Woods conference of 1944. A monetary system in which one of the member states is declared to be the "host" collapses either because the host keeps his guests too dry or because he himself is an alcoholic and seduces them to drink too much. The forecasts of Keynes can be traced exactly. As long as the United States was in surplus—for almost two decades after 1945—it was a host that kept the others dry, and the substance distributed, the U.S. dollar, was rare and popular. The intoxicated guests who needed it had to be written up, if not fined. The landlord was allowed to do this and also to help them with generous economic and development support and military aid. In addition, there was support for the system from the IMF and the WB.

But when the United States itself turned into a deficit country in the late 1960s, the host turned into a drunkard and tried to persuade his guests to drink as well—drinking on a bet. The guests who wanted to stay sober went on strike. They put the host out the door and closed the bar.

This happened between 1971 and the spring of 1973. It had not been a moment of triumph for U.S. diplomacy when U.S. President Richard Nixon—speaking at the moment of the boiling point of international indignation against the host—announced that from then on he would continue to pay his own bills only in dubious paper money. He finally decided on August 15, 1971, to close the last remaining gap in the U.S. gold window: the obligation of the United States to continue to redeem the dollar holdings of central banks in gold. Of course, it was not insignificant that at this time the U.S. government had only a third enough gold to back up its outstanding dollars (see Chapter 2). Nixon's Treasury Secretary John Connally explained the step to other G-10 economic foreign ministers in an accurate, but not exactly confidence-boosting formulation: "The dollar is our currency, but your problem."[1]

However, Nixon's closing the gold window was only a formality: One of his predecessors, Franklin Delano Roosevelt, had already disposed of the full convertibility of the U.S. dollar in 1934. But Nixon's strong step and Connally's interpretation of it fueled a worldwide flight from the U.S. dollar. After a last rescue attempt in the Group of 10's Smithsonian Agreement, the end finally came in the spring of 1973. As we have already seen: It was agreed in a Solomonic manner to end the Bretton Woods system, but not to liquidate its institutions (IMF and WB). A nation may stay in the club, but the rules were abolished! Since that time currencies have been allowed to be traded (even though used at home as "public goods") on the global financial markets like any other normal goods or claims on money: stocks, commodities, or pork bellies. One can speculate on market-determined rises and falls of exchange rates (or prices of money conversions), as with traditional goods with widely fluctuating prices.

This raises the question: Has the idea of a global order for a monetary and exchange rate system forever disappeared from the earth with the end of Bretton Woods as a system?

Living in the "Nonsystem" of Post–Bretton Woods

After his sacking and the closing of his pub, the old Bretton Woods host, or world banker, has not done badly. He landed on his feet. And even though none of his guests had to accept his devalued paper money, most of his old customers remained loyal, and new ones even showed up. Despite its loss of value of more than two-thirds in less than 40 years (as calculated by Euronet), the U.S. dollar lost neither its position as the leading money in the world nor its position as an international reserve currency. No other currency surpasses the dollar in ubiquity, not even the competing euro.

Is there an explanation?

The answer is a very pragmatic one. A world economy of the now almost 190 nations trading in the world, and with hundreds of thousands of goods traded worldwide, cannot do without a common unit of account—unless it becomes acceptable to pay bills with incalculable and unpredictable reciprocal currency exchange rates and for each nation to finance its own costs. Taking

186 currencies alone (the number of IMF members), if settling bills bilaterally, this results in close to 19,000 foreign exchange rates. The accounting would be similar to managing the phone book of a medium-sized town with numbers that can change daily and which would, therefore, have to be reprinted daily. Since ancient times it has been common practice for long-distance traders, international merchants, and bankers to use a binding reference currency for all parties in which they express their prices and conditions for the opening of accounts. Long before the U.S. dollar existed, this role was played by what, for the time, were considered to be major global currencies: the Attic (Athenian) drachma and the Alexandrian tetra-drachma, the Roman Aureus denarius, the Byzantine solidus, gold ducats of Venice and Genoa, Spanish doubloons, Dutch gulden, and the British pound sterling. Thanks to this *"numéraire"* the "trick" was to reduce the already incalculable number of local, regional, or national currencies and their exchange rate parities into a small, easily transparent measure. Based on a common reference currency, there are not 186 IMF currencies, not 19,000 currency exchange rates or individual relations, but only 185—easy for mathematicians to understand: $n - 1$ exchange relationships rather than $n - 1: 2$ at $n = 186$. This brings an overview that can be easily accommodated on a newspaper page or a monitor screen.

The U.S. dollar benefits today from this practical business facility and reasoning of merchants, bankers, and travelers. All currencies of the world are every day, every hour, and every minute "at-a-glance" pictured in comparison with their respective dollar exchange rates. In the gold standard era it was the pound, and before that a host of other currencies served as the exchange rate reference.

But something is troubling from this perspective, dating from the end of Bretton Woods. It is in fact distorted. The commercial measurement of the world-money settlement varies: It is sometimes longer, but usually shorter, than the previous day, week, month, or year, for the dollar yardstick is neither fixed nor authentically calibrated.

Since the end of Bretton Woods this ruler or measure (comparable to the bar of platinum-iridium deposited in a landfill in Paris since 1847, which used to control all meter sizes and folding rulers) of the world economy has gone missing. How, and with what, can it be replaced? Taking a measurement with different, changing yardsticks over time is a deception, and as the ruler becomes distorted it is loathed by the risk-sensitive money markets. One needs to have the right to do such measuring, no less than the right arithmetic.

With the transition to the "nonsystem" of market exchange rates, predictable laws, principles, and arithmetic did not vanish from the world economy. On the contrary, compliance, guarantee, and enforcement have become more necessary than ever, but have been made more difficult without the warranty of a monetary law (such as served by the Bretton Woods system).

It is necessary to charge the Western banking world (as we do in this book) with abusing the newly evolving freedoms both in terms of flight to "lawless" business locations as well as in terms of catastrophic disengagement from the real economy—from both the real savings and investment sectors.

But one reproach cannot be made: that the banking world neglected the issue of taking new monetary and financial risks. On the contrary, it has widely—too widely—expanded. The majority of the newly developed financial products (derivatives, structured credit, credit-default swaps, etc.) serve the individual in terms of protection against these risks. However, the relevant systemic question becomes: What do the sum of all these benefits for individual risk management signify in terms of global acquisitions and private financial sectors, if the overall system can neither calculate nor handle such risks? The system cannot cope even given the necessary state interventions and bailouts in this crisis (which is essentially a bursting caused by risks taken over by a third party).

With the withdrawal of central banks (associated with indirect exchange rate intervention) from control over the currency and capital markets connected with the end of Bretton Woods, the private financial sector has free spaces which those in the old world monetary systems did not dare to dream of. In the gold standard, the "golden brake on the credit machine" (Schumpeter) nipped the proliferation of capital flows and their swelling in the bud. In this system there was no exchange rate and currency speculation, because it was not worth it. The exchange rates were fixed up to the second or third decimal place, and due to the gold parities regulated by law (and therefore difficult to change), revaluations and devaluations hardly ever occurred. In the Bretton Woods system the legal regime took the place of the golden brake.

The system required the intervention of central banks to protect the currency and the exchange rate with the full use of the interest rate weapon and, if necessary, even the currency reserves.

Depreciation or appreciation was the *ultima ratio* (ultimate rationale) of the system and could be done credibly only due to "fundamental imbalances." Without fully exploring these possibilities first, no help was forthcoming. Whether the brake on the credit machine was gold or legal, both brakes were guaranteed to minimize currency and financial risks and kept speculation in check.

The perversion of the nonsystem lies in the fact that it takes a minimum amount of speculation in order to limit the speculation. It gives any international or domestic investors or savers the chance to protect themselves against unpredictable financial risks in exchange for a fixed (and even affordable) fee paid to a professional speculator (bank, fund, or international entity).

But where are the limits for the system? What happens when the volume of these insurance contracts totals trillions greater than the value of what has been insured in the real economy, whether it be exports, imports, or direct or portfolio investments—as visibly occurred in the current financial crisis? Refer back to Figure 1.1.

A financial capitalism without the limits of the real economy on its risk-hedging forms of insurance and techniques will transform itself into a machine from hell. For such a system can neither cover all the risks it creates nor digest them: For this it lacks first the capital and later the profits from the real economy—for these do not exist. This financial system is heading for an abyss that it has itself flung open—a self-summoned *Götterdammerung* ("Twilight of the Gods")! Without a new Bretton Woods it cannot survive.

Keynes with a New Feature: Real (Not Nominal) Fixed Exchange Rates

Many fathers share in the mortal sin of the birth of the global nonsystem of financial capitalism that originated in the West: states, which demanded the return of their monetary sovereignty; a banking world anxious for virtually unlimited freedom; and a scientific perspective (mostly from the neoliberal corner), which wanted to see "prices" in exchange rates and the absence of state standardized "monetary yardsticks." Consider just the pure logic of the question: How, on the one hand, can money at home be a "public good" and, on the other, in global exchange become again purely private and speculative? Can what is taken from national *laissez-faire* be put back into this global *laissez-faire*?

Understandably, the states were fighting for their own affairs, for the priority of domestic objectives: continuation of economic growth, stability of the value of currency, and employment. The banks, like the old Spanish conquistadors, had only one thing in mind: El Dorado (gold). The environmental and economic consequences and costs of their greed were Hecuba to them: Their truth lay mainly in their returns or rents. And science? On both sides of the Atlantic she forgot her public responsibilities: Economics stopped being political science under the force of globalization; it shriveled into management theory, econometric formula of model analysis, or paid contract research for funding partners—even in universities. In Germany, for example, universities drifted away from the Association for Social Policy of 1872, which established a tradition of official duty by economics professors to intervene in the current issues of economic and financial politics—a practice anticipating a distant future. In the United States, natural science became the model for the reductionism of economics, while grantsmanship and corporate consulting began to flourish, narrowing interests to fit the incentives.

In this milieu the "Monetary Disorder" of the post–Bretton Woods era emerged and flourished. The lead institutions of the financial world exterritorialized and decoupled themselves from service to the real economy through their innovations (the new financial products). In doing so they earned in the newly created interbanking markets many multiples of what they would possibly have earned in the old public industrial and passbook bank deposit businesses. They achieved returns that were far above the real gains of the economy, but ultimately had to be paid from there. On the other hand, it was clear where these profits came from— but covered up by science, supervisory and rating agencies, and denied for decades: from the inflation of asset prices ("asset inflation") of the financial world itself.

The build-up of bubbles in the capital markets—in stock market securities, real estate, and other financial assets—became evidence of the success of the so-called investment banking.

It is incredible but true: Those involved in it are large speculators and gamblers, but investment banking became the normal business of the leading institutions of higher finance and its subsidiaries, such as funds and special-purpose vehicles, created for this purpose. In order to expand the new speculative markets, they

seduced inexperienced provincial banks and investors to invest
their money in this paper bubble.

With the bursting of these bubbles, all this vanished into thin
air. In the decade and a half before the outbreak of the financial
crisis in the summer of 2007, there was a single gold rush in values
from, and on, paper, negotiated well only by those who bought
the yellow metal itself in time. Meanwhile, disillusionment has
returned, and once again has begun to find its voice. In the political
and financial worlds as well as in science one acts as if the anarchy in
the global financial and banking sector is only one slip and an
isolated episode, a relapse into the sins of youth, which one has left
behind. Now it becomes a question of the creation of a new global
financial architecture. But which one? The draftsmen of the
blueprint have not yet figured that out. Intoxicated with the old,
they secretly hope something might be produced roughly along the
lines of the former status quo. But that would mean the plan would
lead only to constant replanning—the eternal recurrence of crises
until they come up to the last one, at some point in time.

The global degree of internetworking of the financial world
prohibits any national solution, or any attempt to go it alone. A
global solution is essential, but even that is becoming increasingly
difficult to achieve. The West—the United States, European
Union, and other developed countries of the OECD—has
become too weak to enforce the rules as they did before. And
besides, the West has not come up with a persuasive concept even
for itself. The new, rising world economic actors understandably
would like to liberate themselves from the monetary and financial
dominance of the West. However, they lack the prerequisite
financial infrastructure and necessary know-how. In the new
world bodies (the G-8, the G-20), there is a lot more talk than
action.

However, a set of procedures exists that could form the basis
for agreement by all parties involved: the resubmission of the old

Keynes plan of 1944–1945, supplemented by some important elements derived from our experience since then. A critical review of the historical Keynes model shows that in only one point, albeit a central point, revisions are called for: the method of calculating exchange rates.

An international monetary order, which is just another term for an international monetary law, is inconceivable on the basis of daily fluctuating currency exchange rates, riddled with incalculable risks and speculation. Running such a nonsystem actually invites hyperspeculation. A hair shirt is transformed into a suit. The German idea of stabilizing the market with the help of a national or European legislature is extremely naive. There is always an alternative venue or the ability to pack the forbidden so well that it escapes control—like the decades of experience in the off-balance sheet risks "taken care of" by the banks. Particularly, as theory would have it, when individually controllable risks widen systemically to the point of being out of control.

But the problem is solvable. Drawing precisely from the experiences of the Economic and Monetary Union (EMU), ways can be derived that show how one can resolve the conflict between national goals and priorities of states and a network of fixed currency (metric) exchange rates. When there are differences between real and nominal exchange rates, it should not be a question of the nominal level of exchange rates, but the real level.

No state can or should waive its domestic economic priorities and compliance with them. With nominal fixed exchange rates, the state is threatened with a fatal double conflict: the crisis first imported by the nation, which, in turn, blocks the state's ability to manage the crisis at home—for instance, if the domestic economy declines, but the balance of payments demands high interest rates. This is by no means a rare conflict, and led, as noted, to the collapse of the old Bretton Woods system.

Consider this: It does not have to be like this. The conflict would not arise if the states concerned agree to use their real (inflation-adjusted) exchange rates rather than relying upon the nominal stability (or, more accurately, rigidity) of their exchange rates. This system gives every country the freedom to separate interest rate and exchange rate policies—and still to remain a member of a currency union. An import of depression can be fought with cheap money, as the impending balance of payments deficit is met with devaluation. The real exchange rate remains approximately the same. The threat of imported inflation can be reacted to with currency appreciation rather than with higher and growth-dampening interest; and the real exchange rate likewise remains stable.

Such a system expands the degree of freedom of adjustment strategies for the states involved and they can use either the interest rate or exchange rate method or combine them. This gives them one more instrument at their disposal. The requisite adjustments to exchange rates can be accomplished with different growth paths and inflation tempos; the states remain masters of their domestic policy. This process would connect national monetary autonomy with global monetary integration.

Had this national autonomy element been built into the Keynesian Bretton Woods concept before its abuse by the United States, the world monetary arrangement of the future would have resulted in the following four-pronged approach:

1. The IMF would be extended by the Fund to become a bank, a bank of central banks with its own systemic money, the Keynesian *bancor* in its contemporary form of Special Drawing Rights (SDRs). This bank would be financially independent of the endowments and contributions from its member countries. The IMF country would nominate the exchange rate of its currency to the SDR, which serves thus as a stable

unit of account not subject to devaluation: Currencies can and must have their SDR value go up and down according to demand; a devaluation of the SDR in relation to other IMF currencies would not be possible, because they are the *numéraire* of the system, as, in the past, the U.S. dollar or gold has been. In this respect, the new SDRs would be a "basket of currencies" (as were the old ones) in order to guarantee their value-constancy, and the argument about which currency is in what proportional weight in the basket would become redundant.

2. The IMF members would agree to level, symmetric creditor and debtor rights and obligations. If an imbalance arises, the creditor countries would participate in the compensation credit and assistance from the IMF for the respective debtor countries. System-disturbing or -breaking debt crises would become a thing of the past. The system would be replaced by a built-in weighting or gravity in the direction of balance, and the IMF would be the final arbiter of power and balance of payments, in the last instance intervening with a minimum of new, fresh (and possibly inflationary) SDRs.

3. All IMF nations would commit themselves to real, not nominal, exchange rate stability. Each would retain the right and the opportunity for autonomous economic, monetary, financial, and social policy at a national level. No country would be forced to import inflation or unemployment, as happened in the old Bretton Woods system: The consequences for the domestic value of the currency (inflation, deflation) would be reflected in the external value of the currency, the exchange rate, maintaining transparency in purchasing power. The IMF as guarantor of the system would verify compliance with a rule that ensures the harmonious coexistence of a structural and cyclical nonhomogeneous, state multiplicity.

4. The IMF as the bank of central banks would consolidate agreements with mandatory standards for all IMF member country banks: minimum quotas for capitalization, rules for leverage effects (credit coverage ratios, securing credit risks, principles for setting maturities). Calling on the financial sector to lead in its real functions and duties to serve the economy would be the cause for common action of the IMF and its member central banks, and become the main item on the agenda of future G–20 meetings.

With these steps, the lessons of the severe financial crisis and the construction of a *new* Bretton Woods agreement could become, for the world economy of the twenty-first century, the transformative, fortunate event analogous to the Pax Americana after World War II and the Pax Britannica in the gold standard before World War I. The progress implicit here is that, in the future, the system requires neither old nor new dominant powers with their attendant strife-ridden national egos. The IMF, further developed into a monetary UN, would take over their heritage and their function. It would be an instrument in the service of the global economy of all nations, not favoring just one nation or a privileged group of countries. The world economy would become in reality what it has been up to this point only in theory: a welfare machine for all participating nations.

Chapter 6

Toward a Brave New World Economy

Reducing Debt and Unemployment

Until the outbreak of the financial crisis, it was widely assumed that globalization knows no limits. Markets were more important for future welfare than states. The *zeitgeist* was neoliberal. This became the basis of Reaganomics and Thatcherism, and even shifted the left toward the right (or center) in order to win elections. In the United States Bill Clinton won the presidency twice by focusing on the economy, eliminating the deficit, and initiating a work-for-welfare reform. Meanwhile in Germany it was the "Red-Green" era under Chancellor Gerhard Schröder that reduced the social state through Agenda 2010 and Hartz IV. The economic bibles went from Ludwig von Mises to

Friedrich Hayek on the continent, to the supply-side economics of the Laffer curve (written first on a restaurant napkin) in the United States. This was nothing more than a rediscovery of Jonathan Swift's satirical eighteenth-century observation of basic tax principles: The state that fleeces its citizens the least receives higher tax revenue than the one that squeezes them like lemons. So neoliberalism was not a continuation of the old but a relapse into an earlier era.

The financial crisis stripped away the support for this vision. Paradoxically, the believers of this philosophy of *laissez-faire* were among the first to call for a renaissance of the nation-state. Out of their own interest, poor taxpayers should line up to bail out the biggest and richest banks. For if the financial system collapsed as one of the main pillars of the market economy, the collateral damage for society would be unpayable, according to a chorus of politicians on both sides of the Atlantic, as well as the economists they paid and the media. Clearly there were some important differences in the responses: The United States dealt with the obvious truth that could not be avoided by dealing with the banks, while the EU governments hid behind the euro: It was another act in the play of a currency scandal.

A systemic difference was involved. In the United States there was an unwritten no-bailout clause: The principle that individual states were not responsible for helping each other out of debt was maintained. In the European Union, official written treaties were laid aside and openly and illegally violated. The United States is a federal state that does not want to threaten its existence through such a mortgage, whereas Europe desires to use the crisis to become a federal state. But this would constitute a *coup d'état*!

However, the nation-states of those in high finance who rediscovered the need for them have a serious problem. They have taken it upon themselves to do something they cannot afford to in terms of their democratic and social legitimacy: They must abolish essential rules and values of civil society or risk the legal protection of the property-holder, who is not liable for the debt of third parties, or for the stability and reliability of the currency and public finance. The sums required for the remediation of the banks (camouflaged as "financial market stabilization") are horrendous. These amounts are to be covered either by money that is newly printed by the central bank, or through new state debts piled on the old ones, which are already much too high.

What does capitalism gain when it saves its banks from bankruptcy by driving its states into bankruptcy? It reminds one of the drowning man who clings so long to his rescuer that both go under and drown.

If Western crisis management really wants to identify paths (already partially trodden) out of its biggest financial crisis in decades and not to end in the impasse of a new and equally intolerable socialism, then two reforms will have to be taken on simultaneously in attacking the problem. One reform is on the global level with the aim of submitting the unregulated global economy to a new order, networking the currency and financial markets into a framework of international law: One must bind them to a second Bretton Woods in which the old "golden brake on the credit machine"[1] of the era before 1931 is replaced with a better legal brake (a new monetary law). And the second set of reforms must take place on the level of national law and the welfare states in which the freedom of action from global *laissez faire* is returned to domestic economic, financial, and social politics in a manner in which they are not structurally shattered by two stumbling blocks: the aging of the population and the accumulating public debts that are already far too high.

The longer life span of people has burdened the pension mortgage system of the welfare state more than ever before in its history. The towering national debts of the past (in Germany, for instance, as a partial consequence of a failed policy of reunification) do not give the state much leeway for action.

The nation-state must look for new ways and methods of financing its obligatory tasks and long-neglected "public goods" such as education, infrastructure, and reforms of the social system. It must renew itself from the ground up.

The intellectual groundwork of the reforms of the international monetary system has long been taken care of. In his first handwritten memo sketching out his plans for Bretton Woods (dated August 9, 1941), John Maynard Keynes noted: Only twice in the last 500 years was some measure of harmony to be found between the use of money and the financing of trade between nation-states—in the 50-year reign of Queen Elizabeth and later the 50 years under Queen Victoria. In the first era, stability was brought about by an incredible amount of silver coming from the New World, which transformed deflation into inflation. In the second period, the second half of the nineteenth century, the city of London taxed financial services and shifted the burden of adjustment from the countries in deficit to the states in surplus. Keynes anticipated the end of harmony because of the watering down of his proposals for the historic Bretton Woods system, just as currently the end of the European currency union is probable.

Bretton Woods burst as the United States shifted its burden as world banker onto the new surplus countries in the world (Japan, Germany, and other EU states); the eurozone will collapse sooner or later, since its surplus nations (Germany, the Netherlands, Finland, and Austria) will one day no longer be willing to finance their southern currency partners who are living beyond their means.

Another "golden" era was the period from 1945 to 1965 (albeit without the use of gold as an adaptation and coordination mechanism among the nations driving world trade). The United States played the role of the good banker for the deficits of the rest of the world, as we noted in the preceding chapter. But as the superpower went from creditor to debtor, the road was not paved to slavery à la Hayek, but to the present crisis. Now the crisis threatens not only to plunge all nations in the world economy into a crash, but also to paralyze the democratic and social systems of the Western industrialized states.

The World Economy and Nation: States Are a System of Communicating Pipes

The nations of the West face a Herculean task. On the one hand, they need to stabilize their contributions to the structure of the world economy. On the other, they must be concerned that their rescue efforts do not make the financial system's home unin-habitable for its residents, either by flooding it with too much liquidity (inflation) for the financial sectors or, due to the chain reaction from bank and firm bankruptcies, by causing renters to no longer be able to pay their rent (deflation), pushing them into illegal house squatting or (as happened in Greece) into going out onto the streets. In either case democracy and the welfare state are acutely threatened.

We are already familiar with the measures for stabilizing the world economy and international monetary system. Meanwhile, the IMF has adopted some of the proposals of Keynes: It recog-nizes its own "inside money" (the SDRs) for its operations transactions, and as a reserve currency it uses "outside money" (a euphemism for the U.S. dollar). But before other reform pro-posals can be adopted (see Chapter 5), the IMF must temporarily check back with its members.

Meanwhile, we must clarify how and in which direction the nation–state must be reconstituted so that it can retain its ability to act and, in some cases, extend these capacities. For of what use is the end of global *laissez-faire* and the winning back of state instruments such as setting interest rates and rates of exchange (in the EU, for example) if the larger public debt excludes greater state activity and if the pension mortgage system of the welfare state is on the brink of collapse?

Add to this the special major problem of the European Union: The more competencies and tools of nation-states Brussels pulls into its sphere, the less governments can act on a national level. Although national crisis management is needed more than ever in the postwar period, the European Leviathan has claimed this function for itself. Brussels wants to tackle the crisis as a higher European state. But as the EU's own history shows, it can undertake selective action only above the national level and cannot direct community actions from above. The crisis of the euro states stems from these links to the EU from above. The EU awarded all partners the same creditworthiness despite (often substantial) differences in their existing credit conditions, which resulted in the increasing indebtedness of the Southerners.

The interest rate of the European Central Bank (ECB) was too low for the inflation-and-deficit nations of the EU's zone, and too high for the stability-and-surplus countries. The consequences: extreme inflation disparities and real interest rate differences between the currency partners, deflationary growth victims on the one hand and inflationary growth winners on the other. The integration train still operates today, with individual cars traveling at different speeds.

Democracy Begins and Works at Home

It has been known for a long time that democracy works only nationally, regionally, or locally, as it does in Switzerland. It cannot be Europeanized or globalized. Europe, which first invented the democracy the United States is trying out, does not stand above its democratic values but must abide by them. This means that the EU cannot (and may not) exercise its newly won state flexibility through Bretton Woods II reforms on a communitarian level, but must remain content to do so on the level of the sovereign state.

Nor does the EU need a monetary subsystem that creates more problems than it solves. Least of all does it require an extension of a fiscally financed transfer union that takes away the means the disciplined member states need to alleviate their problems at home.

Unlike the United States, the EU is not a state but an association of independent democratic nations accountable to their citizens. The EU has a mandate to facilitate its member states in "self-help" to cope with the crisis and its effects, to support their own initiatives and not to hinder them. But this self-help and these initiatives begin at home and not through the subsidies from Europe (and as a burden to other nation-states).

In contrast, the United States is a fully integrated federal state, but without regional revenue sharing between the individual states in the federal system. The acute danger of possible state bankruptcy in single states such as Illinois, California, New Jersey, or New York raises the reasonable consideration of a possible change in the federal constitution to alleviate such regional differences. (At the very least one could bring back "revenue sharing" in order to permit states to target federal money they collect more appropriately for their regional and local needs, as economist Robert Shiller has suggested.) For unequal living standards in the same federal state is a contradiction to the basic task of the nation-state: to guarantee the general well-being and assure equal opportunities for life, liberty, and happiness.

This task can be accomplished to only a limited extent by markets through the mobility of capital and work and free access to these (freedom to relocate). If this were not true, these unequal differences, which have been so prominent for such a long time, would not exist. There also would not have been a crisis—neither this one, nor those in the past. Therefore, the task in the United States contrasts with most EU states in the need to change the constitution in order to make it possible to bring about more equality between regions and sectors within the country. This crisis could become a catalyst for such change, which is easier to ignore or to postpone in good economic times.

The fundamental constitutional mandate of the separation of powers invested in the "checks and balances" would remain unaffected. The new provision would respond to market failures and help state governments not to become helpless and have to capitulate to market pressures, whether due to globalization or to regional integration processes.

In general, republican or representative democracy is superior to direct or local democracy (as is Switzerland) for the resolution of national problems, whether ethnic, religious, or regional, as James Madison recognized over 200 years ago (Federalist Paper No. 10). The weakness of this form of government is clearly the possibility of influencing democratically elected representatives by interested parties (pressure groups, lobbyists, big money). Against this there is no panacea. But transparency of government transactions, critical media, and an alert public limit the risks. In counterbalance is the advantage of a government that is conscious of the problems, prepared to govern, and capable of acting. Nothing harms the reputation of democracy more than a government that fails in the eyes of its constituents, whether due to a lack of integrity, of competence, clientelism, or a misunderstanding of elected office as a bastion of patronage.

The national and welfare states of the West are confronted with two old problems and one new one that have become worse due to the crisis. They must guarantee the stability and reliability of the currency, which is the foundation of business for every civil society that is based upon freedom, private property, and the freedom of writing contracts and protecting them. And they must create the social climate for the security of their citizens, first at work and then for the time after that—for old age, which lasts ever longer. Exacerbated by the crisis, the rapid rise in public debt not only restricts the scope of governments to cope with these ongoing tasks, buts expands into a nightmare for the present working generation and their children, for they have principle and interest to repay and an income that has become anything but safe and predictable.

Is this triad of problems resolvable? If so, *how*?

Pillars of Stability and Self-Healing Therapies of Modern Society

In modern society there are legal pillars that are sacrosanct and which one must not touch or soften up, as well as a variety of others with system-immanent, self-healing capacities that one, of course, needs to use if the society is struck with growth disruptions or has problems with taking care of its old people. Money is a "public good" which must never be transformed into a "free good" for those who use it—which is what led to this crisis. The private financial sector reproduced it in huge (inflationary) amounts under the name "credit" and misused it to become richer.

This should never happen again. Therefore the new money constitution, both national and global, is to be based on the real growth needs of people and the world economy, whose natural motor is progress in productivity. The stability of this pillar must not be shaken. This assures that people do not stop saving and do not stop daring to invest their money in their own country, rather than in foreign currencies, which they believe to be safer. The stability of the currency ensures that a country can use its financial resources sensibly, productively, and innovatively. It secures progress and is the natural enemy of every form of currency and financial speculation; for, from currency stability, nothing can be earned.

There is a widespread, but easily refuted, fairy tale that in a society of computer-controlled work, "work runs out," according to Lord Ralf Dahrendorf. Both Keynes in the beginning of the crisis of the 1930s and Schumpeter, looking back from the beginning of the 1940s, were in agreement, as seldom otherwise, that when people are released from "official working hours," no vacuum is created. They can always be used productively "in other ways" (Schumpeter).

Keynes pointed optimistically to the future untapped potential of the leisure economy for the creation of new public goods.

Schumpeter argued from a historical viewpoint. Every phase of overproductivity created new sectors. The overproductivity of the agricultural sector led to the start-up capital for industrialization. And the overproductivity of the industrial sectors was the basis for the development of a "tertiary" service sector. Why, he asked, should it end with just three sectors? In the meantime, the postindustrial society's overproductive high-tech world has created its own "underground" sector—a fourth economy sector.

From "Underground" Work to Lifelong "Retooling"

But what is the "underground" economy? Because official statistics or government financial tax offices do not cover it, it is neither real nor illegal. It creates real value and disposable income and pays its pennies to the fiscal state, only not to the tax office but in the supermarket where the "black market" income becomes "white." The proportion of this underground sector has evolved from close to zero (because there used to be few free hours) up to 30 percent or more of gross domestic product (GDP) today in most developed countries (and in Italy, even more).[2]

So the question becomes: How can one make use of this 20 to 30 percent of GDP and the fiscal economic record? From an economic point of view, one must simply recognize it. Because even if it is not statistically recorded—this private account number of the common man—it has nevertheless supported the economy, relieved the burden on the welfare state, and increased the national wealth through self-created assets. The government could increase its revenues greatly if it decided to tax the spending of its citizens instead of their income, shifting from direct to indirect taxation. And the welfare state would be burdened less if it made a tolerant offer to new start-up entrepreneurs or unregistered solo enterprises: to allow them to contribute to the social and pension systems but not to charge their income against their social benefits. Every citizen who, as a result of his or her own initiative, earns something in the underground economy should be worth more to the state than those who earn legally but, in net, burden the social budget. The standard rates of the official minimum wage (a thoroughly sensible innovation of the modern welfare state) determines indirectly how many workers are "involuntarily" in a position where they may become part of the underground economy. Too high a minimum wage will increase their numbers, while a low one will make it unattractive; why work underground and earn money with your own bills and risk if you can do it as well with a regulated and socially insured job?

It pays for the welfare state to anchor a system of collective learning (and before all else "added learning" or updating skills) securely in the society. The rapid improvements in productivity in the modern, electronic high-tech society not only set workers free, but continually devalue the specialized training and previously acquired know-how in older career paths, leaving their knowledge and skills obsolete. Thereby, the old teaching and learning hierarchy has been turned upside down. It is not the young who learn from the old, but the young who teach the old.

The generation conflict has reached the workplace. An insidious social revolution is on its way. For thousands of years, elderly, experienced hunters and farmers imparted the skills of their professions to their inexperienced children, in the same way that their elders had advised them. Their human capital lay in their practices, in their accumulated know-how over time. In the modern high-tech world, this is turned around. The young come with the latest, updated knowledge to the workplace and replace the inefficient old-timers. Accordingly, the older workers go earlier into retirement. This is cheaper for companies, but expensive for society. If it should become a trend, it will make it impossible to pay for the welfare state in the long term. The companies can cope with the trend by continually training their older workers and absorbing them at the top of the hierarchy. Within firms, harmony is a valuable asset, essential for success.

Ensuring that workers are professionally qualified reduces their fear of losing their jobs. This also pays off for society, because whoever feels secure in his qualifications and does not fear being fired or being forced into early retirement spends more money, consumes more, and saves less. This benefits both the economic and political systems. Long-term plans can be made for the economy with lower risks of unforeseen economic downturns.

It has always been a fallacy to view the amount of transfer income, the resulting continuity of demand, and the value of human capital as burdens for the welfare state. The truth is just the opposite: The more human capital holds its value, the more secure jobs become, and the steadier consumer spending remains, thereby helping to tame the innate volatility of capitalism and its cycles of investment. This sedative effect of the welfare state upon capitalism has been demonstrated by economists from very different camps—from the Nobel Prize Keynesian economist Trygve Haavelmoo (1976) to the father of Germany's social market economy long before him, Walter Eucken. The latter described the "constancy of planning data" as constituting part of the success of the entrepreneur.[3]

The more the systems of collective learning and their methods and programs are based on the dominant traditional and cultural values, the more efficient they are apt to be. "Collective learning" is a social process of distinguishing legitimate patterns of adaptive behavior within a society in order to manage environmental change without losing cultural integrity. Each society is made up of distinctive cultural traditions: patterns or indigenous schemata which become prototypes of meaning in a specific culture used to process information and to "brand" it with particular interpretations. Traditionally, "individual freedom" may be the key cultural schema in the United States, "social order" in Germany, "shame" in Japan, and "status" in France. But governments can adapt to global change and tilt these schema toward important values for the future of the community: "environmental sustainability" in the individualistic United States, "entrepreneurial risk-taking" in the order-conscious German society, "innovation and creativity" in the shame-imbued Japanese culture, and "increased lateral job mobility" in a French culture preoccupied with any loss in status.[4]

Schools, training centers, and the programs of corporate or charitable foundations should focus upon social ethics, financial knowledge, sustainability, political engagement, and tolerance for different cultures in their required teaching or learning materials. A basic concern of collective learning should be to transmit to pupils and trainees that adjustments and alignments to the values and prototypes of other cultures do not mean that one has to surrender one's own or that they must be paid for with the loss of identity: One can accept the foreign without having to give up one's own needs or sense of self. The goal of collective learning should be to make existing pending problems visual (positive transparency) in a context of instructions or policies that create genuine opportunities for solving these dilemmas in a manner that benefits mankind. The opposite, negative transparency, means waiting until one is actually in the midst of disasters, be they floods in Pakistan, smoke from fires in Moscow, or oil spills in the Gulf of Mexico, and then simply giving a statistical description of their consequences without a blueprint or therapy. What matters is to be prepared for such disasters with a positive framework for coping and not to be surprised by them, for they are inevitable. Only then can a crisis management team act quickly and effectively based on preliminary action plans.[5]

Two of the greatest tasks of collective learning that we confront are: how to finance the retirement mortgage the government has taken out, and how to reduce the public debt. Apart from unemployment, developed countries battered by the crisis are most preoccupied by these two ticking time bombs, which threaten the future of capitalism and affect the life planning of the present and the next generations.

The Old-Age Pension Dilemma

With the end of the tribal and family economy, caring for the old people on the basis of kinship has become difficult to impossible. But even in the high-tech age, ancient morality still holds for surviving parents and grandparents: One does not let them perish without care even if they can no longer contribute to increasing the GDP, since this would be a fatal relapse back into the barbarism of the Stone Age. This social contract, or generational contract, is timeless. Each generation is responsible for the former. Only then do they have the guarantee that the next generation will care for them.

The paradox of the modern welfare state is that it permitted the care of the elderly to be transitioned away from the natural family system into an impersonal money-funding regime. The laws of finance are those that determine the form (structure, sequencing) of the retirement system. With the passage of time, a purely private-sector financing of later retirement income comes into conflict with narrow and impassable systemic limits. The amount of "funding" necessary to be applied for untold millions of insured people would be so enormous that it would be explosive for the capitalist social order. The insurance carriers, whether private pension funds as in the United States or state social insurance as in Germany and most other EU countries, sooner or later would raise the largest stock of owners of capital stock and would thus become the effective rulers of the national economy. Capitalism would be abrogated with this method of financing (assuming it works) and would become socialized!

The other limit lies in the risk of each individual relying upon self-provision for old age. There is a common misconception, particularly in the United States, that you must save just enough to be well supplied in old age, free of the alms of charitable organizations or of the state. However, private savings can be transferred as loans in the future, but not at safe values. Even Warren Buffett experiences this, if he now reaches back to his wealth saved from the past in order to live from it. Even he is dependent upon an unknown third party buying the value of his holdings. Whatever the level of savings of those who prepare privately for old age and however they are invested, whether in securities, real estate, or gold, when it comes time to cash them in, there must be someone there to buy them. That there should happen to be a buyer at that particular time and what you might receive are each individual's personal risk. The risk disappears when you put your trust in a state social insurance system with income-based financing. Nowhere is the superiority of the (fairly) secure state clearer over the moody, unpredictable market than in the security (and cost) of old-age pension insurance, called Social Security in the United States. The crisis proved this yet again.

In Germany, the rich self-insurers lost an estimated €180 billion in capital during the crisis (with the grand total still pending).

In the United States, the comparable figure for Americans in private pension accounts—401(k)s—was a loss of over $2 trillion. Meanwhile, the poor "social pensioner"—whose pension is not funded by the stock exchange, but from the income of the insured—was hardly affected at all in the crisis. Those paying into social insurance through their contributions or taxes were assured that the pension could be paid as planned. For what counts for social pensioners is not the vagaries of the stock market, but that those depositing into the social security fund remain fully employed.

The old-age pension is at the heart of the welfare state and holds it together. Germany's social pension system, the oldest in the world (many consider it to be the best), is a striking case in point. Founded in the early 1880s by the "Iron Chancellor," Otto von Bismarck, Germany's social pension has survived all disasters, crises, wars, currency devaluations, and political regimes of the past century and a quarter. Despite revolution, inflation, Depression, Hitler, and the consequences of World War II there was always an army of honest depositors who served to provide all pension rights, 1:1, although not in constant real purchasing power—because that depended on monetary stability.

But this impressive past performance is now acutely threatened by demographics and the turmoil in the world of work. People live longer and work for shorter periods. The number of the insured and the duration of the use of pensions are both dramatically increasing.

At Bismarck's time, the average lifetime of a worker was under 60 years; entry into the retirement age was at 62; on average, five years were covered by the insurance after termination of employment. Today, 20-plus years must be covered by the insurance. In Germany, it is possible to retire at 59, even though the statutory (full) retirement begins at 65 years (transitioning to 67). Companies reduce their labor costs at the expense of social security, a nasty condition that must be solved. The insured live to an average age of 80 or older, and higher for women (including coinsured widows) than for men. In addition, the number of people insured has increased ninefold. In Bismarck's era less than a tenth of the population was insured by the social system; now it is 90 percent. At that time there were 12 workers paying in to finance each pensioner who was insured; now it is only 2.5, and by the middle of the century there will be only one worker for each pensioner, and this one will not have been employed for any long period of time.

Is there a way out of the dilemma in which ever fewer childless people with incomes interrupted by crises and job loss have to pay for the livelihood of ever longer-living contemporaries and fellow human beings (who, in addition, can keep going without worry due to their pensions)?

The solution is adapting work to the increasing life span and to the era of a rising retirement age. Who is retired and when are not determined by the Lord and only in rare cases by the doctor; usually it is decided by the social legislator. If the social legislature raises the retirement age to 70, there are fewer pensioners and a lower pension burden; if it were raised to 80, we would live back in the Bismarck era. So we see that there is a way to solve the problem, or at least to alleviate it, although it is not exactly popular. On the other hand, there are people who would work until death, if they were permitted to—and not just artists, free-lancers, and professors. Many entrepreneurs choose to work no matter what. We should let them be; it brings them joy and society is the beneficiary.

Additionally, one could bring up the number of insured from 90 percent to 100 percent of the working population. Why is 35 to 40 percent of current earned income prevented from being contributed to the pot of the social pension system? For this is generally how high the proportion is of the missing 10 percent of income earners who are privately insured or noninsured—the billionaires, millionaires, entrepreneurs, and freelance professionals in every economy. In the United States, including these incomes may be perceived as socialism, but precisely this "socialism" is practiced in Switzerland. Is Switzerland a socialist state? Its rich do not even get the full value of their deposits paid out, but receive only a token pension, since they should—and do—contribute something for the twilight years of their poorer fellow citizens. The culture of how a society treats its elderly can also be institutionalized—through collective learning.

The consolation in matters concerning old age is that the demographic problems will resolve themselves over time. Already within the next generation, it can be seen that today's "mushroom" of generational stratification (a small base with a broadening upward and outward) will become a "cone," with approximately the same base but rising toward a tip. Then the proportionality of ages in society (the relationship between young and old) will become normalized once more: The pension burden on the economy will decrease, as will the contribution rate of the young for pension insurance. The cost of the old-age culture will fall, particularly if the productivity of the young continues to rise as it has been doing, and the welfare state will recover its ability to act.

The Dilemma of the Overindebted State

This intellectually persuasive formula for solving the pension problems (although politically difficult to implement) is missing for effecting the removal of the other mortgage weighing down the future of states in the West: their overindebtedness. The states and their statesmen have imposed the burden on themselves. Easygoing policies with debt as an inexhaustible source of bubbling "soft" government revenues shaped the politics of Western politicians long before the crisis precipitated a collapse in government revenues and the swelling of rescue expenditures. Since ancient times every politician has paid homage to the maxim: Avoid tax increases, if you can, for they are unpopular. One does not vote for people who raise taxes. But raising indebtedness is a different story. You can always find a banker who makes good business out of it.

However, now the debt resulting in the world of Western nations and Japan from this maxim has exceeded every normal limit in current standards, most of all in Japan, but also in EU countries. Even in the United States, the debt approaches the level of World War II.

One could bail out the immediate consequence of the crisis—the threatened bankruptcy of the top high-finance institutions in the United States and EU—with the debt eruption in recent years, but only at the price that these countries risk moving much closer to their own declarations of bankruptcy. Some EU countries have already had to accept the downgrading of their "ratings" as borrowers, while for others, such as France, this is a situation that may yet evolve. As we have seen before: These debts did not solve the crisis but only served to postpone it.

The Western states face the question of whether they will fall into a crisis *en permanence* as in Japan or there is an emergency exit for them from the impending blockade of their freedom to maneuver.

A comparison with the situation following the October 1929 crash may be useful. At that time, the leading Western states sloughed off the external chain of their internal freedom, the gold standard. They could increase their debts without difficulty and reduce unemployment through "deficit spending" because they had almost none to start with. In Germany, the national debt was less than 10 percent of GDP. But already at the first signs of recovery (in Germany and the United States in the mid-1930s), inflation returned, especially since no cheap imports dampened the rise in prices, as they do today. Exactly the opposite is to be feared this time. The reduction of public debt, a negative "deficit spending," and the pressure of cheap imports keep the scope narrow for price increases. What is threatening is not inflation but deflation, especially since it is easy for central banks to silently gather again the fresh money they created in excess: They need only to raise the interest charges on the minimum reserves of their banks. And they will soon do so.

This time the old way of financing an inflationary boom after the crisis is not open to the countries of the West or, if attempted, can succeed only to a very limited extent. But this path will be completely blocked, as these countries cross over it, on the way to reducing their debts in the already arduous ascent from the valley of the crisis. Billions of skimmed-off tax funds are no longer likely to automatically flow back through government expenditure into the economy and consumer spending, but rather into the accounts of the old traditional state financiers: banks, insurance companies, their foreign customers and counterparties. What happens to the billions is completely uncertain. If the beneficiaries of these funds pay back their own debts or invest them outside the country in foreign currencies, which is probable, they will go missing from domestic economic circulation; this leads inevitably to a new version of the crisis. In this case, the Western nations would not have pulled out of the bottom of the crisis, as they did 70 or 80 years ago, but would have pushed themselves even deeper into it.

What Can Be Done?

The deleveraging of the Western states must be secured by additional conditions placed upon the financial world (the mass of creditors) and by programs of support for the economy (the *real* economy). Only then can we succeed in reducing the state's debt in an economic-and-employment-neutral framework without strengthening the already impending deflationary pressures—which would be catastrophic for the United States and European Union alike.

But how does one avoid this? On one hand, the state creditors (households, banks, financial intermediaries) can be offered an irresistible incentive to steer the money flowing to them effectively into the domestic realm again to ensure that it is not lost for economic circulation. On the other hand (to make sure that there are no remaining deflationary residual effects left), the states can be given the means of financing from the capital markets (i.e., private debt), commissioning an investment-and-infrastructure offensive. For this countercyclical program for a debt relief campaign, however, no public funds in the budget would be allocated, and the state would not take on new debts. The program-financing world of banking would have to be content with a "Contrition Agreement" for the reconciliation of losses that might occur from the full funding of the program by public institutions, constituting a partial warranty for losses during the final accounting.

The shift of government debt during the period of reappraisal of the consequences of the crisis, this time associated more with deflationary than inflationary risks, thus offers the banking world an opportunity to make restitution for the damage the banks caused and are responsible for—including new public overindebtedness. And it would permit, in addition, the resurrection of formerly commissioned state investment and development banks (in the EU countries there are some; in the United States an infrastructure investment bank is under consideration, and investment banks could jump in) to provide credit programs for SMEs (small to medium-sized enterprises), local government, and infrastructure. These banks would seize the use of the "opportunity of deflation" in order to eliminate the structural deficits of the national economy.

It would constitute a new species of "New Deal," which only sounds more complicated than the old one because the situation is different. At that time in the 1930s there was only one risk: An excess of inflation was to be avoided. This time, to walk the narrow path between "real economy" deflation (stemming from weak demand) and "monetary" inflation (resulting from over-liquidity) is not easy, but possible.

The particularly successful development banks, such as the World Bank (WB) or, in Germany, the Kreditanstalt für Wiederaufbau (KfW), have proved in the past that the private financing of public tasks is one of the strengths of modern and enlightened capitalism. It uses the savings potential of the citizens for the successful modernization of its structures and framework. The taxpayer is relieved, because in terms of government costs all that remains are the marginal losses covered by financial institutions, if that should become necessary. But the practices of the WB and KfW demonstrate how this can be avoided: through the restriction of lending to nonprofit projects that are still profitable with revenues coming from modest fees and paying the interest costs of their financiers. There are many such projects in the SME sector, and in the municipal or cooperative sectors. The national welfare state thus would win back its old credibility and ability to maneuver. If the renovation of the capitalist house springs from the regeneration of the "most capitalistic" of all sectors in the debt crisis, then this economic crisis will illustrate how much it follows the path of its predecessors.

For those crises also stemmed from wanting wealth only for some, not for all—but in the end they accomplished the latter anyway. It was a paradox that a fiendishly clever mentor Mephisto once gave Dr. Faust to consider (as we discuss in the Epilogue).

The Three Megatrends of the Global Economy of Tomorrow

Three megatrends will shape the face of the global economy of tomorrow:

1. The number of world actors will increase. There will be more than the current G-7 (G-8) and G-20. In the future world directives will involve more nations than this. The increase in the number of players alone implies that the dominant influence of the West will diminish.

2. The importance of globalization for the prosperity of nations will decline. The mercantilist strategies of "export-led growth" are apt to play a far smaller role than in the past 200 years. Adam Smith's patriarchal wisdom, that the prosperity of nations must be prepared at home, will be taken seriously again. It is above all the BRICs and other emerging countries that will give primacy to their internal markets and structures. Their priorities are called infrastructure development and job creation.

3. The old structure of the world economy, in which the industrialized world pulled out its raw materials from the less-developed world and processed them, belongs to the past. The emerging countries process their own raw materials and build their own industries. Under the pressure of growing scarcity and environmental needs, more and more natural resources (particularly fossil fuels) are being replaced with synthetic substitutes. Herein lies the great opportunity for the old industrial countries to maintain their leadership position in the global economy through innovation and technological advances.

About each of these megatrends, entire books are written. We will limit ourselves to just a few highlights.

The United States faces the historic challenge of creating a modern European–style welfare state with its three pillars: social pensions, health care, and care for the sick. An efficient system of transfer payments must be made between states and "partial states" to offset any significant regional imbalances: The market alone cannot solve this problem.

The EU needs to accept that its mega–integration of some 30 independent, but inhomogeneous member states has failed: It has overextended itself. The powers between EU institutions and member states must be recast. Europe is a democratic continent which cannot be technocratically governed (from Brussels). It is necessary to encourage progress in the domestic development and catch–up process in the peripheral and less-developed EU countries. The relationship with the largest country of the old continent, Russia, must be revised. The exclusion of Russia is a relic of the Cold War and no longer appropriate.

Russia itself has to rethink its role: Will it be a partner to Europe, stay a BRIC member, or remain in "splendid isolation," persisting as a nuclear superpower? Turkey faces a similar dilemma: Will it potentially become an EU member or rise in the tradition of the Ottoman Empire for domination of the Middle East?

The other BRIC countries are under the imperative of building up their internal structures and strengthening them. This applies equally to Brazil, India, and China. Asia's other emerging countries have the great opportunity of avoiding the errors of the EU in their integration models, and not endangering the ability of the state to act.

Japan has been condemned to involuntary isolation in its own economic realm. In its effort to be accepted by the West, it has lost the opportunity for connections closer to home.

Not Japan, but China has become the dominant economy of the Far East. China will not only hold its position but build it further. (Japan shares with England the fate of having overestimated the initial benefits of a special role.) The other emerging country in the region, Taiwan, will sooner or later fall to China, as Hong Kong did before.

Latin America, especially South America, is about to win a private profile; the binding to the "big brother" in the north, the United States with its satellites in Central America, will disappear. Brazil is developing to become the new center of gravity for the region. It is still unclear what progress the Latin American free trade zone dominated by Brazil will make.

The two unknowns in the perspective of the world economy of tomorrow are the Middle East and sub-Saharan Africa, but for different reasons. As long as the conflict between Israel and its Arab neighbors smolders, both will live on grants and public subsidies: Israel from the West, particularly from the United States, and Palestine from the Arabs and the EU. After the expected exhaustion of oil reserves, the rest of the Arab world can anticipate relapse into poverty and serious social tensions. Uprisings of the poor, immigrant workers, or even the seizure of power in some of the uninhabited small states, cannot be excluded.

In Africa, the present can be analyzed, but future development will be difficult to safely predict. The influence of the white elites in the former colonial regions has disappeared. The Western concept of democratic rights and the welfare state—in most emerging markets, a recipe for success—has not succeeded in being able to put down roots in the world south of the Sahara, partly because the tribal structures have stood in the way, and partly because the new local elites have not known how to go about it. The leader, usually with a military background, typically has lacked both political and administrative experience. Weak structures make these countries vulnerable to corruption from within and exploitation from the outside.

The major exception may be South Africa. Here the full adoption of the state structures of the whites by indigenous leaders initially resulted in a small economic miracle. Until recent strikes by the unions and serious increases in unemployment, it influenced its immediate neighbors, for which the country was the largest employer in the area. However, the reach of the South African model is limited to the nearby region. In the "failing states" of the continent, it is not taken seriously. Therefore, it should be a priority concern for the European Union, in particular, to assist these states in their stabilization. This is the only way to counter the undesired immigration of desperate people from these countries to Europe.

If this projected world economy emerges as anticipated, there will be less conspicuous wealth among the world's leading nations and global corporations, but also fewer unfair, competitive practices and beggar-thy-neighbor policies. The curbing of global *laissez-faire* through a binding form of international law and the monetary authority of the nation-states that are concerned about the excessive freedoms taken by the world financial markets is starting to pay off. The future of the world economy could be bleaker.

Epilogue

Faust and Mephisto on the World-Money Stage

Goethe's immortal play *Faust* begins with a prologue in heaven. The Lord God speaks to his adversary, a devil named Mephisto:

Man all too easily grows lax and mellow,
He soon elects repose at any price;
So I like to pair him with a fellow
To play the devil, to stir and to entice.[1]

What is personified by Goethe in Dr. Faust is a researcher with no blinders—a bold, dynamic global innovator, who is advised by his assistant, the opaque Mephisto. It is a drama that lasts for a long evening on the stage, and certainly for several thousand years on earth: the rhythm of recurring economic events, the development

231

and progress of capitalism. Driven by the engine of its financial innovation, which never stands still, and its seemingly endless possibilities and means, it grows and changes continuously. How? Through its successes and failures. The breakdowns emerge unexpectedly whenever people are doing well and become satisfied with their achievements. The crises of capitalism come as a surprise because no one is expecting them. But after they are overcome, capitalism reinvents itself. Human beings are charged with new energy, full of drive, daring, and risk-taking, as if born anew.

So has it always been. The only thing that has changed is the extent of the crashes and what triggers them. In the early years of capitalism, crisis meant hunger and starvation for many people. The triggers or catalysts were either terrible natural disasters (crop failure, disease) or devastating wars. Since capitalism has now reached its later, mature stages of development, the crises emanate from capitalism itself. For a long time it was bad enough that frivolous governments mismanaged their states and their currencies into bankruptcy. Most of the major nations of Europe experienced this as they moved up to the top of the world economy: Spain, France, Germany, and, at last, even England. And smaller nations suffered, too. Each of these state bankruptcies and the consequent currency devaluations transformed millionaires to beggars and forced savers to exchange money where they had their assets invested or to desert it voluntarily because no one accepted it any longer. Although the currency still might circulate for a long time as legal tender, it ceased to be a financial store of value.

However, since the United States emerged unscathed at the end of World War I and took the reins of the global economy out of the hands of war-impoverished, weary Europe, something fundamental has changed: The new and "great" crises of capitalism stem no longer from crop failures or epidemics, or from the more serious consequences of mismanagement of individual states; instead capitalism brings them about on its own in its self-propelling engine room: the private financial sector.

From Paper Gold to Paper Paper

The first of these global economic crises triggered by the financial markets was Black Tuesday on the New York Stock Exchange in October 1929, leading to the Great Depression of the 1930s. It was set off by a crash in stock prices, a loss that was greater than anyone had imagined could occur. The crisis disseminated with the telegraphic speed of light over the globe, shaking the ground of support out from under the gold standard upon which the statutory basis of the leading industrial countries was rooted. Out of "currencies as good as gold" came paper, just paper—first the pound sterling, which until then (1931) was the leading world currency, followed at the end by the U.S. dollar (1934). The consequences of the subsequent destabilization were devastating. The greatest industrial nations of the world experienced the largest outbreak of mass unemployment since the beginning of industrialization and the most severe crash in the world economy since the steamship and railway permitted long-distance travel, extending borders beyond what could be reached by horse-drawn carriages. Almost half of the countries of old Europe sought refuge in distress in political "strong men" and lost their democracy.

What had happened? America's core belief—that the freedoms allowed the brave individual should extend to the free financial sector that loaned him the necessary money to start projects, so that he could use bold and groundbreaking ideas to improve the world—was exposed as a romantic notion. The free financial sector plays the role of Mephistopheles in this capitalist scenario, who accompanies the plans of the dynamic entrepreneurs, investors, and innovators with money and advice, and with promoting his

234 BRAVE NEW WORLD ECONOMY

service ("to stir and to entice"), and obviously thinking more of himself than of the consequences for others. The selfishness of the Mephistophelian financier, however, did not advance the common good. He raised its validity as an open question!

In the stage version of *Faust*, Mephisto offers his diabolical self-promotion: "I am a part of every force, that wants to do evil, and yet creates the good."

But this is never to be taken at face value. Just because he doubted the effect of obvious evil, Mephisto points out his unscrupulous money scam: "The paper here is worth a thousand crowns, it is backed up, with some pledge, by a myriad unpayable goods buried in the king's country."

So it is worthless paper, covered by a fraud—never verifiable as being based on actual mineral resources—and yet it becomes something "good." Faust's life plan (a housing development for "many millions") begins to take off only after he breaks up with Mephisto and chases the devil to the devil.

The crucial issue in the crisis of our time is: Will the West now do the same as Faust? For what is new—in contrast to 80 years ago—is that the creator of the crisis, the big banks of the world, declare themselves to be "systemically important" and their governments believe this to be so. This explains why both the leading, powerful entities of the West—the United States and the European Union (EU)—want to bail out the banks with public funds: throwing more good money after bad; the value of their worthless debt certificates and advance payments should be returned or even restored.

But the simple truth is that the underlying overestimation of the private financial sector permitted the countries of the Western world to fall back into the oldest of all money errors. Whoever does not really know how much fresh electronic money (or credit, its substitute) to advance in order to keep the economy going risks opening the money and credit faucet too far, flooding it with financial means and purchasing opportunities, risking inflation. Or, turning it too tightly in the opposite direction, one remains guilty of not fulfilling one's social contract of transforming the real, enlightened, and available—but ultimately "dead"— capital of savers into financing for productive entrepreneurs, investors, and innovators. A financial sector that does not fulfill this contract or does so incompletely brings the engine of progress stuttering to a standstill; potential economic growth ceases to be fulfilled, and countless people lose jobs, income, and future prospects.

The Narrow Middle Lane of Successful Capitalism

The success of capitalism has always been reflected in the middle lane between the two sides of potential misjudgment by the financial sector. It was arrived at following respective corrections of inflationary overload and subsequent deflationary underuses of potential resources available. In the past, excessive inflationary demands were often predominant, making poor, precapitalist, or early-stage capitalist societies incredibly rich. But in the affluent societies of the West, the protection of the old property began to prevail over new projects to be built. Societies that have become rich want to preserve what has been acquired and not to lose it ("preservation of capital"). Therefore, they emphasize the protection of depositors over the (credit-based) inflationary promotion of new investors and creators of new wealth. Public policy carries the burden of this bill. Therefore, the inflationary investor machine built into early capitalism does not work as smoothly as it did in the past. Whoever operates it or would operate it as before must anticipate significant side effects and risks.

Which ones? A glance at recent history gives us an answer.

The collapse of the Second World communist nations would never have come so quickly and surprisingly if it had had a financial sector available to accelerate capitalist growth and prosperity. But that was not provided for in the communist catechism. Technology alone was not sufficient to surpass the West (as Soviet leaders all mistakenly believed, from Lenin to Khrushchev). The Third World, in turn, still lacks an efficient financial sector today as a power factory to provide "help for self-help." This can and will, of course, soon change. As a nation, it can be an advantage to be a late developer. One avoids the errors and exaggerations of the pioneers of progress. At the same time, this explains why the old success story of the West reached its zenith at the same time it reached its turning point. The "overbanking" in the West no longer guarantees the continuous success of the capitalist system. On the contrary, from its *laissez-faire* emerges a growing danger of crisis *en permanence*. The abundant supply of money and credit no longer automatically supplies finance for real economic growth at higher prices and at still higher and more widely distributed income. The interest of the global financial sector has for some time no longer been in providing funding for new technological marvels, leading to still unknown skilled professions and jobs, and thus assuring the substructure of prosperity for everyone.

The leading institutions in the financial sector of the most developed part of the world economy are less and less interested in doing business with the real economy. Neither does it gain its returns from the deposits of private savers and the economy, nor is its bread-and-butter business the granting of credit to the investing business. Its highest profits are from "in-house business": the debt to other banks based on novel and for the general business community only conditionally suitable financial products (derivatives, securitization, etc.) and upon the lucrative investment of these funds in offshore international capital markets.

With this transformation, the character of traditional inflation has also changed. The abundance of money and credit does not drive the prices of real consumption and investment prices way up;

the increase in the cost of living is kept in check despite the
"feeling of inflation." In place of the old inflation driving progress,
there is now the new "dead capital." The prices for cash investments and assets were shooting sky-high. Rich is the person who
has money claims on real or material assets. But their internal asset
value plays an ever-decreasing role. Thus, the monetary value of a
little clump of gold (one ounce of 31 grams) rose over 30 times in
the past 50 years, from $42 to $1,400! Money claims on real
business assets (shares) and land (real estate property) tell a similar
story. Meanwhile, the gains for real and especially for human
capital (wages, income) remained clearly behind. Still, this
remuneration in the past 50 years has risen significantly in the
United States and the EU, an increase of approximately tenfold.
The result: Large fortunes in Western capitalism are no longer the
accumulated rewards of the hard work of entrepreneurs, but are
rather "earned" with the help of the financial sector. This
advancing trend, leading through intermediate crises that repeat-
edly correct "asset inflation," has become both a symbol and an
alarm bell of Western capitalism. But the question raised here is: Is
not this ringing already sounding its own death knell?

From Gold to the G-20

Two impulses for global demand stimulated the dynamics of the
world economy established after 1945 under the aegis of the
United States (which heavily diluted the plans of John Maynard
Keynes): the need for reconstruction of war-torn Europe, economically subsidized then and for quite a while thereafter by the
still-intact United States, and the catching up of the decolonized
Third World. Keynes brought the poorer nations onto the world
economic stage as players, naming them the "developing countries" and giving them their own institution for financing: the

World Bank. They thus became official partners in the global political discourse.

At that time the upscale Bretton Woods system was brought into being, ensuring that the postwar world economy remained in global balance and never overextended its financial resources; it was not Mephistophelian from the point of view of either investment or statute, nor should it have been. The United States did not live beyond its means—at least not at the time. Its sizeable current account surpluses covered the needs for subsidy of the Europeans; the Marshall Plan, the World Bank, and other loans provided the financing. The Third World had long been financially self-sufficient: The countries could rely on the financial reserves they had accumulated during the war. The world economy expanded under these conditions, without being endangered by global tensions.

But at the end of the 1960s, the golden age of the first two postwar decades faded away. In the West, the focus shifted: Europe and Japan returned to the world economy, while the United States fell back. Tributes had to be paid, first for the Cold War, then for the "hot" wars that the United States led, building up its military accordingly. Third World nations had consumed their reserves, and increasingly became dependents in the system. The "development aid" invented in the early 1950s did not fill the ever-widening hole of their current account balances, but rather financed it, thus holding it in place. Whether the increasingly pervasive inflation in developing countries was "structural" due to lack of savings or the result of weak, incompetent, corrupt governments is open to interpretation. The growing deficits of the developing world initially caused far more stress for the order of Bretton Woods than the slow onset of the dollar's decline. In the last decade of this system, the IMF had to approve far more devaluations of Third World currencies than ever before. They punctured the principle of fixed exchange rates before it was officially abandoned. Paradoxically, these downgrades served now and again to "stabilize" the U.S. dollar.

Two storm surges brought the already fragile Bretton Woods system to the point of collapsing: First, the separation of the U.S. dollar from its gold parity in August 1971 undermined the trust of foreign central banks in the currency, which up to that point had remained intact. The dollar was no longer a reserve asset "as good as gold." Second, the oil or OPEC shock of the fall of 1973 established overnight a second informal, "private" world monetary system. It dethroned the IMF as the central bank of central banks and as lender of last resort, replacing it with the global, dollar-based financial system. This financial system demonstrated its effectiveness and efficiency by easily succeeding in closing emerging gaps caused by the oil price escalation (tenfold by 1980, and twenty- to thirtyfold to date) in balances of current accounts and balances of payments in the First and Third Worlds by recycling petro dollars.

But this recycling was nothing but the establishment of a gigantic global customer credit machine! The oil consumers bought on credit and became indebted. OPEC was able to assert its dictation of oil prices with the help of its trusted bankers. To this day, the global financial community continues to finance this credit system: since the end of Bretton Woods, there is no longer what Joseph Schumpeter called a "golden brake on the credit machine" for governments, central banks, or the global banking and financial system itself.

This perpetual system (or rather nonsystem) is Mephistophelian *par excellence*! It permits all states and central banks in the world to print endless supplies of their paper money—as much and for as long as they deem it necessary to revive economic cycles, to finance domestic benefits, or to plug holes in balances of current accounts or of payments. In this monetary environment, the global banking community has to fear a liquidity squeeze only if it brings it on itself by greatly overestimating the productivity of its once-in-a-century innovations, that is to say, of the internal system of interbanking or the derivatives market, which then can unexpectedly break down as in 2007–2008.

For almost 40 years the Western-Mephistophelian post–Bretton Woods system has taken its momentum from the real overconsumption of the West, especially that of the United States, and from the uninterrupted ability of the Western financial sector to provide the necessary means (until recently). From the customer credit machine meant for the payment of oil bills, a system of financing has emerged for the excessive Western standard of living. The current account of the United States (a permanent identity card of its overconsumption) has slipped from decade to decade deeper and deeper into deficit. But despite the sharp decline in world market share of the United States, the U.S. domestic market has become a receptive bazaar for exports from all over the world: at first primarily German and Japanese industrial products, and later including goods from China, South Korea, India, and other emerging nations of the world economy. The export-led mercantilist economies of these countries would collapse if the United States closed its bazaar, declared the dollar to be a national currency, and fully addressed its unresolved domestic problems. But this danger is not too likely. The U.S. financial sector, which is globally oriented toward its customers abroad, knows how to prevent it.

Nevertheless, the BRICs and the other G-20 nations must confront the fateful question as to whether and how long they can and want to accept *this* global economy. While it ensures the survival and growth of its existing export sectors, this comes at a high price. The nations making a living from exports need to make a large share of their national savings from export surpluses available to foreign countries as credit, especially to their customers in the United States. Only then can the "balance of imbalances" be maintained, meaning that some nations consume and others save to make it possible. It is the "recycling" of the Western banking system that secures these financial transfers.

Still, the BRICs and other non-Western nations of the G-20 have to pose the question of what is better for them: using their savings to invest capital abroad (in foreign money, financial products, or direct investment) or putting it to work for the benefit of their own people at home, by shifting to a market-oriented development strategy. For with this money, new industries and infrastructure projects can be financed.

But for the West, there is also the fateful question of whether and how long it can live with a financial system that permanently seduces it to live beyond its means—at least as long as it still is creditworthy abroad or remains so because of its currencies (the U.S. dollar and euro) and investment securities (stocks and bonds), for which there are still markets, either as central bank reserves or in the form of private capital formation. The Western banking system may continue effectively to market Western currencies and asset accounts. But sooner or later, governments and central banks of the West will confront the crucial question of the limits of growing external debts—at the latest when the resulting transfer burden, the solvency of the state, or the acceptance of the currency come into question.

This problem is more acute for the United States than for the EU. On the one hand, the United States profits from continuing high revenues from its substantial external assets and from the fact of the continued, unabated acceptance of the U.S. dollar as reserve medium and as a "safe haven" for investors from countries where monetary and inflationary risks are high. But this may change. In the long run, the sword of Damocles of a liquidity crisis, caused by excessive transfers to foreign countries, hangs over the United States, its domestic economy, its market capital, and its public finances, as is the case with any debtor country. Even if for the time being the "net" is listed as less than the "gross," the catastrophe will occur when gross and net become identical!

For the EU, namely for the eurozone, the same problem arises domestically. The eurozone, originally planned as a currency union, has been transformed by the debt excesses of its southern members (plus Ireland) into a transfer-union not provided for in the EU treaties: *de facto* by means of aid for deficit budgets and possibly also *de jure* by means of the newly proposed rules to prevent state bankruptcies. The burden of these internal transfer mortgages to protect and save the euro also diminishes the ratings of the euro countries that are still healthy, and which subsidize these mortgages: Germany by itself guarantees the continued existence of the euro and the euro's standing in world financial markets with 70 percent of its federal tax income. As long as the crisis simmers over the euro, its prospects to replace the dollar as the leading international currency are not great. Even an end to the failed monetary experiment cannot be excluded in the future.

The G-20 countries and their opinion shapers (to whom this book is dedicated) are thereby faced with a difficult decision on changing course: Should they wait and see if the U.S. dollar will once again stabilize, as was the case several times in the post–World War II period, maintaining the status quo of the world monetary-financial system, however fragile, for whatever period of time—or should they act in anticipation of a collapse that can no longer be avoided?

What alternatives are available?

The global flight to gold—a popular uprising of depositors against the Mephistophelian policy of states and their central banks—has increasingly led conservative and neoliberal politicians (including the current World Bank president) to call for a return to the gold standard: The private gold standard of investors and the public one of the currencies would become united again. No matter how justified the motives of savers or how understandable the objectives of politicians may be, the realization of this plan would have disastrous consequences for the global economy and even more so for the national economies that constitute it!

The available amount of gold worldwide must be sufficient: It would have to be multiplied by nearly 40 times or the price of gold would need to be raised by 4,000 percent. Historical experience is not encouraging when attempting such an experiment. The global and national economies are dependent on the money and credit supply that orients itself by its real growth potential. An always possible lack of money and credit must not be permitted to brake the prosperity machine or even to lead to its collapse, as was seen after September 1931 in England, when the nation was forced to abandon the gold basis for its currency (the pound sterling being a worldwide valid gold certificate, unlike the dollar, for which redemption was limited to central banks) in order to rescue the British economy from the damage caused by monetary and credit withdrawal.

At that time, the world economy broke down; not because, as today, it was suffering from financial overdose (inflation and speculation), but because of the opposite, a financial underdose caused by the shortage, the one-sided distribution, and the happenstance geological discoveries of the yellow metal—the "barbarous relic," as Keynes once called it. A return to gold would bring the few gold-producing countries of the world unjustified profits while, in the rest of the world, a fight for gold would break out, in the form of an even more conflict-prone export mercantilism than we have today in order to keep the financial flexibility for domestic growth, employment, and social policies at home.

A world of high-tech and other potential sources of modern productivity is incompatible with a medieval monetary system based upon mining. A systemic solution for the contemporary global economy looks much different from that!

The future must belong to only one world currency system, which carefully weighs and rebalances the legitimate interests of its participants against each other. The West can no longer insist on the advantage that its monetary and financial system is the only one that is responsible for the world economy: the only one in which international economic transactions (exports and imports) can be carried out, and trade and the global movement of capital (direct and portfolio investments) can be financed.

Emerging and catch-up nations must learn that without currencies and efficient financial sectors equivalent to those of the West, they will inevitably have to "lend" a large part of their savings to the West—and to leave their money to work there and to build up assets in foreign denominations instead of their own. The collapse of communism should serve as a lesson for all Third World nations as a case in point. To catch up with the West from a backward position requires not only modern technology and an army of planning bureaucrats on the drawing board, as all the Soviet leaders, from Lenin to Stalin to Khrushchev, had believed. It requires a financial sector that realistically assesses the daring ideas of entrepreneurial pioneers of progress, and also funds them if they pass the test of their calculations. Helping people to help themselves can function only in this way.

The West must learn to get better control of its "overbanking" in order to prevent future financial crises like the present one. The Third World (to which large parts of the former communist Second World now also belong) must overcome its underbanking. Only then can it optimize its rich potential in natural resources, human capital, and real savings and achieve parity with the West.

In the world monetary system of the future—as described in Chapter 5—the dollar will once again be the national currency of the United States and no longer a medium for world reserves. Its place will be taken by the Special Drawing Rights (SDRs) of the IMF, a general coupon valid in all the currencies of the world. For the old-world banker, the United States, this will signify neither waiver nor abdication, but liberation from a burden. Freed from these obligations, future U.S. governments will be able to turn again to focus upon the long overdue reforms of their own country. Should the euro experiment come to an end, Old Europe may be represented with a multitude of currencies in the global concert. The currency that shows itself to be the strongest and most stable in the competition with other European currencies will determine the "standard pitch" for all Europeans in the "orchestra" just as the Deutschmark (DM) did before the advent of the euro.

The sooner the G–20 comes to a mutual understanding on this new, improved version of a Bretton Woods II, together with the corresponding domestic reforms in member countries, the greater the probability of returning more quickly to those golden times that Bretton Woods I facilitated in its early phase. Since then everything has expanded: the insight into the system, its opportunities and constraints, the productivity of new technologies and their markets. What is missing is the restoration of the stability of currency and finances. In contrast to communism, capitalism has always survived each of its many crises because it was capable of learning. Why should it be different this time?

Invitation

Further explore the themes in this book with updated contributions by the authors at their web site/blogs:

http://BraveNewWorldEconomy.blogspot.com
http://Geldherrschaft.blogspot.com

Notes

Manifesto: Democratization of Capitalism

1. Joseph Alois Schumpeter, *Capitalism, Socialism, and Democracy* (New York: Harper Perennial, 1950; orig. pub. 1939), 31–32.

2. Ralf Dahrendorf, "Is the Work Society Running Out of Work?" *Omega*, 8:3 (1980): 281–285.

3. Robert Rubin, former Treasury Secretary, Economist Buttonwood Conference, New York, October 25, 2010.

4. Joseph Alois Schumpeter, *Die Kreditwirtschaft. 1. Teil. Kölner vorträge*, Bd. I (Leipzig: G.A. Gloeckner, 1927), 80–106. Reprinted as Joseph A. Schumpeter, *Aufsätze zur ökonomischen Theorie*. Ed. E. Schneider and A. Spiethof (Tübingen: Mohr, 1952), 158–184.

5. Joseph Alois Schumpeter, *The Theory of Economic Development*, trans. Redvers Opie (Cambridge, MA: Harvard University Press, 1934), 74.

6. Fritz Karl Mann, ed., *Das Wesen des Geldes* (Göttingen: Vandenhoeck & Ruprecht, 1970).

Chapter 1: Midas Reveals How to Create Money through Credit Fraud

1. Joseph Alois Schumpeter, *Die Kreditwirtschaft. 1. Teil. Kölner vorträge*, Bd. I (Leipzig: G.A. Gloeckner, 1927), 80–106.

2. John Maynard Keynes, *Treatise on Money* (1930) and *General Theory* (1936). It was Keynes who on the eve of the outbreak of World War II warned the world of states against using the war as an alibi for opening the locks of inflation (*How to Pay for the War*, 1940). And it was he who designed the world monetary order after the war (*Proposals for an International Clearing-Union*, 1943–1944), which had the potential to ban the Midas cult once and for all. Those of his proposals to the Bretton Woods Conference that failed after the war could become reality after the current crisis. We return to this in Chapter 5.

Chapter 2: The Great Bluff

1. Cited by Jason Zweig, "What History Tells Us about the Market," *Wall Street Journal* (October 13, 2008), W1.

2. John Dewey, "The House Divided against Itself," *New Republic* 58 (1929), 270–271: "Anthropologically speaking, we are living in a money culture. Its cult and rites dominate."

3. Matt Taibbi, "The Great American Bubble Machine," *Rolling Stone* (July 9–23, 2009), 1.

4. John Kenneth Galbraith, "In Goldman, Sachs We Trust" Chapter 4 in his book *The Great Crash* (London: Penguin, 1954), 69–90.

5. Taibbi, "Great American Bubble Machine," 7.

6. "Inside the Gold Mine," *Sunday Times* (London) magazine (November 8, 2009), 8.

7. Robert Isaak, *The Globalization Gap: How the Rich Get Richer and the Poor Get Left Further Behind* (Upper Saddle River, NJ: Financial Times–Prentice Hall, 2005), chap. 1.

8. Marcus Brunnemeier, "Deciphering the 2007–2008 Liquidity and Credit Crunch," *Journal of Economic Perspectives* (Spring 2008). The preceding section draws from Brunnemeier's lucid analysis.

9. "Timeline: Credit Crunch to Downturn," *BBC News* (August 9, 2007), http://news.bbc.co.uk/2/hi/7521250.stm.

10. Thomas Friedman, *The Lexus and the Olive Tree* (New York: Anchor Books, 2000), 142.

11. Rich Miller, "Is the Federal Reserve Running Out of Tools to Fight the Credit Crisis?" *New York Times* (March 17, 2008), Business Day, 1.

12. Robert Shiller, "What Would Roosevelt Do?" *New York Times* (August 1, 2010), BU, 5, New York edition.

13. David Leonhardt, "Obamanomics," *New York Times Magazine* (August 24, 2008), MM30, New York edition.

14. David Cho, "Bank Loophole for Wall Street Remains in Financial Regulation Bill," *Washington Post* (May 19, 2010), Post Business, 1.

15. Jeff Madrick, "U.S. Financial Regulations: Plugging Holes in a Faulty Dam," *Triple Crisis: Global Perspectives on Finance, Development, and Environment* (July 26, 2010), www.triplecrisis.com.

16. Lawrence H. Summers, "Technological Opportunities, Job Creation, and Economic Growth," remarks at the New American Foundation on the President's Spectrum Initiative, National Economic Council, June 28, 2010, www.whitehouse.gov/administration/eop/nec/speeches/technology.

17. Dan Ariely, *Predictably Irrational* (New York: HarperCollins, 2009), 25–31.

18. Jenisha Watts, "Former Motown Exec Helps Bury Dead," Essence.com (January 4, 2010), 1.

19. Fareed Zakaria, *GPS*, CNN (July 4, 2010), www.livedash.com/transcript/fareed_zakaria_gps/4998/CNN/Sunday_July_4_2010/247160/.

20. Data from www.BabyCenter.com, Cost of Raising Your Child calculator.

21. David Leonhardt, "America's Sea of Red Ink Was Years in the Making," *New York Times*, A1.

22. Ned David Research (2010), www.ndr.com.

23. Daniel Di Salvo, "The Trouble with Public Sector Unions," *National Affairs* 5 (Fall 2010), 3–19.

24. "Companies' Cash Piles—Show Us the Money," *Economist* (July 3, 2010), 65–66.

25. Judith Warner, "The Way We Live Now: Dysregulation Nation," *New York Times Magazine* (June 20, 2010), MM11.

26. "The Morning After: A $3 Trillion Consumer Hangover," *Economist* (June 26–July 2, 2010), 97.

27. See Alberto Alesina and Silvia Ardagna, "Large Changes in Fiscal Policy: Taxes versus Spending" (NBER Working Paper No. 15438, revised January 2010).

28. IMF, "Will It Hurt? Macroeconomic Effects of Fiscal Consolidation," chap. 3 in *World Economic Outlook* (October 2010), www.imf.org/external/pubs/ft/weo/2010/02/pdf/c3.pdf.

29. "CBO Report: Debt Will Rise to 90% of GDP," *Washington Times* (March 26, 2010).

30. Fareed Zakaria, *GPS*, CNN (August 1, 2010), www.livedash.com/transcript/fareed_zakaria_gps/49/CNN/Sunday_August_1_2010/266746/.

31. Alan Blinder and Gordon Rentschier, "How the Great Recession Was Brought to an End," *Moody's Analytics* (July 27, 2010), www.economy.com/mark-zandi/documents.

32. *Quest Means Business: Q&A*, CNN (August 3, 2010), http://questmeansbusiness. blogs.cnn.com/category/Q&A/page/2/.

Chapter 3: Giant with Feet of Clay

1. Eugen von Böhm-Bawerk, "Macht oder ökonomisches Gesetz?" in *Zeitschrift für Volkswirtschaft, Sozialpolitik und Verwaltung,* Bd. XXIII (1914), 205–271. Reprinted by Duncker & Humblot (Berlin, 1975).

2. One of the coauthors along with his colleagues has submitted such a complaint to the German constitutional court.

3. Wilhelm Hankel was Karl Schiller's Director of Money and Credit.

Chapter 4: The *New* New World

1. Mario Lettieri and Paoloa Raimondi, "BRICs Drive Global Economic Recovery," *IMF Survey Magazine* (July 22, 2009), 1.

2. Goldman Sachs, "Dreaming with BRICs: The Path to 2050," Global Economics Paper No. 99 (2003), www.gs.com. See http://advisoranalyst .com/BRICMarket.php#99.

3. Keith Bradsher, "China Uses Rules on Global Trade to Its Advantage," *New York Times* (March 15, 2010), A1.

4. "The World Turned Upside Down: The Charms of Frugal Innovation," *Economist* (April 18, 2010), 1–14.

5. Robert Isaak, "Making Economic Miracles: Explaining Extraordinary National Economic Achievement," *American Economist* (Spring 1997), 59–69.

6. Thomson Reuters, based on data in "Counting Their Blessings," *Economist* (January 2–8, 2010), 24.

7. Markus Jaeger, "Demographic Outlook for BRIC Countries Differs Sharply," Deutsche Bank Research (February 26, 2010), www.dbresearch.com.

8. "Emerging Asian Economies on the Rebound," *Economist* (August 13, 2009), Briefings, 2.

9. "The Rising Power of the Chinese Worker," *Economist* (July 29, 2010), Briefings, 2.

10. Interview with Fareed Zakaria, *GPS*, CNN (June 21, 2010).

11. Ibid.

12. "Great Wall Street: China's Banks," *Economist* (July 10, 2010).

13. "The Charms of Frugal Innovation," *Economist* (April 18, 2010), 1–14.

14. McKinsey & Company, *India Banking 2010: Towards a High Performing Sector*, www.mckinsey.com/locations/india/mckinseyonindia/pdf/india_banking_2010.pdf.

15. Eric Hobsbawm, *The Age of Extremes* (New York: Abacus/Time Warner, 2002), 577.

16. "How to Get Children out of Jobs and into School," *Economist* (July 31, 2010), 17–18. Such collective learning policies point the way toward a more "civilized capitalism" (see Chapter 6).

17. "Brazilian Banking System Outlook Is Stable," *Moody's* (June 15, 2010), http://imarketnews.com/node/15011.

18. Courtney Weaver, "Price of a Presence in Russia," *Financial Times* (July 27, 2010), Companies-Technology, 1.

19. Henry Paulson, *On the Brink* (New York: Hachette Book Group–Business Plus, 2010), 161.

20. McKinsey Global Institute, "Debt & Deleveraging: The Global Credit Bubble and Its Economic Consequences" (January 2010), www.mckinsey.com/mgi/publications/debt_and_deleveraging/index.asp.

21. Rebecca Wilder, "Two BRICs: India versus Brazil," *News N Economics* (January 7, 2010), www.newsneconomics.com/2010/01/brics-not-equal-and-not-necessarily.html.

22. Timothy Shaw, "Theory Talk #10," www.theory-talks.org/2008/06/theory-talk-10.html.

23. *Financial Times* (September 12, 2010).

Chapter 5: Time for a New Bretton Woods

1. John Connally at G-10 Rome meetings (1971), www.project-syndicate.org.

Chapter 6: Toward a Brave New World Economy

1. Joseph Schumpeter, *Die Kreditwirtschaft, 1. Teil. Kölner vorträge*, Bd. I (Leipzig: G.A. Gloeckner, 1927), 80–106.

2. Wilhelm Hankel, *Gegenkurs: Von der Schuldenkrise zur Vollbeschäftingung* (Munich: Siedler Verlag, 1984).

3. Walter Eucken, *Grundsätze der Wirtschaftspolitik* (Tübingen: J.C.B. Mohr, 1952).

NOTES

4. Robert Isaak, *Managing World Economic Change,* 3rd ed. (Upper Saddle River, NJ: Prentice Hall, 2000), 20–22.

5. Ibid., 281–284.

Epilogue: Faust and Mephisto on the World-Money Stage

1. Johann Wolfgang von Goethe, *Faust*, trans. Walter Arndt (New York: W.W. Norton, 2001), 11.

Bibliography

Ariely, Dan. *Predictably Irrational*. New York: HarperCollins, 2009.

Brunnemeier, Marcus. "Deciphering the 2007–2008 Liquidity and Credit Crunch." *Journal of Economic Perspectives* (Spring 2008).

Dahrendorf, Ralf. "Is the Work Society Running Out of Work?" *Omega* 8:3 (1980): 281–285.

Eucken, Walter. *Grundsätze der Wirtschaftspolitik*. Tübingen: J.C.B. Mohr, 1952.

Friedman, Thomas. *The Lexus and the Olive Tree*. New York: Anchor Books, 2000.

Galbraith, John Kenneth. "In Goldman, Sachs We Trust." Chap. 4 in *The Great Crash*, 69–90. London: Penguin, 1954.

Haller, Max. *Die Europäische Integration als Elitenprocess: Das Ende eines Traums?* Wiesbaden: Verlag für Sozialwissenschaft, 2009; English version: *European Integration as an Elite Process: The Failure of a Dream*. New York/London: Routledge, 2008.

Hankel, Wilhelm. *Caesar: Weltwirtschaft des Alten Rom*. Frankfurt: Ullstein Sachbuch, 1992.

———. *Die Euro Lüge . . . und andere volkswirtschaftliche Märchen*. Vienna: Signum Verlag, 2010.

———. *Die Euro-Illusion: Ist Europa noch zu retten?* Mit Wilhelm Nölling, Karl Albrecht Schachtschneider, und Joachim Starbatty. Hamburg: Rowohlt Taschenbuch Verlag, 2001.

————. *Die Euro-Klage: Warum die Währungsunion scheitern muß.* Mit Wilhelm Nölling, Karl Albrecht Schachtschneider, und Joachim Starbatty. Hamburg: Rowohlt Taschenbuch Verlag, 1998.

————. *Gegenkurs: Von der Schuldenkrise zur Vollbeschaftingung.* Munich: Siedler Verlag, 1984.

————. *Das große Geld-Theater.* Deutsche-Verlags-Anstalt, 1995.

————. *John Maynard Keynes: Die Entschlüsselung des Kapitalismus.* Munich: Pieper, 1986.

————. *Prosperität in der Krise.* Vienna: Verlag Frtiz Molden, 1979; English version: *Prosperity amidst Crisis.* Boulder, CO: Westview Press, 1981.

————. *Weltwirtschaft.* Dusseldorf: Econ Verlag, 1977.

Hankel, Wilhelm, and Robert Isaak. *Die moderne Inflation: Ein Fall für Exorzismus oder Moderation?* Köln-Deutz: Bund-Verlag, 1981. English edition: *Modern Inflation: Its Economics and Its Politics.* Lanham, MD: University Press of America, 1983.

Hankel, Wilhelm, and Gerhard Zweig. *Volkswirtschaftliche Grundfragen der Sozial Reform.* Köln-Deutz: Bund Verlag, 1956.

Hartz, Louis. *The Liberal Tradition in America.* New York: Harcourt Brace, 1955.

Hobsbawm, Eric. *The Age of Extremes.* New York: Abacus/Time Warner, 2002.

Horsefield, J. Keith. *The International Monetary Fund.* Vol. I, *1945–1965.* Washington, DC: International Monetary Fund, 1969.

Huxley, Aldous. *Brave New World.* London: Chatto & Windus, 1932.

Isaak, Robert. *American Democracy and World Power.* New York: St. Martin's Press, 1977.

————. *American Political Thinking: Readings from the Origins to the 21st Century.* New York: Harcourt Brace, 1994.

————. *European Politics: Political Economy and Policy Making in Western Democracies.* New York: St. Martin's Press, 1980.

————. "From Collective Learning to Silicon Valley Replication: The Limits to Synergistic Entrepreneurship in Sophia Antipolis." *Research in International Business* (2008). doi:10.1016/j.ribaf.2008.03.006.

————. *The Globalization Gap: How the Rich Get Richer and the Poor Get Left Further Behind.* Upper Saddle River, NJ: Financial Times–Prentice Hall, 2005.

————. *Green Logic: Ecopreneurship, Theory and Ethics.* West Hartford, CT: Kumarian Press, 1999.

————. "Making Economic Miracles: Explaining Extraordinary National Economic Achievement." *American Economist* (Spring 1997): 59–69.

———. *Managing World Economic Change*, 3rd ed. Upper Saddle River, NJ: Prentice Hall, 2000.

Isaak, Robert, with Ralph Hummel. *Politics for Human Beings*, 2nd ed. Belmont, CA: Wadsworth, 1980.

Keynes, John Maynard. *The Collected Writings*. Vol. 25, *Activities, 1940–44—Shaping the Post-war World: The Clearing Union*. London: Basingstoke, 1980.

———. *The General Theory of Employment, Interest and Money*. New York: Harcourt, Brace & Co., 1936.

———. *How to Pay for the War*. London: Macmillan, 1940.

———. *Treatise on Money*. London: Macmillan, 1930.

List, Friedrich. *Das nationale System der politischen Oekonomie*. J.G. Cotta'scher Verlag, 1842.

Nölling, Wilhelm, Karl Albrecht Schachtschneider, und Joachim Starbatty, eds. *Währungsunion und Weltwirtschaft: Festschrift für Wilhelm Hankel*. Stuttgart: Lucius & Lucius, 1999.

Paulson, Henry. *On the Brink*. New York: Hachette Book Group–Business Plus, 2010.

Reinhart, Carmen, and Kenneth Rogoff. *This Time Is Different: Eight Centuries of Financial Folly*. Princeton, NJ: Princeton University Press, 2009.

Schumpeter, Joseph Alois. *Capitalism, Socialism, and Democracy*. New York: Harper Perennial, 1950.

———. *Die Kreditwirtschaft. 1. Teil. Kölner vorträge*, Bd. I (80–106). Leipzig: G.A. Gloeckner, 1927. Reprinted as *Aufsätze zur ökonomischen Theorie*. Edited by E. Schneider and A. Spiethof (158–184). Tübingen: Mohr, 1952.

———. *The Theory of Economic Development*. Cambridge, MA: Harvard University Press, 1934.

———. *Das Wesen des Geldes*. Edited by Fritz Karl Mann. Göttingen: Vandenhoeck & Ruprecht, 1970.

Taibbi, Matt. "The Great American Bubble Machine." Last chap. in *Griftopia*. New York: Random House, 2010.

von Böhm-Bawerk, Eugen. "Macht oder ökonomisches Gesetz?" In *Zeitschrift für Volkswirtschaft, Sozialpolitik und Verwaltung*, Bd. 23 (1914): 205–271. Reprinted by Duncker & Humblot, Berlin, 1975.

About the Authors

Wilhelm Hankel is a consultant to central banks and governments the world over, from Costa Rica to China, from Egypt to Georgia, and in the past year in Syria and Iraq. He is an international economist renowned for trying, along with three colleagues, to stop through legal action the introduction of the euro, as well attempting to stop the recent bailout of Greece by the German government. His creative theories of money, the world economy, and recovery recipes for stalemated political economies are illustrated in 14 books, including *Prosperity amidst Crisis*, *Weltwirtschaft* (*World Economy*), *Caesar: The World Economy of Ancient Rome*, *John Maynard Keynes*, and most recently *Die Euro Luge und andere volkswirtschaftliche Märchen* (*The Euro Lie and Other Economic Fairy Tales*). Director of the Department of Money and Credit in the German Economic Finance Ministry under Economics Minister Karl Schiller (where he was instrumental in the creation of *Bundesschatzbriefe* and SDRs), Hankel was also president of the Hessische Landesbank in Frankfurt, and has taught monetary theory and development economics at the University of Frankfurt and at many universities, including Harvard, Georgetown, The Free University of Berlin, Dresden, and Johns Hopkins University SAIS in Bologna, where he published *Modern Inflation* (coauthored with Robert Isaak).

Robert Isaak is a political economist specializing in international management. He has written 11 books on behavioral theory of collective learning, comparative political economy, globalization, comparing cross-cultural efforts to replicate Silicon Valley, and promoting ecopreneurship internationally. Guest Professor of International Management at the University of Mannheim, he is The Henry George Professor of International Management at Pace University in New York, and has previously taught at New York University, the University of Heidelberg, SUNY at Purchase, Franklin College in Lugano, ESC Grenoble, SKEMA School of Management at Sophia Antipolis, and Johns Hopkins University SAIS in Bologna. Isaak has served as a consultant for Siemens, Technicon, Prudential Intercultural, and Global Intercultural, and his most recent books include *Managing World Economic Change*; *Green Logic: Ecopreneurship, Theory and Ethics*; and *The Globalization Gap: How the Rich Get Richer and the Poor Get Left Further Behind.*

Index

Acton, Lord, 62
Africa, 178–179, 229
Age demographics of emerging
    market countries, 155
Agenda 2010, 205
Aging of population, 208,
    218–222
Agricultural Bank of China, 162
AIG (American International
    Group), 71, 75, 85
American International
    Accounting System (IAS)
    controls, 48–49
American International Group
    (AIG), 71, 75, 85
American spending habits, 58–59
Anglo-American capitalism, 144
Anti-Western trends, 144–145
Aristotle, 151
Article 125/126, 111

Asset-backed securities (ABSs),
    43
Asset inflation, 6, 40, 47–48, 128,
    198
Austerity vs. stimulus, 92–97

Bailouts, 12–13, 50–51, 70–71,
    76, 89, 120–123
Balanced budget laws, 87
Bancor, 188, 190
Bank capital, 32–36
Bank failure costs, 37–38
Bank for International
    Settlements, 82
Banking Act (Germany), 36–37
Bank lending policies, 28
Bank of America, 85
Bank of Canada, 70
Bank of Japan, 70
Bankruptcies, 123–124, 133, 232

Bankruptcy *vs.* exchange rate
  adjustment, 133
Bank supervision, 16–18,
  49–50
Bank-to-bank liabilities, 42–43
Bear Stearns, 69, 71, 75
Bernanke, Ben, 70, 73
Bismarck, Otto von, 220
Black market labor, 7–8, 19
Black Tuesday, 35, 233
Blinder, Alan, 73, 94
Bloomberg, Michael, 151
BNP Paribas, 70
Böhm-Bawerk, Eugen von,
  117, 123
Brazil. *See also* BRIC countries
  (Brazil, Russia, India, and
  China)
  age demographics, 155
  economic development in,
    166–168
  effects of financial crisis, 154
  future challenges for, 229
  productive capacity, 172
Bretton Woods agreement, 62
  debtor/creditor equality of
    treatment, 188
  economy after, 193–197,
    239–240
  end to, 191–193, 239
  new version, 13–16, 200–203,
    244–245
  original *vs.* new, 13–16
  pillars of stability of, 187–189
  principles of, 185–187
  purpose of system, 184–185
  reasons for failure of, 185–191

BRIC countries (Brazil, Russia,
  India, and China), 139–179.
  See also individual country names
  debt *vs.* investment and savings
    in, 171–172
  demography of, 155
  and exports to United States,
    240–241
  extreme savings of, 145
  future challenges for, 228
  global imbalances and, 172–174
  growth characteristics of,
    157–158
  household debt in, 172
  imitating past successes, 141–143
  population growth in, 177
  rise of, 143–147
  trade and investment in Africa,
    178–179
British Petroleum, 91
British pound, 114
Brown, Gordon, 76
Budget deficits, 77, 89–90, 93
Buffett, Warren, 64
Bush (George W.) administration,
  62, 83, 85, 89
Bush, George W., 60, 61

Capitalism:
  characteristics of modern, 2–3
  "civilizing" of, 97
  vs. communism and fascism,
    144
  crises of, 174, 232–233
  democratization of, 1–24
  effects of aging population on,
    218–219

effects of welfare state on,
    216–217
role in *New* New World, 148
structural defects of, 35–36
Western changes in, 235–237
Capitalism, Socialism, and Democracy
    (Schumpeter), 7
Capital of banks, 32–36
Cardozo, Fernando Henrique,
    166, 176
Central bank, 17
    control of interbank market, 47
    importance of, 20
    independence from, 42–43
    role of, 182
Characteristics of *New* New
    World, 147–149
China. *See also* BRIC countries
    (Brazil, Russia, India, and
    China)
    age demographics, 155
    banking system, 161–162
    currency appreciation, 100
    economic development in,
        158–163
    economic miracles, 153
    educational development, 163
    export-led growth strategies
        of, 141
    export markets, 161
    export policies of, 145–147
    future challenges for, 229
    national health care in, 159
    population growth in, 177
    rural finance, 160
    stimulus package of 2008,
        158, 160

China–ASEAN Free Trade
    Agreement (CAFTA),
    162
Chrysler, 85
Citigroup, 85
Citizens' security, 212–213
Clearing Union, 186
Clinton, Bill, 31, 36, 205
Clinton, Hillary, 142
Clinton administration, 62
Collateralized debt obligations
    (CDOs), 43, 64
Collective learning, 18–19, 217,
    222
Cologne Herrstatt Bank, 37
Communism, 144, 240–241,
    244
Competitiveness of United States,
    100–103
Conditional cash-transfer (CCT)
    programs, 167
Congressional Budget Office
    estimates, 88–89
Connally, John, 192
Consumer confidence, 74
Contagion, 69
Copenhagen Climate Summit,
    142
Corporate executive bonuses/
    compensation, 85
Corporate hoarding, 90–91
Credit:
    levels of control, 182
    overreliance on, 234–235
Credit bubble, 198–199
Credit-default swaps (CDSs), 43,
    69

Credit derivatives, 32–33,
    42–43, 55, 69
  and financial reform, 81
  Greenspan's justification for,
    66–67
Credit fraud, money creation
    through, 25–51
Credit market controls, 31
Credit risk controls, 193–197
Crises of capitalism, 232–233
Crisis management, 210, 218
Currencies. *See also* Deutschmark;
    Dollar; Euro
  alternatives to current euro,
    125–129
  bankruptcy laws, 123–124
  "concubinage" of, 132–138
  elimination of competition, 128
  euro rescue package, 113–115,
    121–123, 138
  euro survival, 117–120
  exchange rate adjustments,
    133
  key reserve currencies, 97,
    100–103, 149
  post–Bretton Woods, 193–197
  and SDR values, 201–202
  stability/reliability of, 20,
    213–214
  transition to euro, 109–112
Currency risk and
    competitiveness, 110
Currency risk controls, 193–197
Currency stability, 212

Dahrendorf, Ralf, 7, 214
Debt culture of America, 85–92

Debtor/creditor equality of
    treatment, 188
Decoupling theory, 154–157
Deficit reduction, 86, 92–97
Deflation, 12, 208
  and elimination of structural
    deficits, 225–226
Democracy *vs.* plutocracy,
    151–152
Dependencia theory, 176
Deutschmark, 109, 125–127
Deutschmark zone, 125
Developing nations, 237–239. *See
    also* Emerging markets
  interior development *vs.*
    outside capital assistance,
    175–176
  redistribution of economic
    growth to, 157
Development aid, 238
Dewey, John, 56
Dodd-Frank Act, 81
Dollar:
  as currency of last resort,
    97–100
  devaluation of, 59, 61–62
  as exchange-rate reference,
    193–194
  maintaining key reserve
    currency status, 100–103
  place in new world monetary
    system, 244
  post–Bretton Woods, 193–197
  removal from gold standard,
    239
Dollarization, 97–100
Dot-com bubble, 62, 63, 66

Economic and Monetary Union (EMU), 15, 116, 119, 122, 125, 132–135, 183, 200

Economic miracles, 153

Economic reforms, 207

Education, types and importance of, 21–22

Elderly, care of, 218–222

Emerging markets:
  and decoupling theory, 154–157
  demographic trends, 155
  redistribution of economic growth to, 157

EMU. *See* Economic and Monetary Union (EMU)

Eucken, Walter, 216–217

Euro:
  alternatives to current, 125–129
  bailout plan for, 120–123
  guarantee by Germany, 242
  lessons learned from, 135
  and national currencies transition, 127–129
  question of survival of, 117–120
  rescue package for, 113–115, 121–123, 138
  transition to, 109–112

European Central Bank (ECB), 70, 106, 118, 120, 130, 210

European Central Bank system (ESCB), 112–113, 130

European Court of Justice (ECJ), 106

European Monetary System (EMS) of 1979, 110, 133

European Parliament (EP), 106

European Stabilization Fund (ESF), 120

European State Bankruptcy Law, 123–124

European Union (EU):
  citizenship in, 106
  Commission and Council of Ministers, 106
  compared to United States, 107
  constitutional fidelity of institutions, 116–117
  continuation, as hard currency block, 125–126
  crisis management in, 210
  and democratic processes, 108
  effects of end of euro on, 129–132
  external debt limits, 241–242
  future challenges for, 228
  future view of, 129–132
  and German Democratic Republic (GDR), 108–109
  indebtedness of member nations, 118–120
  national currencies transition, 127–129
  overview, 105–107
  and promises of peace, 107–108
  as soft euro-currency union, 126–127
  southern countries, with euro-currency union, 126–127
  transition to euro, 109–112
  withdrawal from, 125

European Union Commission, rescue program, 120

Exchange rate adjustments, 133
Exchange rate mechanism
    (ERM), 126, 191
Exchange rates:
    adjustments, 133
    and currency risks, 183–184
    dollar as reference for,
        193–194
    fixed rate system, 190–191
    floating, 191–193
    real fixed rate system, 200–203
    real *vs.* nominal, 200–201
Export-led growth strategies,
    140–141, 227

False accounting, 49–50
Fannie Mae, 71, 75
Fascism, 144
Federal Deposit Insurance
    Corporation (FDIC), 31
Federal Reserve Bank:
    interventions for economic
        recovery, 80
    quantitative easing program,
        95
    and subprime mortgage crisis,
        69–70
Financial crises, reasons for,
    181–182
Financial crisis beginning in 2007,
    27–28. *See also* Credit
    bubble; Credit derivatives
    bailouts, 12–13, 50–51, 70–71
    compared to previous crises,
        3–7, 39–41
    conclusions from, 47–51
    events leading up to, 32–35

government intervention in,
    75–76
historical basis for, 1–3
Obamanomics, 76–85
origins of, 65–72
remediation of debts from,
    206–207
responsibility for, 35–36
securitization of assets and,
    68–69
Financial crisis of the 1930s.
    See Great Depression
Financial "experts," 56–57
Financial illiteracy, 92
Financial innovation, 39–41
Financial market unification,
    42
Financial reform stumbling blocks,
    208–209
Financial reform package of
    2009, 81
Financial reforms, 45–46
Financial regulators, innovation
    and, 39–41
Financial sector, effects of
    globalization on, 3–7
Financial systems collapse,
    37–38
Financing and risk costs, 183
Fitch, 48
France, 115, 118, 122
Franco-German condominium, 2
Freddie Mac, 71, 75
Free-market fundamentalism,
    65–66
Free trade agreements, 100
Frugal innovation, 164

Geithner, Timothy, 79, 80, 100
General Motors, 85
Generational conflicts, 5–6,
    215–216
Germany:
  acceptance of euro, 111
  Banking Act, 36–37
  effects of euro on, 135–136
  effects of transition to national
    currency, 127
  and euro depreciation, 118
  and euro rescue, 114–116,
    122
  German Democratic Republic
    (GDR), 108–109
  guarantee of euro, 242
  and national currencies
    transition, 127
  old-age pension system, 221
Gerrymandering, 152
GIPS countries (Greece, Ireland,
    Portugal, Spain), 135–138.
    See also individual country names
Glass-Steagall Act, 17, 31, 36,
    57–58
Global banking, fatal innovations
    of, 41–45
Global finance, revolutionizing of,
    58–60
Global imbalances, 157, 172–174
Globalization:
  Anglo-American vision of, 53
  effects on finance, 58–60
  effects on leisure time, 152–153
  limitations from, 4–5
  technology and, 57
Global laissez-faire, 13–16

Goldman Sachs, 57, 63–65, 79,
    81, 83
Gold standard, 133, 150
  advantages of, 45, 47
  currency control with, 196
  overview, 26, 184
  reasons for failure of, 116
  return to, 242–243
Governance models, 150–154
Government investment/
    development banks, 21
Government overindebtedness,
    222–224
Government transparency, 212
Great Bluff, 53–55, 79–80, 94–96,
    102–103
Great Depression, 27, 30–31, 35,
    45, 233
Greater Mekong Subregion
    (GMS) agreements of
    economic cooperation, 162
Greece, 107–108, 112–115,
    118–120, 135, 172
Greenspan, Alan, 55, 65–68
Gross, William, 94
Group of 20 (G-20):
  and global imbalances, 172–174
  summit, 80

Haavelmoo, Trygve, 216
Harmonized price of living index
    (HPI), 118
Hartz, Louis, 152
Hartz IV, 205
Hayek, Friedrich, 206, 209
Health care reforms, 86–87
Hegemony stability hypothesis, 62

High-frequency stock trading, 147
HIRE Act Jobs Bill, 83
Hoarding, corporate, 90–91
Hobsbawm, Eric, 166–168
Housing bubble, 62, 63, 69–70
Human capital potential, 155–156
Human capital value, 216
Human labor force, 7–8

IKB, 70
Ikea, 169
Illinois fiscal problems, 87
Income inequality, 86
Income maldistribution, 40
India. *See also* BRIC countries (Brazil, Russia, India, and China)
  age demographics, 155
  agricultural dependency, 164
  banking intermediation, 165
  economic development in, 163–166
  educational development, 164
  effects of financial crisis, 154
  energy/resource dependence, 165–166
  population growth in, 177–178
  productive capacity, 172
Industrial Loan Companies, 81
Inflation, 12, 85, 235–237
Infrastructure development, 227
Initial public offerings (IPOs), 64
Intel, 92
Interbank market control, 47

International Bank for Reconstruction and Development. *See* World Bank (WB)
International Monetary Fund (IMF), 58
  as basis for credit and exchange rate calculation, 187–188
  and emergency rescue plans, 121
  introduction of, 186
  loss of power of, 31
  and PIIGS rescue program, 120
  Special Drawing Rights (SDRs), 14–16, 140, 190, 209, 244
  U.S. assistance from, 189
  voluntary compliance rules, 146
International monetary order, 199–203
International Refinancing Window, 186
Investment and infrastructure offensive, 225
Iraq War, 61, 87
Ireland, 106–107, 112–114, 118–120, 135
Islamism, 144

Japan, 228
Jefferson, Thomas, 56
Job creation, 79, 92, 227
Johnson, Lyndon, 61
JPMorgan Chase, 57, 75, 80

Keynes, John Maynard, 5, 14,
    213–214. *See also* Bretton
    Woods agreement
    and "aid for development,"
       174–175
    on developing countries,
       237–238
    on historical periods of financial
       harmony, 208
    interpretation of philosophy,
       50–51
Keynesian model, improved
    version, 200–203
Key reserve currencies, 97,
    100–103, 149
Kreditanstalt für Wiederaufbau
    (KfW), 226
Kreditwesengesetz (KWG), 36

Laffer curve, 206
Laissez-faire, 13, 152, 210, 230
Landesbank Baden-Württemberg,
    70
Landesbank Sachsen, 70
Latin Coinage Convention,
    116, 126
Latin Monetary Convention, 133
Lehman Brothers, 71, 75, 79
Leisure economy, 214
List, Friedrich, 22–23, 177
Long-Term Capital Management
    (LTCM), 72–73
Loopholes in regulation, 80–82

Macroeconomic controls, 47–48
Madrick, Jeff, 82
Marshall Plan, 238

Materialism, 96–97
Medicare costs, 87–88, 90
Medvedev, Dimitry, 154, 169
Megatrends of future global
    economy, 227–230
MERCOSUR, 168
Merrill Lynch, 81
Midas, 28–29
Middle East, future of, 229
Military spending, 60
Mint Union, 133
Mises, Ludwig von, 205
Mobility limitations of employees,
    4–5
Models of governance, 150–154
Money and goods economy,
    182–183
Money creation, government role
    in, 30
Money development through
    credit fraud, 25–51
Money progress *vs.* money
    fraud, 29
Moody's, 48
Morgan Stanley, 81
Morgenthau, Henry, Jr., 185
Motorola, 169
Mukherjee, Pranab, 164

National bank regulation, 47–48
National Coinage Act, 133
National monetary autonomy, 201
Negative transparency, 218
New Century Financial, 69
New Deal, 226
New New World characteristics,
    147–149

New world monetary system, 14–18, 200–203, 244–245
NINJA (no income, no job or assets) loans, 68
Nixon, Richard M., 192
No-bailout clause, 111, 137
Nominal exchange rates, 200–201
Nordic Monetary Union, 116
Northern Rock, 70

Obama, Barack, 1, 31
  campaign promises, 86
  at Copenhagen Climate Summit, 142
  economic theory of, 80–81
  efforts at financial reform, 81–83
  and financial crisis beginning in 2007, 76–85
  key economic promises, 78
  and long-term deficit reduction, 86
  policies leading to current budget deficit, 89–90
Obama administration:
  budget gaps, 93
  freeze on discretionary federal spending, 100
  policies, 53–55
Off-balance-sheet risks, 49–50
Oil bubble, 64
Oil price escalations, 239
Old-age pension system, 88–89, 218–222
O'Neil, Jim, 143
OPEC, 140–141, 239
Organization for Economic Cooperation and

Development (OECD), 55, 159, 163
Overconsumption, 58–59
Overproductivity, 214

Paulson, Henry, 65, 71, 73, 170
Pension account losses, 219–220
Pensions, 8–11
Piggyback mortgages, 68
PIIGS countries (Portugal, Ireland, Italy, Greece, and Spain), 111, 112–114. See also individual country names
  indebtedness of, 118–120
  rescue program for, 120
Plutocracy vs. democracy, 151–152
Politics (Aristotle), 151
Population dividend, 156
Porter, Michael, 64
Portugal, 107–108, 112–114, 118–120, 135
"Power or Economic Law?" (Böhm-Bawerk), 117
Prebisch, Raul, 176
Productive capacities, 172
Public debt, 212, 222–224
Putin, Vladimir, 153, 169

Rand, Ayn, 65
Rating agencies, 48–49
Reagan, Ronald, 61, 66
Reaganomics, 205
Real estate bubble, 64
Real exchange rates, 200–203
Regional revenue sharing, 211
Regulation of national banks, 47–48

entschier, Gordon, 94
epresentative democracy, 212
Reserves of foreign exchanges and
    gold, 146
Residual reserves, 140–141
Resources, potential underuse of,
    235
Retirement, 218–222. *See also*
    Old-age pension system
Revenue sharing, 210
Reverse engineering, 164
Rostow, W. W., 177
Rubin, Robert, 66
Rural finance, 160
Russia, 168–171. *See also* BRIC
    countries (Brazil, Russia,
    India, and China)
  age demographics, 155
  commodity export dependence,
    168–169, 170
  economy of, 153–154
  future challenges for, 228
  need for viable economy, 178

Safe harbor currencies, 121
Sam's Club, 91
Schröder, Gerhard, 205
Schumpeter, Joseph Alois, 7, 17,
    18, 20, 214, 239
Scotland, 115
Securitization of assets, 43,
    68–69
Self-employment, 19
Shanghai Cooperation
    Organization (SCO), 140
Shaw, Timothy, 174
Siemens, 91

Silva, Luiz Inácio Lula da (Lula),
    167
Smith, Adam, 227
Smithsonian Agreement, 192
Social security, 8–11, 87–88,
    219–222
South Africa, 229
Spain, 107–108, 112–114,
    118–120, 123, 135
Special Drawing Rights (SDRs),
    14–16, 190, 201–202, 209,
    244
Special purpose vehicles (SPVs),
    44, 68, 198
Stability Pact, 111, 137
Standard & Poor's, 48
Start-ups, 18–19
State bankruptcy, 123–124, 133,
    232
Stimulus package of February
    2009, 78–79
Stimulus *vs.* austerity, 92–97
Stock Market Crash of 1929, 35,
    233
  Goldman Sachs and, 64
  public debt following,
    223
Structured investment vehicles
    (SIVs), 68
Structured products creation,
    68
Subprime mortgages, 44–45,
    69–70
Summers, Larry, 79
Supervision of financial markets,
    45–46
Systemic crises, 45–46

Taibbi, Matt, 63–64
Taiwan, 229
Tax cuts, Bush-era, 83
"Taxflation," 35
Teaching/learning hierarchy, 215–216
Tea Party movement, 85, 152
Term Asset-Backed Securities Loan Facility (TALF), 80–81
Term Auction Facility (TAF), 80
Tertiary service sector, 7–8
Thatcher, Margaret, 66
Thatcherism, 205
Toxic waste mills, 44
Transparency, 20–21
Treaty of Amsterdam, 111
Troubled Asset Relief Program (TARP), 94
Turkey, 228

Unemployment, 79
Unfair competition, 22
Unification of world financial markets, 42
Union wages, 90
United States:
  continuing competitiveness of, 100–103
  events leading up to decline, 55–58
  external debt limits, 241
  financial power of, 60
  foreign investing in, 101
  future challenges for, 228
  household debt in, 94, 172
  and IMF assistance, 189
  loss of status, 150

need for regional equality, 2?
privileged position under Bretton Woods agreement, 189–191
as world banker, 189
U.S. savings and loans crisis, 37

Vietnam War, 61
Volcker, Paul, 61
Volcker Rule, 81

War costs, 87
War in Afghanistan, 61, 87, 96
War on Terror, 61
Washington Mutual, 75, 80
Welfare state:
  challenges of, 5
  effects on capitalism, 216–217
  role of, 23
Western economic model, 145
Western education, 21, 22, 96, 101–103, 150
White, Harry Dexter, 185
Working-age populations, 155–156
Workplace generation conflict, 215–216
World Bank (WB), 175, 226, 238
World monetary systems. See Bretton Woods agreement; Gold standard; New world monetary system
World Trade Organization (WTO), 145

Xin, Zhang, 160